SEVENS HEAVEN

SEVENS

The Beautiful Chaos of
Fiji's Olympic Dream

The Beautiful Chaos of Fiji's Olympic Dream

BEN RYAN

with Tom Fordyce

WEIDENFELD & NICOLSON

First published in Great Britain in 2018 by Weidenfeld & Nicolson
an imprint of The Orion Publishing Group Ltd
Carmelite House, 50 Victoria Embankment
London EC4Y 0DZ

An Hachette UK Company

1 3 5 7 9 10 8 6 4 2

A CIP catalogue record for this book is
available from the British Library.

ISBN (Hardback) 978-1-4746-0825-1
ISBN (Export Trade Paperback) 978-1-4746-0826-8

Typeset at The Spartan Press Ltd,
Lymington, Hants

Printed and bound by CPI Group (UK) Ltd,
Croydon, CR0 4YY

www.orionbooks.co.uk

For Dad, gone too soon but who inspired me to believe in better. When the whistle went, when the final was done – you were right there with me.

And for the people of Fiji – you will never know the difference you made. *Lolomas.*

VANUA

NABOUWALU LANDING

BURESALA WHARF

ST. JOHN'S COLLEGE

LEVUKA

OVALAU

LAUTOKA

NADI

VITI LEVU

NAULUVATAU

NADROGA

NASINU

NAVEYAGO

SUVA DOMAIN

SIGATOKA

VOTUA

PACIFIC HARBOUR

Frigates

BEQA ISLAND

ONE

Sometimes instinct takes over. Sometimes you just know, within the first two seconds. Sometimes a choice just seems right.

And sometimes when you make that decision, you have no idea where it will end up taking you, of how the next 30 years have just flipped around on those two seconds, of how nothing in your life will be quite the same ever again.

Late summer, 2013. I am 41 years old, a successful rugby coach, a man five years married and with a just-big-enough house in a just-good-enough part of London. I have been offered a job that will provide a decent salary, long-term stability and an acceptable level of stimulation. I am sailing untroubled waters, and the breeze is at my back. With one message from a friend, one 140-character post on Twitter, I decide to jump over the side instead.

There is no safety net, no lifeline, no guarantees of rescue or second chances. Just the faint outline of a dream, the first note of a song yet to be written. Man overboard. Man a long way from the shore.

I began as a player, became a teacher and grew into a coach. In seven years with England's rugby sevens team I had taken them to World Cup finals and Commonwealth Games, building a reputation as an innovator, doing things differently, bringing in diets and training that no one had seen before and that soon became staples in every other dressing-room on the sevens circuit.

It had come to an end both slowly and quickly. England rugby is seen as a business, and a serious one at that, and all in the system must treat it that way. I threw everything into it, because that is my way; I looked for the little forgotten advantages that others might have neglected, and nothing I have done has come without hard work and commitment. But underpinning it all must be pleasure and fun and excitement. You play rugby to test yourself physically and mentally against others. You play it to express the way you feel, to burst free of the prosaic constraints that can hold you back in the real world. You don't play to spend days staring at reruns and never-weres on a laptop, or to be lecturing players for hours in a classroom, or to be stuck in meetings far away from the pitch. And you play to treat those around you properly, to let sport develop the best of your characters, not to be lost in Machiavellian struggles for power and influence and to have people above you who can only be trusted never to be trustworthy.

Slowly that had become my life. Quickly I'd found myself on the outside. You always hope you can keep your integrity even while those around you are losing theirs, but I could feel myself changing. And so when the end came, the bullet fired by a man whom I felt I could no longer trust, there was a sense of relief combined with the disillusionment.

UK Sport is the support network behind Great Britain's Olympic revolution, and the job they offered after I left England looked interesting and secure, even if it would also take me away from hands-on coaching towards long-term planning, from an itinerant life in planes and foreign cities to nine-to-fives in rural Buckinghamshire.

It was all in place, the next three years laid out neatly and predictably in front of me. And then, within hours of their confirmation coming through – you've got it, when can you start? – so too did a text message:

Ben. Seen this on Twitter? The Fiji sevens job is up.

Each rugby nation has its special charms. New Zealand play with miraculous pace and precision. England are the aristocrats with the biggest house and the largest support. In Wales they marry the muscle up front with cavalier dash in the backs. Ireland use the wind and rain to pin you back and stretch you out. France are a smoking blend of menace and madness, Australia are the attack-minded upstarts, Argentina hard-nosed and flamboyant in equal measure. Don't cross the South Africans, and don't underestimate the fire that lights up Scottish bellies.

And yet none of them play rugby like the big men from the little Pacific nation, just as no one plays football like kids from the Brazilian favelas, or no one runs as fast as the boys from Jamaica's boondocks, and nowhere is the beautiful chaos of Fijian rugby distilled in sweeter form than in its sevens.

Runners coming at you from everywhere. A conjuror's

sleight of hand on a bulldozer's chassis. Sidesteps and shimmies, battering-rams and blistering pace. Skips and dips,
offloads and smuggled-away passes, smiles and songs and
a pleasure in it all as if the only things that mattered were
having fun and cutting loose.

All around the world, Fiji have always been every rugby
supporter's second team. On the islands themselves the
players are the folk heroes and the warriors, the meal
ticket and the great distraction from cruel poverty and
relentless political instability. Every child in every village
plays, every adult is obsessed. They learn with anything to
hand – balls of scrunched-up paper, empty plastic bottles
– and often with nothing on their feet except wet red
mud or golden sand. It is brutal and beautiful, intuitive
and unstructured, both the spiritual home of the short-
form game and a quarry mined incessantly by greedier,
richer nations, the best players enticed overseas by pro
contracts and short naturalisation periods, Fiji itself left to
battle on with minimal resources, shoddy equipment and
compromised coaches.

You cannot ignore Fiji. You cannot prevent your heart
doing a little jump at the mention of a coaching vacancy,
or your mind racing ahead with the possibilities and problems, and how you, more than anyone who's tried before,
might be the one to unleash all that untapped potential.

I took a breath. I had a winning record for England
against Fiji. I knew that gave me clout. I knew too that
serendipity was on my side: while Fiji had never won an
Olympic medal of any colour in 60 years of trying, the next
Olympics in three years would feature the return of rugby
for the first time in 92 years and the seven-a-side version
for the first time ever.

The fact that the deadline for applications had just passed seemed less important than all that emotion and instinct. I sent a short email, no CV asked for, simply an expression of interest, and the reply came promptly back: *Can you do an interview over Skype at two in the afternoon, Suva time?*

Two in the afternoon in Fiji's capital is two in the morning in London. Fine – I like espresso. Staying up late was no problem. I did a little basic prep. I knew the current team's strengths and weaknesses from my time with England, when we had played them in the annual World Series and beaten them several times, so I could talk about those with authority. I understood it would be madness to try to change the way they played, but I realised too that if I could add a framework, to make them consistently brilliant rather than intermittently outstanding, and get them fitter and even faster, and put in place selection strategies that weren't just based on who you knew and which province you came from, as rumours said they were, I could make a difference. If I could convince the blazers of that too, the same officials who sacked coaches as regularly as they emptied the bins, it might get interesting.

At 2 a.m. I was wide awake and good to go. Instead I had my first exposure to 'Fiji Time', less a degree on the international date line than a state of perpetual possibility. I would come to understand Fiji Time in detail: something is scheduled to happen; it probably will, at some stage, although there's no rush, and there's no certainty around when, and if it doesn't . . . well, something else has come along instead, and maybe it wasn't meant to happen anyway, otherwise why didn't it?

So 2 a.m. became 2.30 a.m., became 3 a.m., became lying on the sofa with my laptop on my stomach and the early-morning flights into Heathrow starting to thunder past overhead. Somewhere close to that late-summer dawn the Skype beeps sounded. I sat up, fired up the video link and rubbed my eyes.

My face was being projected onto the wall of chief executive Manasa Baravilala's office, and I had the sense this was not established procedure. People who were not board members, people who seemed uninvolved in the actual interview, kept popping their heads in to have a look and say hello. I was repeatedly asked if I knew Jonny Wilkinson, the great hero of England's World Cup win of 2003, and if I'd met the Queen. I thought it went OK. I asked a few questions. I didn't fall asleep. I had at least met Jonny.

Much later that morning, after a long frazzled lie-in, I went online, keen to learn more about Fijian culture and life. I knew all about the rugby, but I knew little of anything else. Had you given me a map of the Pacific and asked me to point to Fiji, I would have gone north of New Zealand and just hoped not to pick Tonga or Samoa instead.

The first headline I saw on the *Fiji Times* website announced that Manasa Baravilala had been sacked.

Right. Game over before the game had begun. That was Fiji for you, and Fiji would clearly be for someone else. Bisham Abbey would be my new playground, and that would be fine – part of Britain's push to the Rio Olympics, medals an indirect result of what I would be trying to do. UK Sport had never been better funded; in the four years up to those Games in Brazil it would have almost £350 million to spend. My life would be calm, and it would be comfortable. We could bring in the best coaches and the latest equipment to work with athletes who needed little motivating and were already close to the finished article.

And it would not be the Rugby Football Union, awash in power battles and personal rivalries, and led by a boss who in seven years had rarely come to see the sevens team he was ultimately responsible for, training at a ground two miles from his office. I had been told, towards the end, that my job depended on England's performance in the next two tournaments and the subsequent World Cup. When we reached the semi-final of those tournaments, handing out a record-breaking defeat to Fiji along the way, and then made the World Cup final, it was something of a surprise to be sacked anyway.

I had found it impossible not to be dragged down by it all. My strength was completely spent from worrying about the boss. Calm and comfortable might be rather easy to get used to.

Two weeks later, sitting in an Italian restaurant in south-west London with my wife Natalie, my mobile started ringing. I recognised the dialling code.

+679. Fiji.

I jumped up and strode outside, into a little side road that ran towards Richmond Green. It was a warm evening, still light at 8 p.m., well-heeled Londoners out for a gentle stroll, others throwing Frisbees about on the grass, comfortable lives and solid wealth everywhere you looked.

Hello, Ben? It's Berlin Kafoa. I'm the acting CEO of Fiji Rugby.
Hi, Berlin, what can I do for you?
We're just about to have a press conference.
About what?
About how we've appointed you as our new coach.
A silence, a frown, a jolt of adrenalin.

Appointed me? Do I get any say in this?

Of course. You have 20 minutes. Please call me back.

I walked slowly back into the restaurant, red tiles on the floor, carefully exposed brick walls, contentment in the air. There was so much easy affluence that the décor had been designed to look shabbily chic – tables like old school desks, carefully tatty wooden chairs, old leather books on the shelves. Thick-rimmed wine glasses in front of us, a bottle of Valpolicella half-drunk and ready to be poured for more.

We talked first about the sensible stuff: moving to a place neither of us had ever been to before, moving thousands of miles from friends and family, from one of the world's great cities to a nation whose population could have fitted into one London borough. We talked about Natalie's job and career hopes. We talked about commitment and changes of heart. I hadn't yet signed a contract with UK Sport, so I still had time to give them a grateful no thanks. We talked about the possibility of keeping options open, of going over there for a look, of simply flying home if it wasn't working and felt like it never could.

We talked about all that. But instinct had already kicked in. Berlin had given me 20 minutes; I'd known after two seconds.

Those sorts of sped-up moments bring their own rush. It's two espressos in one mouthful, it's a sudden sharpening of your senses. When you jump overboard, the water is cold. I phoned Fiji back. We drank our wine and felt light-headed even before it had kicked in.

It was good to enjoy that feeling, because it wouldn't last long. Soon the text messages started arriving: *Congratulations, but you do realise...? Great news Ben, aren't you worried about...? Blimey, you're brave...*

World Rugby called and told me that all funding to Fiji had been suspended while they investigated where it had been spent. Fiji Rugby, a union traditionally strapped for cash, was now effectively bankrupt. Again.

Gut feelings do not tend to run due diligence. There had been no discussion of terms, or salary, or how long the deal might actually be for. It had simply been, can you get here in about ten days' time? Pay for your own flights, we'll reimburse you when you arrive. We'll sort everything out then.

I had taken them at their word, rather than asking for a day or two so I could discuss it with my agent, or a contract in writing so my lawyers could examine the small print as well the large details. I'd just said, yeah, OK.

I'd had a pay-out when I left England. At some level I knew that I could tick over for a while without losing the house. But the hangover from the big rush came sweeping over me all the same, walking up the Thames towpath up to Hammersmith the next soft, balmy morning to see my chiropractor. And not just a few reservations but an absolute panic – a sick feeling in my stomach, a wave of regrets and what ifs and what on earth have I done?

I called my agent. Can we get out of this? I've known Mark for a long time, and with him there is no being nice for the sake of it. He was sympathetic but firm: to quit now, when it had already been in all the newspapers, would look terrible. It would damage my chances of getting any other job. To pull out saying I wasn't being paid enough would make me look even more stupid – shouldn't I have found that out before signing? The earliest I could realistically hope to leave was after a year. It was a 12-month minimum sentence.

I walked all the way back from Hammersmith to Brentford. Along the Thames, that's a good few hours. It must be getting on for six or seven miles. Past the old Watney Brewery in Chiswick, on towards Barnes, heading north again towards Kew, and every step, thinking, Shit. Shit. Shit . . .

Had Mark said he could get me out of it, I would have been gone, filled with the happiness of a liberated man. Instead I was like an unhappy kid trying to get out of school. Could I pull a giant sickie? Could I blame it on Natalie?

It was Natalie who talked me down. Let's just go there and see what happens. If we don't like it, we come home. We'll get a nice hotel, we'll have a proper look round. The first tournament is on the Gold Coast in Australia, a week or so after we're scheduled to land. We do that, fly back to London, and make our decision. Think of it as a holiday with benefits. Don't think of it as for ever.

Fiji is a nation of 300-odd islands, spread over more than a million square kilometres in the lonely South Pacific. New Zealand's North Island is 2,000 kilometres to the south. That's a lot of ocean for a kid brought up on Field Lane in Brentford. It was 10,000 miles from the city where I had always lived, from my 81-year-old mother, from my two sisters and my friends and Natalie's family.

I did a little bit of the research I should have done before. Even the RFU hadn't seen as many coups as the Fijian government, or been under siege for two months from its own security force. The Fijileaks website was awash with stories of corruption and bribery, of police brutality, of prisons stacked with political opponents.

Then there was Frank Bainimarama, the military chief who had seized power once in 2000, and again after the most recent coup in 2006. He was now the prime minister; the governments of Australia and New Zealand had preferred to describe him as a dictator. Sanctions had been imposed and the country had been suspended from the Commonwealth after he had backtracked on a promise to hold elections. It was why there had been no Fiji sevens team at the Commonwealth Games in Delhi in 2010, where I had taken my England team to the semi-finals. You read stories about Bainimarama that you hoped weren't true, and you read stories about him that seemed impossible. You could believe that he still played touch rugby every morning; he was Fijian. But had he really postponed that final coup by 24 hours so that a big rugby match involving his Army team could go ahead as scheduled?

So much for calm and comfortable. So much for soft landings.

You fly to Fiji from London, and you're flying for ever. You get jetlag, and then go so far that your jetlag gets jetlag, and a day later you're still travelling. It's always daylight and you can never sleep. If you're excited about what's at the end of it, it's an exhausting experience. If your head is full of doubt and regrets, it's an awfully long time to be feeling sick.

Nadi International Airport is on the far west of the biggest and most populated island, Viti Levu. Natalie and I staggered off that final plane like zombies, red-eyed, stiff-limbed, desperate to lie down, desperate to lie flat. We dragged our heavy suitcases through Customs, straight into a whirlwind – girls running over to drape garlands of flowers round our necks, a huge banner, *Welcome Home, Ben!*, some sort of ukulele orchestra starting up, journalists rushing over for interviews. Two hours of mayhem were followed by another flight to Suva, the capital across the other side of the island, and eventually on to the Novotel in Lami, a few miles west along the coastal road, and this time the full board of the Fiji Rugby Union was awaiting us in reception: more cameras, more television crews, a great feast prepared for us, and all the time the panic rising, and the doubt and heavy exhaustion dragging us down.

We lasted about 20 minutes. Apologies and handshakes, pleas that we had been awake for almost three days, promises that we would do it all properly in the morning. And then I was sitting on the edge of the bed in the hotel room with Natalie, the world outside a cage of total darkness, nothing to offer perspective on where we were or what we were doing. Suitcases dumped in the corner, nothing taken out except a toothbrush, the heat prickling our skin, the lassitude of crossing those latitudes heavy on our shoulders, all the doubts and fears and regrets filling up the room around us. We sat there looking at each other. Shit...

Dawn came early each day. Sitting on the hotel bed, looking left, it was a shimmering wall of blue – all sea, all sky, one reflecting the other, the horizon hard to find. Open windows let in a little waft of frangipani. Dark-green islands in the distance. That one was called Mosquito Island and another Snake Island were the sort of details that were best learned later.

The ANZ Stadium in town was hosting the annual Oceania sevens, a geography lesson for me as much as a sporting one. Hello Tuvalu. Welcome to the Cook Islands, American Samoa and the Solomon Islands. Papua New Guinea, Samoa, I promise that one day soon I'll be able to place you all on that vast Pacific map.

Alongside the main event was an invitational tournament for club sides from across Fiji and a select group of nations – the USA, France, Argentina. Natalie and I were guests of honour, sweltering even in the shade of the grandstand, doing nothing more than observing.

I noticed him before the summons came: big, over six feet, thickset, a stern look on his face, there in the middle of the stand, bodyguards either side of him, jacket and shirt despite the heat, and no one getting anywhere close.

Frank Bainimarama.

I made my way over, aware that the entire stadium was watching us, that everyone knew everyone else was watching. It felt strangely like being 16 again and getting ready to pick up your new girlfriend from her parents' house for the first time, knowing that as soon as you knock on the door you will come nose to chest with her terrifying father.

I knew he would want to keep me close. I was the big arrival, even if no one knew yet how temporary I wanted the stay to be. Rugby was his game and the nation's game. I knew too that his support would be limited, in case I made a mess of it all. Be nice, I thought. Make a couple of neutral comments, walk away after a respectable period of time. Talk less and listen more.

He held my stare. I was conscious of not holding his too long. Television cameras had moved carefully into place. I could tell he was wearing his neutral expression, even if his neutral was most people's third-gear intimidating.

13

He welcomed me. The cameras stayed on him. I thanked him. The cameras backed away.

He looked at me again. 'You're going to get a lot of advice out here,' he said, neutral face locked on. 'Don't listen to any of it unless it saves your life.'

He chuckled. His bodyguards leant back, allowing the butts of their guns to slide out from under their shirts, and chuckled too.

There would never be a meeting I would have with Frank when I wouldn't leave thinking, Ben, be careful. I knew I would have to watch every public step, every word I said. I would find out that he took things personally, that he held grudges, that he made things happen. I would see the hidden ruthlessness emerge, and I would see it work for me: a problem of mine that he would hear about, met with one comment – *Don't worry, I'll sort those sons of bitches out* – and terminated with one phone call. There would never be any point when I thought I could challenge him, when it could be anything else than him in charge.

Bright sunshine overhead, storm clouds coming in. A few matches later, right in front of us, one of Fiji's new stars, Kalepi Namoua, went down heavily with a broken leg, a bad one, a spiral fracture.

I drove up Laucala Bay Road to the Colonial War Memorial Hospital with the team doctor, as much to see what happened in Fiji when you suffered a serious injury like that as to help in any way. Kalepi's parents arrived as he was being assessed. And then they took him away, before he could be operated on, to take him back to their village, where the witchdoctor, who called himself a healer, would later push the bones back through the skin and wrap leaves around his shattered leg, which would then get infected.

I watched him being carried away, thinking, if this guy doesn't get this leg set in this public hospital, forget about whether I pick him again, he's never going to play rugby at this level ever again.

Storm clouds and sunshine. At the same hospital, where Fiji Rugby's CEO was presenting a new scanner to help diagnose heart problems in young kids, something came over the young patients as the nurses whispered to them that this red-haired, red-eyed man in the corner was Fiji's new sevens coach. It didn't seem to matter that the only thing I'd done was eat a couple of hotel buffet breakfasts and be significantly unsettled by their unelected leader. A first positive thought: if merely meeting a pasty, equivocating coach could have this effect, what would happen if we could get this team to win? What would an Olympic gold medal mean to a country raised on rugby but starved of success?

With the first of the nine legs of the Sevens World Series due to begin on Australia's Gold Coast the following week, the hard work would have to begin imminently, even if the team selection would not be mine, nor their fitness. The pitch where they were due to assemble was in the middle of an Army camp, mosquitoes feasting on the boys, players getting ill because of the poor sanitation. They were here not because it worked for training but because it worked for the Army officers who could stand around watching and boasting about their own importance. There was no training kit and no water bottles. The few rugby balls they had were so old and worn that there was no grip on them at all. It was me and a whistle and nothing else.

With Kalepi crippled, I needed to choose a replacement for the squad. Four names were given to me. Three of them

I had never heard of. The fourth, Osea (nicknamed Oscar) Kolinisau, I had seen in action before and rated: 27 years old, not tall at 5ft 9ins but solid at more than 14 stone, an explosive runner, dangerous on the wing or counter-attacking from full-back in the 15-a-side game. I submitted his name to the Fiji Rugby Union and came up against the next unforeseen speedbump.

Osea? No, you can't pick him.

Why?

He's a trouble-maker.

How?

He just is. You can't.

Osea, I found out, had spoken up for the players in the past. When training had been going badly, he had complained to Fiji Rugby's board, and now the board was complaining back. I was happier to hear it, because a team full of yes-men gets you nowhere. There must be honesty, and a coach must know how his players feel if he is to do more than just issue instructions and assume each will process them in exactly the same way.

When I drove to Osea's parents' house in Suva and spoke to his father Tui, a pastor in the local church, a different back-story emerged: that when Osea had been dropped from the national squad, he was so stricken that it took all his father's persuasion and prayer to get him to continue his university education, let alone his rugby career.

You need players who care, who understand what they might lose if they do not produce their best, and so I made time to talk to him. Within a few seconds my instincts kicked in again: I can trust this man, I can feel a connection. I couldn't put my finger quite on what it was – maybe his tone, his manner, the way he looked at me – but I felt it immediately. You and I are going to be fine. You and I are going to get on really well.

Against the advice, I brought him into the team. To widespread shock, I then made him my captain. Of all the things I did in that first year, all the punts and cute calculations, that was the one that paid back most handsomely. That was the start of it all.

That was the start, but we were beginning a long way down. To the Gold Coast of Queensland, training at a local club, turning up in our kit, the heat dry, rising up through the parched, bleached grass. Face and arms smeared with white sun-block, late-morning sun sending sweat down my back and into my eyes. I set up a fitness assessment, a simple standard called a yo-yo, similar to the bleep test, designed to gauge your aerobic endurance, running between two cones in a gradually decreasing number of seconds.

I won it. The 40-something coach beat the cream of Fiji's rugby talent. I stood there in the bright sunshine, feet sweating in my rugby boots, the smell of the sun-cream and sweat in my nostrils. This was my team. This was what I had gambled it all for. I walked off in search of water and realised we had none.

They appeared mentally shot, too, ready to drop out straight away, puzzled as to why they were even being tested. They never trained for sevens, just played it, sometimes up to 50 tournaments a year, almost one each week. No training, no building fitness progressively over the season, no recovery. None of them had thought, maybe I should stay in shape to impress our new coach. Instead the thinking had been, wait and see who it is, if he's from my province I'm getting picked anyway, if he's from another island I've got no chance whether I can run like Usain Bolt or a three-toed sloth.

That had to change. I took aside the long-standing and long-suffering team physio, William Koong, and told him what we needed: physical intensity, and fast. We would have to break some players to get others where we wanted them.

William was smart, much more so than he liked to let on. He was from the village of Sawani, out on the west coast of Fiji's second island, Vanua Levu, but he under-stood the wider world and how to navigate through it. As a physio, he would take a large metal trunk on all our trips to overseas tournaments, filled with medical necessities, with strapping, with bandages and pads. On the last day of training I would sometimes be surprised by how much strapping the players were wearing, fearing an outbreak of muscle strains and injuries. William would wink and show me what had replaced it all in the trunk: gifts for home that otherwise wouldn't make our luggage allowance, expensive memory-foam beanbags lent to us on long-term lease from other tournaments. If you can be creative with mere luggage, you can be creative enough to make young men run a little further and faster than they had been used to.

We didn't tank in that first competition. Fiji never could, not with the ability in those fingertips, not with that in-built balance and strength. But we lost to Wales in the group stages, something which said more about where we were than where that Wales team might be heading, and up against England in the quarter-finals, a team I had pushed to their fitness limits myself, honed at the world-class facilities of the English Institute for Sport, we couldn't get close. Beaten by my old team, the gap between what I had left and what I had taken on stark before me, the doubts and panic rising again.

I could see the whole thing was a mess. There was only one thing I could salvage from it, and that was that the wreckage would not be witnessed by others. I'd seen in the past what happened to Fijian teams when they lost badly: they would go out that night and drink badly too – big lads on the sauce who don't do it enough to handle it and have too much energy and warrior spirit stored up for it to end up any other way.

So I banned them from booze until they were home and far from my eyes. I literally sat downstairs in the hotel foyer with Natalie and made sure that no one was coming up or down the stairs drinking. I needed one small victory from the carnage, not just for that week but to take into the bigger battles ahead, and that would be it.

The problem would never fully disappear. Over the next three years I would see key players banned, hotel rooms in flames, crying girlfriends and broken marriages. Sometimes it would not be the players' fault. An uncle or tribal relative would roll into town, or be part of the ex-pat community in the city where we were playing, and when the older man decreed it was time for beers, the younger man culturally could not refuse. I understood too that they needed an outlet for all that pent-up emotion, which was why I not only let them hit the fast food after the tournament but paid for it from my own pocket. It would make no difference to their performance at that point, and I found it quietly amusing to see them being joined, surreptitiously, by players from other countries trying to sneak a dirty burger under the radar. Kiwis, Samoans, Tongans and Fijians, all together under the Golden Arches.

And I began the process of making them feel good mentally as well as physically. You will all be invited to our first training camp back home. You will all start off with an 'A' star. It's up to you to lose your place. You have a head-start over everyone else from the islands, but your behaviour is pretty important in determining what happens next. I tried to be just as positive in my own thinking. Even if some of them had been pretty terrible in that tournament, well, look, that's off the back of minimal fitness, with a coach who has barely started to coach, and years of mismanagement and underachievement. Someone somewhere must have thought you were half-decent, even if there was some fiddling around with selection because your village head was owed a favour by someone higher up, or your cousin happened to be talking to the right selector at an opportune time. Some I knew were far better players than they were showing, like winger Samisoni Viriviri, who played domestically for the police sevens side and had shown glimpses for the national team before. Sami's grandfather had been a star, capped in the 15-a-side game against Australia and England, part of the legendary Fijian XV that had beaten the British and Irish Lions in Suva in 1977. Sami loved his fast food and he loved his booze. You could see both on his 6ft frame, slowing him down, blunting his silhouette and his attacking edge. He was also so shy that no coach had tried to get through to him. I knew there was better to come from him, and that I had to start by showing him support.

Coach for a while and it becomes a subconscious business. Even as we had been falling apart on the Gold Coast,

I was figuring out the little steps and the small gains, hunting the easy wins that might lead to much more. At the invitational tournament I'd seen back in Fiji, there had been kids playing for the clubs whose talent was extraordinary. Argentina, USA and France had all been beaten by local teams. I could lose four of the current squad, bring in four callow replacements from that level and get an instant uplift, especially if that quartet included a 23-year-old giant called Semi Kunatani, a flying flanker from the Yamacia club and a rampaging off-loading maverick named Pio Tuwai I'd spotted at the Coral Coast tournament. I could hit their diets, replacing starchy carbs with lean protein, and adding pace and power as a result. The set-pieces – scrum, line-out, penalty moves – were being done as little add-ons the day before matches. We could hone those. The kicking was woeful, random in direction at best, technically flawed. I could improve that by 10 per cent in a few weeks. Defence? Defence was like collective suicide, broken charges from what should have been a solid white line, whacking the opposition round the head because they had been brought up carrying the ball high, getting yellow cards for those infringements and others on top because they were unfit and tired and making bad, bad decisions as a result. There were hundreds of little things like that, everywhere I looked. What would happen if we got all those elements right?

I was back in London for only eight days after that first spell in Fiji. All that time my brain was ticking over with ideas and names and thoughts and schemes. Natalie would stay at home, at least until the New Year. I couldn't wait to get back to Fiji.

Instinct against logic, precedent against the present. I

had still not been shown a contract. My flights and hotel bill had not been reimbursed. Maybe I should have realised that I was just being told what they thought I wanted to hear, that Fiji Time was about to meet Fijian finances to leave me with nothing for a whole lot longer. But had I known that there would be no contract waiting for me, that I would not be paid a single cent for another six months, would I have gone back to Fiji at all?

TWO

My best friend has gone, and I don't know how to find him. Me and Noel, tighter than I have ever been with anyone. Together at school, side by side on the rugby pitch, out in the back garden playing every sort of game invented and several we made up ourselves. Sleeping in my school uniform so I can get up quicker and get down to the table-tennis tables left out in the playground, Noel the number-one seed, me pushing him every morning at number four.

Summer holidays together, taken by my mum and dad, with Noel's parents so far away and his guardian a man who you know you don't want to spend too much time with. Watching rip-off VHS videos of big-hit films and chasing each other round the streets of Brentford on cheap versions of proper BMX bikes. Baths together, top-and-tailing in the same bed, all the photos of me as a kid with Noel alongside.

And then he begins to slip away. Other kids on the scene, man-boys with troubling habits and crueller games and an attitude to the world that says fuck you and let's fight rather than explore and escape and excite. Noel getting pulled away, being changed, growing in a different way. Getting together and feeling something is slipping. Getting together and feeling doubt and apprehension, and wanting to do something about it but knowing you are powerless against these colder, bleaker currents. Something forever there between you that should never be broken, bad luck and bad decisions taking one of you one way and the other somewhere else.

You move on and you move away. And then you come back, and you want what you used to have. You want to sit down again and admit all that was there before, even as you understand it can never be the same again. In my head there's never anything wrong with Noel. He is perfect and so are we. You know that has gone, but you want it to be superseded by something different and still deep.

And so I start to look again. I go to old haunts and old acquaintances. I pull favours and I ask myself questions.

Searching for my best friend. Searching for what I'm missing.

I began our first significant training session back in Fiji with 20 players gathered around me. It would be a serious session to deal with an acute lack of fitness: 100m sprints, a jog back and then go again, a 200m run in 30 seconds or less, then 60m more hard running, 30m, cutting the recovery times between each effort.

I ended the session with three players. The rest were hiding in the bushes at the far end of the pitch, or at least hiding as well as 17 men with an average weight of 15 stone could behind a few fronds and glossy leaves.

When it happened the following day, I threw the bush-babies out of the session and began again. You get fit, you get in the team. You don't get fit, you don't get in the team. I just want you to give it your best. Together we're going to get better.

The only one talking to me was Osea. The rest were saying yes, but only, I sensed, from a fear of saying no. Osea, having thought his career might be over, had already glimpsed the other side and not liked what he'd seen. He knew he needed someone to push him, and he trusted me to do it. I trusted him to bring some of the others with him. To all of them I sent a careful message via the two national newspapers, the *Fiji Times* and the *Fiji Sun*. These are good players. I'm going to work them hard. We're going to be fitter for our next tournament, and if we get that right, the nation will have more to feel good about.

Everyone in Fiji reads those papers: players, their parents, the coaches, the partners, the tribal chiefs. By spelling it out so publicly, I was making the responsibility a collective one.

They would have to change, but so would I. I set up a 40m sprint test, one I had run in England with high-speed cameras, an electronic wind gauge, GPS trackers tucked between each man's shoulder-blades and laser timing, the video clip of each effort instantly Bluetoothed to the players' complementary iPads. In Suva the boys started by one of the coconut trees and finished at a plastic cone. I timed them on a hand-held stopwatch.

It was the slowest I had ever seen sevens players recorded. It made no sense. The boys had no endurance, but Fijian players always had immense top-end speed. Where was it? Had that gone too?

Physio William strolled over, all wisdom and worldly knowledge. Ben. Get them to chase each other.

Why?

Just try it.

I began again, this time with one man by the coconut tree, another five metres behind him. When I blew my whistle it was like watching a pair of synchronised explosions.

William came over again. Give the guy in front a ball.

I did. The explosions blew past on fast-forward.

Sports science had taken me a long way, but I was a man up a creek trying to use a laptop as a paddle. Running 40 metres for no reason made no sense to a Fijian. It wasn't far enough to count as a workout. It wasn't anything at all. Make it a chase, make it a competition not to get caught, and suddenly the pitch came alive. Give Fijian men a ball, ask them to score a try or save one to win a match, and they were forces unleashed. The flaw had been mine.

Fiji sprawled around me, complicated, contrary, dark hills piling up inland, reefs and breakers rolling in from the empty ocean. Coaching players in England had been easy; I knew how they felt, because I had been one myself. I ate the same things and I listened to the same music. Here I was a stranger, off my charts, out of my depth. I needed to leave the Novotel and its breakfast buffet and its bar serving Fiji Gold in chilled glasses. I couldn't change Fijian rugby without Fiji changing me first.

I had spent a few late nights in conversation with a sevens obsessive named Culden Kamea, who ran the country's big rugby magazine, *Teivovo*. Culden was from Fiji's second city, Lautoka, over on the west coast of Viti Levu. His son Randall had been capped by the national sevens side before taking a professional contract over in France. It bemused him that no previous coach had bothered leaving the main island to see what talent might lie undiscovered in the hundreds of islands and villages, that team selection was made from the comfy office of the Fiji Rugby Union in Suva, rather than the real guts of the nation.

I needed to understand Fiji, and needed Fiji to understand me. And so a few mornings later Culden and I packed up and set off: four and a half hours north from the capital up Kings Road, through Korovou and Lodoni, hugging the coast, Pacific to our right, rainforest stretching away to our left, to a little dusty town called Natovi Landing. A small ferry tied to the jetty, buses being loaded into the hold alongside cattle and motorbikes, one ramshackle café on the quayside with people drinking sugary tea inside or sitting on cases and lugging parcels outside, kids running around barefoot in shorts and faded rugby shirts, hawking warm *roti* bread or petrified-looking fried fish. Big cakes for sale, smothered in luminous icing.

I bought a little of everything and ate a little bit less, before heading onto the boat and a chugging voyage eastwards to the Lomaiviti islands, Ovalau in our sights.

Ovalau is not big – maybe 10km wide at its broadest point, 13km long, a huge blown-out volcanic crater in the middle cradling villages and cool lakes. It has steep forested hills down the east coast, rolling grassy hills to the north, a scattering of tiny coral islands hanging off its southern tip and 9,000 inhabitants, all of them clinging on to a dusty existence, most of them in old rugby shirts.

I felt out of place. As we were dropped off at the jetty at Buresala Wharf, I was the only one in socks and shoes. I was also the only one with red hair and freckles, and the only one smearing himself with Factor 100 sun-cream. There was no traffic as we jolted and bumped along the dirt road, through the mahogany trees and around limping dogs, past the homestead of the Patterson family who ran the ferry service, a TV in one of the open-sided buildings showing an old Fiji match. Warm puddles in the road splashed brown water up the side of our jeep, a sticky heat sending sweat creeping down my back and the runny sun-cream into the corners of my eyes.

Levuka had been Fiji's first capital, albeit at a time when capitals could consist of two streets, five pubs and a load of drunken whalers. It still looked paused in an ancient era, single-storey clapboard houses alongside corrugated shacks, a solitary sealed road running from the tuna cannery at the south end of Beach Street up past the dark tower of the Catholic church. Narrow alleys climbed up the hills, houses set on the grass alongside.

There was one hotel, the optimistically named Royal. We stayed instead at a guest house, the New Mavinda Lodge, no air-con in the room, just a creaking fan and a mesh over the window to keep the flies out. From the front porch you could look out over the ocean at the sinking sun and see the silhouettes of long, thin boats chugging in on rattling outboard motors, men with kit-bags on their laps coming ashore for the rugby tournament that weekend.

Breakfast the following morning was less a meal than a meet and greet. Word had spread that the new Fiji coach was in town; heads came round the door, bodies and helloes followed: *Bula! Bula!* In an escalating convoy we trekked up a hill to Wainaloka village, the grass on the pitch uneven and harsh, creaking wooden bungalows nestled close to the touchlines. I was led to the halfway line and a large sofa with a rug laid on the turf in front of it. A parasol was stuck in the ground behind me and angled forward. On my left on a wooden table were two big metal urns of tea. I took a sip from the cup that was offered to me; it had so much sugar in it that the teaspoon almost stood up straight. To my right was another table, this one creaking under the weight of the cakes that various women in *sulu-i-ras*, Fijian sarongs, were bringing over, the icing fluorescent once again. Behind us, under the trees, the old boys were sipping something from old coconut shells, kicking back with grins and chuckles and nodding of heads.

The talk came from every direction. Would you like to try this cake? Maybe some more of this one? Which one would you say was best? Several large and competitive ladies all leaned in with worried expressions awaiting my opinion.

I watched the games hammering past in front of me. Each village had their own team, picked from a pool that was big in talent if limited in size, 50-year-old men lining up outside 14-year-olds. All of them had brand-new shirts, saved up for over the past year despite life teetering along the breadline, to be worn around the village for the next 12 months too. The tackling was brutal, wild shots aimed up high, necks and heads taking a battering and the referees letting it all go, but the offloading was sensational – players wrapped up in the tackle somehow finding a way to flick the ball away to a team-mate steaming in from behind, the ball never going dead, no one ever taking the easy option or the ball to the ground.

It was patchy. Not every outrageous pass or step or dummy came off. But when it did, the tries that followed were sublime, seven men linked up at thundering pace, running angles that made no sense until they suddenly did, the ball cosseted and then smuggled away, speed from men who should have lost it long ago, awareness and imagination from kids not old enough to know better.

Talking all around me – watch this player, this is the village out the back, another slice of this one? Questions from me too – Who's that number 6? – and first a name coming back and then his family brought over, everyone excited that maybe this kid was going to get invited to the capital to train with the big boys. Maybe that referee could step up to work with us. Maybe that guy over there, the one organising his village's team and kit and food, could be the manager I needed for our next tournament away.

Ovalau had a reputation. In the 15-a-side game it was a tough place to go. Big teams from the bigger islands would travel over on the boat, arrive seasick, struggle on the tight, bumpy pitch and go home a few hours later with a chastening defeat to take back with them. In sevens, Ovalau's various teams took players from where they could. There was a team of wardens from the local prison, their star winger one of the inmates. You might not think a load of prison guards would want to let fly a man convicted of violent assault, but where was he going to run to?

I began to learn how players might be discovered and promoted. If you played well for the wardens' team, you would find yourself given a job at the main prison in the capital, Suva, and with it a place in their higher-profile team. It was the same with the police team, or the army. Rugby was the magic conveyor belt that took you from your dusty home towards the brighter lights in the far-off distance. There were few smooth rides; the dashing inmate looked good enough for my nascent squad, but with his criminal record he could never get the visa he needed to play overseas. Talented kids in the Army would be released from official duties at the first hint of a rugby call-up, yet they could also get lost in boozing and fighting when on leave with the regulars. Bright sunshine and storm clouds.

That night I was called to the elder's house, up steep, broken steps through the middle of the village, all the natural light gone in a fingersnap. Dogs asleep on the warm stone, tails to be stepped over if you could make them out. One large room, coconut matting on the floor to sit on, no glass in the windows and people standing patiently outside or staring in. This was a *talanoa*, the time for stories, for sharing experiences and thoughts, for speaking with warmth and with welcome.

All the men sat at the front, the women busy with pots and ladles in the back. Food was brought forward, the explanations careful and slow. You have to try this... We call this one *kokoda*.

There were huge tubs of curry, chicken on the bone, heavy hunks of lamb, meat that I couldn't recognise by smell or taste, bobbing around in sauces thick with fat slices of chilli. Some sort of seaweed dish, piles of *roti* bread being torn apart, lumps of sticky rice taken in handfuls and dipped in.

I asked for a knife and fork. Discreet laughter followed. I tried a few words – *vinaka vakalevu*, thank you very much – and the laughter burst out through the cracks. Trying to pick out the bones with a knife and fork proved as troublesome as you'd expect in a room full of people using their fingers.

I was exhausted, jetlag on top of the previous day's travelling and sketchy sleep and a day in the sun on full alert. In England I would have slipped away with a quick goodnight. Here, where else was I going to go?

A cold beer would have been perfect. There was no cold beer. Instead, as the plates were cleared away, another big tub was brought into the centre of the circle. It was *kava* time.

The *tanoa*, a bowl, looked like it was full of muddy water. I would learn the secrets behind it over the forthcoming months: a root, grown for three or four years, sold on the roadside by kids on Friday and Saturday nights, bashed down into a powder, the strength of it depending on which island and soil it came from and whether it had been cut with anything cheaper. Wrapped in a cloth, or an old sock if the new Fiji coach wasn't in the room and there was nothing else to hand, soaked in warm water like a giant intoxicating tea-bag until all the juices had been extracted and all the good stuff was in there.

Kava brings people together. *Kava* creates the warm vibes and the talkative, contemplative moods that make a *talanoa* happen. As the guest you get served first, your half-coconut acting as a *bilo*, a makeshift cup. There are two claps, the *cobo*, one hand on top of the other, a greeting in Fijian, and then you reply with a clap of your own and a *Bula!* – to the village, to the elders, to the province.

I took my *bilo* in two hands and knocked it back as instructed. Three claps, a shout of *Maca!* after another nudge in the ribs. The *bilo* had been three-quarters full, what Fijians call a high tide. A half-full *bilo* is a low tide, a *bilo* filled to the brim is a tsunami. The tides kept coming for me, and with them a sense of soft relaxation, of feeling at home all these miles from familiar shores. Smiles all around, talk of rugby, talk of coming back again soon.

Maybe the RFU should have invested some of their millions in a supply of ethically sourced *kava*.

But then again, maybe not. Later on I was struck down with vomiting and diarrhoea. This *kava* was made with local water, and my London guts couldn't cope with it. (At later *talanoas*, the white guy with the red hair would be offered bottled water in his *kava*.)

As I lay there that night, churning, blanching, I was bitten by a spider on the arm that was probably thrown theatrically over my pale face, and I awoke sweating to see my limb swollen up like a balloon animal. Man overboard, man down.

Feeling awful, I went for a walk along the dirt path northwards from Levuka, an invitation from the night before in my mind. St John's College was seven kilometres away, a Catholic school as old as the one I'd left behind in Ealing so many years before, long wooden dorms around the rugby pitch on the grass plateau above the sea, a tall church like something plucked from rural France, if it hadn't been made of whitewashed blocks of coral stone.

The kids there could play well, and they could talk rugby like old men in West Country boozers. Quite a few would be picked to represent Fiji in the Commonwealth Youth Games a year and a half later, including five of the girls. They were fit, and each term the teacher in charge – a priest named Father John – would take them all on a brutal trek to the highest point on the island. They cared about the national side almost more than its coach did, which was one of the reasons why I would bring the team back to train there 12 months later for a camp that connected the superstar players with the grass roots in a way unimaginable for any other elite team.

33

I had never been a teenage traveller. In my gap year between school and university I'd broken my ankle in training and so spent the time working at Twickenham rather than away with a backpack; there'd been a little Interrailing, and a couple of months in Zanzibar in my early 20s, and with England I had gone from Sydney to Hong Kong to Dubai, but always in short bursts and in good hotels. Out here, on the other side of the world, my aim was to stay open to all the fresh, disconcerting experiences. I didn't want to be the bloke who gets full tribal tattoos in his first week and is then working in the City a year later, but I also wanted to avoid the slow death of the expat embrace – cocktail parties with people I had nothing in common with except a passport, a curious attempt to recreate the dullest parts of English or Australasian culture in a place twice as intriguing.

If I couldn't deal with Fijian customs, what really was going to change? When I sat down for breakfast at St John's with kids eating white bread and tuna from the cannery, telling them I was off simple carbs wouldn't really work. When the instant coffee came round I couldn't push it away and insist on my usual double espresso. I had assumed the food was prepared with unwashed hands, and I found out quickly that the handshakes were constant and always dusty. I had a little tube of antibacterial hand-gel in my pocket, but I realised just as rapidly that getting it out and rubbing it all over my hands after every greeting was as rude as baring my backside.

Showers in rural Fiji weren't hot. Toilets encouraged you to get in and out as quickly as possible. Guest-house fans sometimes worked and frequently didn't. But there could be no complaining, because I was always given the best.

Meals would be served on Fiji Time, and with a vast supporting cast. I would be told to sit down at a certain hour, and the food would arrive two or three hours later, after all the friends and relations of the hosts had discussed rugby selections and tactics with me, when I had passed through my initial hunger and started getting hungry instead for the next meal down the line. There was no requesting a specific dish or asking for it to be cooked in a particular way; you ate what you were given, when it arrived, and you understood that this was a gift that, after one lacklustre tournament and a headful of doubts, you barely deserved.

On that first trip to Ovalau my bag was full: a laptop with a couple of movies downloaded onto it, a solar charger, smart-phone. The smart part of the phone was the least utilised part of it; there was enough network to send a text message and no signal nor wifi for anything more. The laptop stayed in the bag, because there were people to talk to and meals to wait for. By the time I came back with the boys the following year the bag was a third of the size and there were no trainers on my feet either. Your feet dried off more quickly without them, and your feet washed more easily than white pumps. Only the sun-cream stayed, part of a huge box my big sister had sent over for me, its application rather like that famous story about painting the Forth Bridge: you started smearing it on at one end, and by the time you'd reached the other end, it was time to start again.

Back on the main island, five weeks to go until the next leg of the World Series, I needed a training pitch away from the army's heavy gaze where I could push the players' physical conditioning to its limits. Forty minutes west along the coast from Suva, just off the main road in Pacific Harbour, was a small resort called Uprising. The owner and I got on immediately, laughing when he told me that the plot had originally been stacked with marijuana plants, tonnes and tonnes of them, and when the police had come to burn them all down there had been significant gatherings of locals in the downwind direction. The pitch wasn't great – no padding at the base of the posts, no flags in the corners, not particularly flat – but Rene was keen to improve it. There was also a little *bure*, a cottage, where I could stay. No more Novotel, a little less distance between me and sea and mountains.

There was also no training kit, no water and only a couple of balls, yet William and I worked the players relentlessly. In that defeat to England on the Gold Coast we had never looked like winning, no matter that the scoreboard suggested there were only a couple of tries in it. Even the points we had scored had come from a little glimpse of individual brilliance rather than the sort of creativity and togetherness that could be maintained.

We were due to play England again in the group stages, which in Dubai was particularly bad news. I had won the tournament there with them twice, the combination of the relatively short flight from London, the lack of jetlag, a typically serious England pre-season of training and the large expat community making a blend that other teams struggled to match. Fiji, by contrast, always underperformed there – the last ones in on the cheapest flights, out of shape after a summer doing whatever paid a little money, often a new coach on a short-term charge picking players he was familiar with and ones pushed his way from people and places he knew.

This new coach understood that there was a limit to what I could do. The fitness came first, then adding to the squad some of the in-form young talent I'd spotted on my brief travels, among them that giant kid Semi Kunatani I'd seen tearing it up at the Coral Coast tournament. Kick-offs were the next simple fix. Rather than spraying them anywhere, without any thought of what might follow, I got them to aim at Semi. Anyone could have done it before, but no one had. And then the most uncomplicated of defensive strategies: keep all seven men on the pitch. Don't try to take your opponent's head off, don't try to test the flexibility of his neck, don't give the referee any reason to confirm the stereotypes he has of casually violent Pacific islanders and start waving his yellow card at the team in white.

The creativity, for now, would have to come away from the pitch. I had a friend in Abu Dhabi who ran the city's Harlequins club. Andy liked me and he loved Fiji, so from his own pocket he paid for us all to fly over a week in advance of the tournament rather than a few days before as usual, putting us up in a hotel. All he asked in return was that the boys came down to coach the kids at the club and then played a no-contact game against the first VII. It wouldn't have worked with England; the players carried with them too much natural reserve, were too conscious of looking stupid when messing around with the kids or coming up against keen if limited amateurs. To my Fiji team it came as second nature; village life was all about playing rugby with kids, making fun of themselves, playing against any age and at every opportunity. Rather than looking to swerve the extracurricular efforts, they would ask when they could come back to coach the kids again.

That universal love for Fiji would touch us wherever we went. In almost every city we visited supporters would want to help however they could. A few months on, when our Emirates pilot found out none of us were getting paid, he organised a whip-round among his fellow pilots to send us home with a couple of hundred dollars each.

It all made a difference. The lack of money meant our training camps could only be short, and short training camps meant the players going back to their villages to continue eating the diet they always had. Sometimes that could mean one meal a day, breakfast skipped, all the hidden sugar in the bread at lunch sending them crashing in the afternoon, some lads coming to training having not eaten for 24 hours.

As we eased up on training in the last few days before the Dubai sevens began, the deeply ingrained bad habits began to resurface. At the hotel breakfast buffet the lads would find a long loaf, a great slab of white bread that might last a family in England a week, slice it in half lengthways, fill it with butter and just start munching. If there were sausages they liked them fried in coconut oil. Rather than use a mug to fill up from the tea urn, they would take the bowl left under the tap to collect drips and fill that instead, enough tea to keep a building site going all day.

I spotted one of my new players, Mosese Mawalu, strolling back to his table with a tower of ten *pains au chocolat*, each with a fried egg on top. He gave me a big grin. 'Eggs are good, right? Bread is good!'

I kept it easy: show me a colourful plate. Oranges, banana, avocado, a couple of eggs not balanced on a pastry underneath. I gave them rest, tapering the hard sessions off so their bodies could absorb the benefits while bouncing back fresh for the matches to come. I took away the free sports drink that was given to every team in the tournament; the boys, assuming they were healthy, were necking them late at night, adding even more sugar to a diet already drenched in the stuff.

They responded. Fiji had never won the Dubai sevens in more than 25 years of trying, but we were too good this time for England, by a solitary try at least, and then, against reigning world champions New Zealand in the semi-final, all that beautiful chaos suddenly came together in 14 rampaging minutes.

In the dressing-room beforehand I hadn't been sure. The players were singing and dancing, something none of my England players ever did until the Christmas party. They were joking around with each other, relaxed, not thinking about our opponents at all. I had also given them Red Bull for the first time, which had felt a bit like giving a can of it to your mother. The outcome could not be entirely predicted, but it would certainly be interesting.

We absolutely blitzed them. Everything we touched came off – tries from everywhere, rugby that had you whooping, the most successful team in World Series history so stunned that they were shouting at each other on the pitch, which was bad enough among the seven of them but was even worse when they accidentally put eight on the pitch instead.

We won 44–0. New Zealand's heaviest-ever defeat. Eight tries to nil, Osea and Semi on the board and brilliant. Kiwi coach Sir Gordon Tietjens so furious afterwards that he walked away without shaking my hand.

Into the final, South Africa dispatched 29–17, two of their tries coming with the match long since gone. By that stage it almost didn't matter. New Zealand had always been the yardstick for Fiji – multiple World Cup and Commonwealth gold medal winners, the country where so many Fijians went looking for work, the nation that nabbed so many young Fijian talents and naturalised them to play in black instead of white. The issue I now had was keeping expectations in check, because none of these players were contracted, and all of them could be poached by other clubs, as had happened so many times before. We also had no backroom team or sponsor and thus no money for kit, and pitches, and water, and rugby balls, and travel to the remaining seven tournaments. This is not going to be the norm, I told celebrating players and giddy journalists. Don't expect sunshine all the time, you're going to get showers as well. But you can see what happens with a little preparation: if we can instil some of the stuff that's missing, just imagine what we might be able to do.

The old sporting cliché says that you learn more from defeat than victory. But I was learning plenty from limited success too: that when the boys were relaxed and having fun, they played to their best; that I would have to herd them to their meals and then navigate them past the sugary trapdoors; that you had to put a water bottle in their hands after matches, or they would forget to drink anything until just before the next game when it was far too late.

There is always a temptation for a coach to over-prepare. You can spend two hours with your players in a classroom, picking out multiple opposition players to watch and all manner of different plays, reviewing previous matches in slow motion and from every available angle, turning a few key points into a blizzard of white noise and feedback. It can make you feel better about yourself as a coach. I'm doing my job – must be, look at the hours of scrutiny I'm putting my players under. It makes your boss feel better about himself: look at all this money we're spending on analysts and laptops and cameras on drones. Less can never mean more.

Except it can. A game of sevens takes 14 minutes, two halves of 10 minutes in a big final. If you can't see something having watched it back once, you're not watching it properly. If you can't condense your instructions into three or four key points, you're creating a fog rather than shining a light.

With Fiji I now knew I had to keep it simple and deliver it in a way that worked for them rather than the England team I had left behind. Four things to think about before a game: this is the line-out that we can use; this is the kick-off that we'll do; this is how we're going to defend this; and by the way, he's their star player, so keep an eye on him. Not sitting the boys down in front of a whiteboard or a big screen, but sitting down next to them with a piece of paper: look at the kick-off, see how their defence is set up, see the hole here. Then I would go to the next player and do exactly the same. As my relationship with Osea developed I would show it to him first – look, we'd get a bit of change out of attacking here – and he would talk to the backs while I talked to the forwards.

It was often a slow buy-in. The young players would need a little reminder just before a game, and so I might reinforce the message again by asking an open-ended question and getting them to come up with the solution, or asking the player running the water on at breaks to mention it once more. Always the tactics were simple in execution, and always limited in number.

It turned out that Fijian coaches had never bothered replaying clips of matches to the players, either because they didn't want to review them themselves or because they saw no point. The first time I did it, when we were away at a tournament, sticking one game on in the dinner hall and wandering off to get a coffee, I came back to find them watching it like a movie – not with a frown, pointing out what had gone wrong, but laughing uproariously at mistakes and standing up and cheering at the tries, taking the mickey out of anyone who missed a tackle or an over-lap. New Zealand and England were looking in to find out what all the laughter was about.

I loved it. A little part of me wanted to tell them to learn from it as well as enjoying it, but I soon realised that was happening regardless. Why get stressed about something that should end in entertainment and fun anyway? Routines can suck all of that away – finish a game, bang, get in the ice baths, stick on your recovery tights, here's your protein drink, here's your food, now sit down and listen to your coach drone on about that last match and then the next one for the same endless time. No wonder players and coaches get burned out. No wonder I had almost forgotten the simple pleasures of the game.

In that big RFU machine, it had all felt so robotic and arti-ficial by the end. It wasn't me. As a scrum-half at Cambridge and Nottingham and West Hartlepool, I had loved to play off the cuff, and as a young coach, mentored by former Bath, Ireland and England coach Brian Ashton, it was the creative rather than the pre-programmed that excited me. I would tell stories to get points across to players – *Star Wars* analogies for some, for others the climax to the film *Seven* to understand that every action has a consequence. I loved having to find unusual methods to get diverse characters to flourish. Here was a chance not just to find something new but to rediscover the old me too.

THREE

Noel and I meet when we're nine years old. We are in the same class at school. I'm a little bit taller than him, but he stands out in other ways, one of three black kids in the whole year. I'd gone to Strand-on-the-Green primary school, our annual school photo showing faces much more representative of this diverse part of west London, but my new school is predominantly white as well as strict. I'm there on a scholarship, feeling out of place, and Noel is there on his own, sent over from Zambia by his parents, living in a flat down the road with an unmarried, older guy who knows his dad through some work they did together out in southern Africa.

This man looks after Noel for a small fee. I'm not sure how much fun it is, because Noel is always with me and my family. When we play rugby we are in partnership at half-back, me scrum-half, getting him the ball, him fly-half, deciding how the team should use it. We have a PE teacher who is straight from central casting – Welsh,

sportsman's moustache, permanently tracksuited – and he coaches
us well, realising that kids who get on make better team-mates and
that being team-mates only strengthens a young friendship.

Noel uses my house as his own. Tea after school, lunch after
rugby for Richmond minis on Sunday, scoffing it down so we can
get back out in the garden to spin flat passes to each other or volley
the football against the fence. Half-term weekends he comes away
with us down to Fishponds in Bristol, summer holidays we all pile
down to Weston-super-Mare, the huge expanse of sand at low tide
perfect for football and rugby and tennis and running races.

We're together all the time. I can't imagine how we couldn't be.

Approaching Christmas in 2013, three months after the
phone call on Richmond Green, two months after that
jetlagged landing, I was settling into some sort of broken
routine at the little cabin at Uprising resort in Pacific
Harbour.

Natalie was still in England, and while we would try
to speak most nights on the phone, the time difference
made it difficult, one of us wide awake and full of chat
while the other was heading into or out of sleep. There
weren't many others around – sometimes Rene, the owner
and also a good sevens coach himself, James, the hotel
manager, occasionally a few random guests at the resort.
I missed espresso and I missed the buzz of London, the
non-stop action and the mates to hook up with for a drink,
the sense of being at the centre of everything even if you
weren't directly involved, of soaking up new music and
new looks and ideas almost by osmosis. I had music stacked
up on playlists on my phone and I had a few books, but my
working days were so long that the nights came in early
and fast. As dusk fell great bats would come squealing in

over the mangroves, black against the sky like swooping kites. I would have a hot chocolate outside as the world turned and be asleep by 9 p.m., exhausted by the heat and heavy thoughts.

Days began with the natural alarm call of animals and bright sunlight. Out of bed at 5 a.m., wandering outside, stretching and yawning, sitting down on the sand with my back against the trunk of a coconut tree and a coffee made with beans I'd brought over from Borough Market in south London.

The beach stretched for a few kilometres in either direction, grass and sand in front of my cabin and then a slope down to the water, flat and calm inside the distant reef out in Rovodrau Bay. On a clear morning I could see Beqa island, 12km offshore. It was known by the locals as *Daku*, or Shark island, because of all the tiger sharks and bull sharks, silvertips and nurse sharks lurking in the sudden drop-off outside its wide lagoon, hills up above where the Sawau tribesmen would dig big pits of charcoal and walk the white-hot coals. To its west lay Yanuca, a low-slung hang-out for surfers chasing the Frigates Passage break.

Coconut trees all around me, dull thuds if a nut fell to the sand or rhythmical hacking if one of the villagers was up there bringing down breakfast. No cars going past but plenty of noise as the huts came to life, shouts of *Bula!* – Greetings! I would pass 20-odd cooks and cleaners and bar-staff on the short walk to the resort dining room, and all of them would stop to say hello and how are you – Jone (who looked like a Fijian Marvin Hagler), Nancy, Mia.

I had been given a team manager for that first tournament on the Gold Coast, an affable old boy who had never done the job before and was primarily there for a free

47

holiday. It transpired that his home province had voted in the new Fiji Rugby board, and this was his reward. All the logistics we needed, all the administration and flight booking and bus sorting, all that was left to whoever might pick it up in his absence. In our little unit he considered himself chief of the village, because that's what he was at home, so the idea that he might need to work never occurred to him.

The next guy, a former international prop forward called Paula Biu, was friendly and helpful to me and Natalie, but was always bringing his mates into camp, and was more suited to the 15-a-side game than the pastoral side of sevens. We used him for a while but moved him on when we could.

And then came the third one, Ropate Kauvesi, the only one who had actually applied for the job. He was a man who could always lift my mood. He was naturally big, pushing 180kg, vast arms and paws on him, so ursine that I would end up calling him *Bear Levu*, Big Bear. His father had been the mayor of Suva, but after backing the wrong coup, he had been placed on a travel blacklist and left his role. Ropate had grown up in Raiwaqa, a notorious neighbourhood in Suva, and was now living in the roughest part of town, continuing to put on weight.

He had a backstory. As a kid he had been some player, star of the annual national schools tournament with the powerhouse Ratu Kadavelevu School in Suva, a good enough back-row forward to go on tour to Australia and then get a rugby scholarship to Scots College in Wellington and be converted into a mobile front row. He was good enough to become a future All Black too. Instead he had stayed on to study, working as a predictably effective bouncer in bars in Wellington, working in a bank during the day. When he had first arrived at camp I assumed he was simply another government plant. Keep an eye on Ryan, enjoy yourself while you're there.

Instead he came on tour and excelled. Immediate rapport with the players, relaxed and funny, incredibly organised. We would get to the airport to find him charming everyone at the check-in desk and somehow getting all the boys upgrades. You'd find out later that he'd been there the day before with some sort of sweetener, all above board, before staying up late fine-tuning his Excel spreadsheets and looking into the worst-case scenario for bus times from the hotel to the stadium. On the training pitch he would start doing the warm-up with the team and have them all in stitches with his slow-motion skills and tricks.

Everyone he met seemed to become his friend. Introduce someone to him once, let them spend five minutes with him and for the next year they would always be asking you, How's Ropate? Hanging out with him over breakfast or during the evening at his place, I would just sit back and absorb all the jokes and stories, both of us sipping a Milo milkshake. Fijians, I was learning, loved to talk. Gossip and rumours would fly about the islands on what they called the coconut wireless – rapid word of mouth, exaggeration and tittle-tattle. Ropate seemed to be both broadcast studio and bass speaker.

In a very short space of time I became very close to him. One night he knocked on my door.

Ben, I think you've got a sore throat. I noticed in training that you didn't look very well.

Ropate, I'm fine.

No, you're ill. I've got you some tablets – make sure you take one of these every day.

He winked, handed me a six-pack of giant chocolate bars and grinned.

He and William would sneak off after dinner at tournaments and come back later smelling of fish and chips or KFC. The two of them were getting closer the more time they spent in each other's company. In the gym I could hear the boys asking mock-innocent questions the next morning – Ropate, where did you go last night, we missed you... William, is there a fried-chicken place in this part of town? Ropate loved it, a friendly uncle to them rather than a martinet, a manager they would all obey instantly because they liked him so much.

Stress didn't seem to affect him. He could deal with delays and cancellations with a shrug and a smile. By doing so he chilled me out as well. I'm not someone who finds physical intimacy easy, but he quickly became a man I loved to hug.

Ropate off the pitch, Osea on it. My captain lived about an hour away in the opposite direction to my burgeoning manager, staying at the family home with his mother and preacher father. I relished how he challenged himself each day in training, setting an example to the others even as he was standing up to those above him at Fiji Rugby, and I soon moved him in from the wing to fly-half, to have him right in the middle of things, as much of a link between me and the players as that position made him the fulcrum between the forwards and backs.

We had to bond in a different way to the way Ropate and I did. There could be no beers with Osea, with any of the players; that was where I established the boundary between ally and mate, even if we would have been rock-solid friends had rugby not been around. Instead that intimacy, that sharing of emotion and openness, came from something that I had left behind years ago.

It's hard to pin down exactly what *lotu* is. It's Christianity, but in multiple contradictory forms; it's prayer, but as much about sharing your hopes with those around you as asking God for special favours. It's hymns, but more about communal singing, a potent mix of male-voice choir and beautiful harmonies rather than stodgy, plodding Victorian moral fables.

The players were all believers. They just believed in whichever blend of local myth and imported catechism worked for them, or whatever missionary had reached their village first in the colonising scramble of the late-nineteenth century. There were Catholics, Anglicans, Methodists, Seventh Day Adventists and the Church of the Latter Day Saints. Most of the Fijian population with Indian roots were Hindu.

Each morning before training, always at tournaments and often after training too, we would have a *lotu*. All of us sitting together, sometimes a local minister or one of the players' elders leading it, hymn-books passed round, singing that was deep and melodic and stirring. It was never too structured and it seldom lasted more than 20 minutes, a collective pause in a frantic physical day, deep breathing and mindfulness and team bonding wrapped up in a language that signified more.

I was brought up Catholic. My dad and grandad had grown up in working-class Manchester, part of the great Irish industrial diaspora, my grandma spending Saturday nights down a local Irish Club full of songs and beer. The religion had come down through the generations; at my secondary school, run by the Jesuits, you were made to put the initials AMDG at the top of each page of work: *ad majorem Dei gloriam*, for the greater glory of God. That sort of thing becomes instinctive – I was still habitually writing it on my essays at university until I realised what I was doing – but the rest of it gradually became oppressive to me. Church on Sunday, again on Wednesdays at school. By my late teens I would tell my dad I was going to the last mass on Sunday to postpone the tedium as long as possible, walk past the church and keep going, walking for as long as the service should roughly take, sticking my head in on the way back to see who the priest was, in case I was asked when I got home.

So *lotu* shouldn't have worked for me, but it did. In the mornings, sat on mats outside one of the rooms, the prayer might be that we were going to have a good day and that we'd all look after each other. There would be a song, we would all hug, and then go to breakfast. In the evening the prayers would include thanks for the day we had shared together, rugby threaded through it all. If a player wanted to say something to the group they would stand up: I'd like to apologise for being rubbish in training today; thanks to you for the water at the end. It became almost like a team meeting, finishing with a few practicals: training at 10 a.m. tomorrow, boys, breakfast at 8 a.m., *lotu* 7.30 a.m. If there were guitars, one of the players might strum a few chords while the rest of us clapped along and tried to harmonise in thirds.

I would sing along. Three big hymns – 'Au Rei Vei Kemuni', 'Tou Cakacaka Tiko Ga', 'Isn't the Love of God Something Wonderful'. Osea gave me his old song-book, and I would mangle some of the words and whisper questions about others – What does that one mean? – Oh, love... The boys would laugh when I started singing in Fijian or got words wrong, and it all added to the informality and relaxation. Word spread further that I was joining in, that I was learning some of the bigger tunes off by heart, and the surprise and respect started reverberating back down the coconut wireless.

Occasionally on a free Sunday I would go to the local church with my landlady's mum Sophie, just for a few songs and a glimpse at another part of Fijian life, to be told which players I should select by 60-year-old women who could reel off the team that had won the Hong Kong sevens a decade before. When the mass finished a few decorations round the building would come down and a couple of others would go up and the Latter Day Saints gang would come in for their service.

That first year had to be an education, but it also had to be about boundaries. By absorbing as much of the local culture as I could, I hoped to be able to sieve out what could drive us on and what was holding us back. *Lotus* worked. They connected us as a group. When village elders came into camp overnight or to tournaments en masse, it fractured us instead.

It had always happened. An elder deciding to lead his own *lotu*, everything delayed by an hour. Relatives coming to the hotel where we were staying for a tournament and sleeping in the players' rooms, two or three of them on the floor, bringing their own friends or others from that province to join in too. With it came the *kava* ceremonies – an intrinsic part of Fijian life, but out of context in a hotel in Cape Town at two in the morning with a match later that day, so many high tides and tsunamis that what they called a wash-down followed to flush all that natural sedative away, alcohol from the bar and out of suitcases, beer following *bilo* until the *tanoa* had been emptied.

If an elder or older uncle is with you, you cannot leave until they say so. If you mix *kava* with booze and players who have been training hard and sweating all morning on the training pitch, you get trouble – fast-food wrappers in the bins and corridors, arguments and aggression, women who aren't wives or partners, bars getting smashed up.

Culture could be a cover for so much. A minister coming into camp to lay hands on the players, telling them he is inspiring them to blessed new heights, instead waking them up in the middle of the night for prayers so he can go back home and show his mates the photos of him with Fiji's sevens team. Keeping the players apart from all un-announced visitors caused a lot of consternation: it's not easy saying no to an ambassador, or a man who runs an island, or a minister who is used to his words opening doors and bowing heads.

Life in Fiji also brought frequent spells of simple magic. Sitting out on the thick, coarse tropical grass around the pitch after training, locals coming round with a big bag of fresh green coconuts, three cuts from the machete and off with its head, passing the coconut round and taking big slugs of the cool sweet juice, laughing and joking with the boys, all of them shattered but happy from working so hard.

There was so much I had to fix, so much we didn't have. In those moments of togetherness it all felt worth it. It drove me on. I wasn't being paid, and my own savings were going on new rugby balls and petrol for the team bus. I had problems with the board and worries about the government. Natalie was thousands of miles away and distant emotionally on bad days too. Under the palm trees, wind coming off the lagoon, shirt stuck to your chest with sweat and smiles all around, you could let some of that go.

And some of things they could do in training… I had a little drill that I plagiarised from Barcelona FC, called *El Rondo*, where they would have five or six players in a circle, two in the middle trying to intercept and everything one touch per man. My rugby version had three attackers, two defenders, a small square of pitch to play in and tries to be scored. It was designed to promote deft touches, ingenuity, steps and swerves, and it soon became a showcase for the best of the Fijian way. Slow, slow, quick, quick, bang – one ridiculous pass, an offload designed to beat it, another to top that one. It was mesmerising to watch, the tricks when I put them against each other one on one – I'll kick the ball to you, you try to beat me, I try to bring you down – enough to make you whoop. A sidestep that put the defender on his backside would be met with explosions of laughter. Someone would then try to come up with a better one. All the time pushing each other, all the time learning, every bit of it fun.

The World Series continued with mixed results: beaten comfortably by Samoa in the quarter-finals in Port Elizabeth; beaten by New Zealand and Australia in the group stages out in Las Vegas. For all the rapier work in training, there were also many chinks in our armour. After every tournament another player I was trying to develop would be poached away by an overseas club, offering a contract where we had none, offering wages for his family when we could provide nothing but coconuts. The ones who stayed with us were being called back into the police or army or wardens' teams, forced to play in competitions a couple of days later and coming back to us injured or exhausted.

It made my increasingly regular meetings with Frank all the more fraught. I knew he watched every game, and I knew he had people in his ear telling him that this foreign coach was clueless, that I was trying to rebuild a broken reputation off the back of Fijian talent. When he would summon me to his house in the Domain part of Suva, just below the parliament buildings and the foreign embassies, I would have to observe all the correct formalities in exactly the right way. No eye contact when he was speaking, making sure I was barefoot, a simple reply to his initial greeting: Very nice to meet you again, sir. Letting him dominate the grip when we shook hands, his hand on top, always being physically below him, murmuring, *Tolou, tolou*… (derived from 'too low' in English) if I had to stand up to leave while he was still seated on the mats.

In our private conversations I could call him by his first name, although that took time. He made it clear that I would be given the same chance as his ministers: this is your area, do it properly and I'll leave you alone. That made sense; his life was based around clear leadership and tight control. At the same time, knowing you were nominally free to go to the Sports Council to try to negotiate some sort of budget was somewhat compromised by the fact that the head of the Sports Council was his daughter.

Litiana was actually extremely pleasant and good at her job too. There was also a New Zealander named Peter Mazey who worked with her who was always very understanding. But I was glad I found out who Litiana was before my first trip there, before I sat down to complain about my missing salary or that Frank's brother-in-law on the rugby board was being a pain in the backside. All the time I would be looking out for these hidden trip-wires, trying to understand the real mapping at work, knowing that anything I said to anyone could find its way back to Frank on the coconut wireless. It made me cautious and it made me listen all the more. I would see someone surprising getting a plum job and slowly work out that there was a cousin in common somewhere along the line, or that the conditions of the post included guaranteeing a certain number of votes when the time was right. I realised too that there was nothing to be gained by being critical or publicly cynical. It was happening whether I worried about it or not, and allowing myself to get sucked into the internal machinations would either drive me round the bend or flush me down it.

At least you knew where you stood with Frank. In some ways he was a supersized version of a headmaster I'd come across early in my teaching career, a wizened old disciplinarian who ran his school with the same manifest authority. A note in your pigeonhole summoning you to his office would pump up the heart-rate; walking in, as he sat there in his leather-bound chair, whisky in hand, oil paintings on the wall, made you wonder what might have been overheard in the staffroom. You were never directly told that your job was in danger, only that we should make sure the first XV beat our rivals at the weekend, or else the disappointment really would be widespread.

Thick though the smell of danger around Frank was, it was also preferable to the dog days at the RFU. If I kept Fiji winning, Frank would keep me going. Winning with

England made little difference. You never knew where you stood except that it was slippery and a slope.

In those warm sunlit dawns at Uprising or travelling the interior with Ropate chasing leads about promising players, Fiji could feel like paradise. I had to remind myself of the darkness that came after the sunlight, while never forgetting that it could be that way in the West too. In Britain you can ignore the black undercurrents if you're rich or lucky or naive enough. There are too many degrees of separation between an ordinary life and the ugly stuff that happens at the margins. In Fiji there are no secrets. The wireless may be coconut but it's a fast broadband for rumours. Stories flow around the *talanoa* and come leaching out in the *kava*. Some of it is gossip, some of it made up. The truth surfaces too, benign or strange or menacing.

In those distant cities on World Series trips I would meet Fijians working abroad, some of them from economic necessity, some because Fiji had become a problematic place for them to live since the coup. I would hear murky tales of corruption, shadowy stories about the wrong sort of politicians in prison cells where the light bulbs had been removed and the windows were shuttered. On the Fijileaks website I would be shown photos and documents suggesting all that and more.

To navigate that chaotic world with imperfect knowledge was almost impossible. At the Corrections Centre in Suva, a charity ran the Tagimoucia art gallery, filled with the works of prisoners who were behaving well enough to be allowed access to paint and canvas. I was asked if I would mind one painting my portrait. He seemed a lovely kid – friendly, talented, wise. Aged 18, pissed up and full of teenage anger, he had killed another man in a fight. Now he was all regret and doing a life sentence, no matter how much he changed.

Through the British high commissioner's wife I was introduced to a young Indian girl. She had been caught trying to smuggle a kilogram of cocaine out of the country and into New Zealand. I asked her why she had done it; she said there had been death threats against her family in India had she refused, that she wanted to train as a nurse or maybe even a doctor, and the money was going to pay for her training and living costs.

She was serving 12 years in the toughest prison in the country. Each time I visited, if we could find a quiet corner, she would reveal a little more – that the shame was so great she had not even tried to tell her family where she was, that when she did get out she feared for her life anyway.

I had told my players that the standard you walk past is the standard you become. That was what I held on to now. If I ever saw anything bad or negative with my own eyes and I failed to influence it in the right way, I would have to go. Against the rest I was flotsam on the tide.

FOUR

The sporting day starts early when you're obsessed. Up and already dressed, onto my black, white and silver Raleigh five-speed bike and over to Northfields to meet Darren Fenton, then on to Ealing and the school. There for 7.30 a.m., bikes in the rack and on to the table-tennis tables, four of them in a row, the kids who lived closest already playing. A rankings ladder for us to battle over, always trying to knock off the kid one rung up. A school team to take us on travels and adventures, Noel number-one seed and me topping out at four, pushing each other on, bits of free kit and drinks and food if we were doing well.

An asphalt playground with markings for every kind of sport painted in different colours. Playing football on brighter mornings, playing late into the dusk before getting back on our bikes to get home before all the light had gone. White Sondico footballs with red hexagonal panels. If the goals were up, you'd use them. If they were down, the gap between two fence-posts with the stiff metal mesh was the net. If you got moved on, goals were imagined out of other street furniture – a set of steps, a bench, a bin and a schoolbag lobbed nearby.

Monday-to-Friday life for me and Noel. Rugby on Sunday mornings and those big lunches back at Mum and Dad's. Noel's guardian would be there sometimes. My dad didn't like him, although I never found out for years.

Noel's old man was a photographer in Lusaka, and he did a deal with the guardian: Noel would get the benefit of a British education, the guardian would be sent money each month to keep him at school and a little more on top for housekeeping.

And slowly it fell apart. Money coming up short, money slipping away between the cracks. Noel beginning to change. Noel coming to school less, playing less rugby. Me starting to wonder. The friendship starting to stretch and shift.

Leaving for World Series tournaments with England had been an uneventful affair. The team hotel was half an hour from Heathrow. We met in our branded training kit, got on the coach, arrived, checked in and departed without a fanfare or leaving party.

In Fiji we left with every player's family in attendance – parents, brothers, sisters, wives and girlfriends. If it was a kid making his debut the extended family would be there too – cousins, uncles and aunts, all dressed as smartly as possible, as if they were off to Sunday church afterwards. Journalists from the *Fiji Times* and *Fiji Sun* would interview the mother and father.

The players felt that support and they paid it back. Your family had looked after you, put food on the table, kept you clean. When you grew up it was your turn. When the players were being paid they would ask for the next week's daily allowance as a lump sum. It would be handed straight to the family, and a small portion handed back for absolute essentials.

Except the players weren't being paid. The families were turning up and leaving empty-handed. Even the vague promises I'd been given back in the autumn had evaporated, unattributable and impossible to chase down. Neither was anyone who came in contact with the team getting what they were due. The team manager before Ropate had asked for the bill when we were out for lunch, called the waiter over and told them to send it straight to the FRU. He'd walk out, laugh and admit it would never get paid. Hotel bills went the same way. It was all done on a wink and a dodge. Everyone was getting burned.

I had been back to London that first Christmas to see Natalie and bring some more clothes over. When I had left Suva it had been to a promise that a contract would finally be waiting for me when I landed at Heathrow. That deadline was not met, and I had no idea when that contract would become a reality. I talked to World Rugby, and they suggested they might be able to pay me as a consultant for three months while the FRU sorted themselves out.

As bills came in for the villa I was now renting in Pacific Harbour it went very quiet, and then suddenly rather loud: World Rugby, frustrated by relentless evidence of financial mismanagement, announced that they were suspending Fiji's entire £1.5 million annual grant.

No salary, no sponsor, no players contracted, no balls, no assistant coach, no money to even travel to the next tournament in Wellington, the shortest and cheapest trip on our annual itinerary. My counterpart on the 15-a-side team, Inoke Male, lost his job.

When we sold our house in Teddington that Christmas it had seemed both liberating – we're free, we can move anywhere! – and logical: we had just converted it from one bedroom to two, and thought the London property market had hit preposterous heights that could surely not be topped. In the few months since the new owners had already seen it go up in value so much that they could have paid my year's wages on the additional equity alone. Meanwhile emails were arriving from mates back in England – I'm going into this Premiership club to talk about a potential role for you, just give me the green light.

I began to wonder if I could base myself in London and do the Fiji job part-time. Then I looked at the cost of the flights. It would be the most expensive and exhausting commute in world sport.

With England I had access to a gleaming rugby-specific gym, strength and conditioning coaches, nutritionists, psychologists, a team of physios, MRI scans, GPS tracking, an iPad per man and a hotel on the banks of the Thames with a rugby pitch in the grounds, a 25m swimming pool, a well-stocked bar and a pitch-and-putt course. All I could cling on to in Fiji was that no matter what the resources, you still had to pass the ball and make your tackles.

Still the storm clouds swelled. Emails from old coaches telling me I had to get them on board, that they could drag performances from this inconsistent team that I could not. Emails from journalists telling me they had quotes from former coaches putting the boot in, and how would I like to respond? Stories on the coconut wireless of trouble behind the scenes with the board, that a foreign coach had been the wrong choice because he couldn't understand the Fijian way and Fijians couldn't understand his complicated tactical instructions in English. He'll say one thing and the boys will do another.

To great fanfare the board announced a new sponsorship deal: £12.5 million over five years with a Vodafone consortium, all our problems solved, the board covering themselves in glory. Except this was a Fijian deal. Most of the deal wasn't actual cash but free sim cards and network contracts. Not enough money to sustain rugby in Fiji but a misleading enough headline for World Rugby to say, OK, you clearly don't need any financial support from us any longer. It was actually worse than no deal at all.

I had to fight the feeling that the odds were stacked against us. Fiji had never before lost two of their three group games in a leg of the World Series, but the way that had happened in Las Vegas fitted in with the madness that was all around. Leading against Australia with time up, our scrum-half threw the ball straight into touch. Maybe I should have reminded him at some point in training that this was against the rules, but he was a Test-match scrum-half who had been playing sevens all his life. I might as well have told him an oval ball wouldn't always bounce in a straight line. Australia kicked the resulting penalty to win.

The Sam Boyd Stadium is a horseshoe-shaped bowl of red seats, hot desert air blowing through it from Sloan Canyon or the Valley of Fire national park, the sky always a deep blue and the cool of night a sweet relief. New Zealand came at us like wild bobcats. The two Fijian-born players in their team, knowing what was planned and hating it, let it slip to Osea in advance: we're targeting your playmaker Pio

Tuwai, we've been told to get him off the field, whatever it takes. It was brutal. Endless penalties to us, Pio off injured under a hail of late tackles and cheap shots, the referee letting their hitmen hit all they wanted.

In the aftermath one of their players would be banned for nine games for eye gouging and another for two games for a spear tackle, picking one of our boys up by the legs and dropping him unprotected, head first, into the hard Nevadan turf. It was too late to save our tournament and just enough to turn up the heat back in Fiji. The coach can't coach and he can't protect our boys. We're getting picked on again and the Englishman is letting it happen.

There was an insecurity about Fijian players that had less to do with the rugby skills they possessed than the cultural history on their shoulders. With travel across the frantic world came the fear that people from a tiny cluster of dots from a cartographer's pen were almost second-class citizens. White people run the world, they're obviously better than us. And then the counterpoint: we can't have a white man running our sevens team, our pride and joy, because this is the British Empire all over again. This is colonialism with a whistle and slightly better sunblock.

I could understand all of that. But that self-doubt could be exploited by opportunistic locals too, and it made it all the harder to protect the players from the storms that had wrecked them before.

Of all the tournaments across the world, nothing meant as much to Fijians as the Hong Kong sevens. Rugby had been played in Fiji ever since the early 1900s, introduced by an itinerant plumber from New Zealand who took a job at the Grand Pacific Hotel in Suva, but it was the inaugural Hong Kong competition in 1976 that had sparked the nation's love affair with sevens – taking Fiji's domestic stars to the world, leading to the establishment in Suva of the Marist sevens, the country's first formal tournament.

Fiji triumphed in Hong Kong in 1977, 1978 and 1980, and again in 1984. Then, at the same time that the national television network was opened and began beaming live coverage across the islands, along came Waisale Serevi, a 5ft 7in explosion of side-steps, shimmies, acceleration and daring, a man who could beat three men on his own or throw a 40m one-handed pass to put a team-mate away to score instead. With Serevi in the side you could do any-thing. Three Hong Kong wins on the bounce from 1990 to 1992, three more from 1997 to 1999.

Here we were, going back to Hong Kong, and here was Serevi – now in his mid-40s and many years retired – get-ting involved in every way he could. I liked him as a man and I'd loved him as a player. His influence on the team was rather more nuanced.

As a player, he had sometimes fasted during tourna-ments. It had worked for him, so he believed, and that strange gospel soon spread. From having to make sure my players weren't eating too much I was now having to check they ate anything at all. I had to count them into the dining room and count them out again afterwards. I found out one player hadn't eaten for two days. When I asked why, he just grinned and said, Serevi! He claimed to be lighter because there was no food inside him. He was also slower and tired all the time for the same reason.

When we were successful Serevi was always suddenly around. He developed an ability to appear from nowhere when a trophy was being presented. 'The boys asked me to come up,' he would say, lifting a cup he had done nothing to win, and such was his status that none of the boys liked to say anything. I didn't mind at all. He was happy to be with the team; he was part of the Fijian sevens family.

But with Serevi came others who just wanted to be with Serevi. In Hong Kong that meant the head of the Fijian High Commission in China. Together they woke the players up at 2 a.m. for an ostentatious *lotu* that left the players who weren't exhausted by unnecessary starvation shattered from a lack of sleep.

It effectively derailed our final day. Having scraped through the quarter-final against the USA, we were awful in the semi-final against England and lost badly. The Hong Kong sevens loves fancy dress and it loves getting it drenched in beer. Surrounded by Minions, the Village People, high court judges and hundreds of Elvis clones, we were unrecognisable. There was no need to ask the Where's Wallies. They could have told you: it was the coach who prepared his team on four hours' broken sleep.

It was probably the worst sevens match I was ever involved in with Fiji. Under those famous curved grand-stands, on holy ground for Fiji sevens, the players were rugby ghosts, nothing in their legs or minds, soft targets the opposition could run through with ease. I felt like I needed to get a cardiac machine to get them moving.

Fijians still love Serevi and they always will, but they needed this team to be successful too. An Olympic gold medal would do things for the country that even all those Hong Kong titles couldn't touch. I had to sit him down for a conversation that I didn't want to have but categorically needed to. We love you. If you were even ten years younger you'd be in my team. Come to see us when it's all over. It'll be easier for all of us.

I gave everyone a chance. The ambassador in Hong Kong would not be allowed back the following year. The Fijian ambassador in the US, by contrast, took me out for dinner when we arrived and asked what he could do for us. He gave the boys pocket money because he understood the contract situation and the difference those funds would make to their families. He made sure the expat community gave us their support but didn't invade the hotel and sleep on floors. And so he became an ally in the years that followed. Each time we landed in Vegas I could think, great, I've got this man on my side.

In Tokyo at the end of March 2014, free of distractions, we hit our sweet groove again. With victory there came a win bonus of 25,000 Fijian dollars, about £8,000, which split between 12 players, Ropate and a few hands at the FRU, did not go far. I became used to seeing the big cardboard cheque at the airport on our return and then hearing the quiet complaints from the players weeks later that it had still to land in their own accounts.

The most precious thing that win bought me was a little more time. I now had victories in two of the first six World Series legs. We had beaten New Zealand well a couple of times; I'd capped a lot of new young players who had great promise. All of it with no money, most of it with only a little help. Although the knives were still out, not all of them were coming for me.

In Scotland and London, the final two tournaments of the 2013–14 series, we reached the semi-finals. I caught up with mates and family and marvelled at how busy southwest London felt. New Zealand beat us both times, winning with the last play of the match each time. It gave them the overall title, their fourth on the bounce. Our own winless record stretched back almost a decade. But we were alive.

That summer, in my solitary dawns and on evening walks along the beach at Pacific Harbour, I tried to take stock of what I had and of what we needed. As soon as the season had ended I'd lost seven players, Pio Tuwai taking his impossible offloads and four team-mates to the Sri Lankan Army team for a short-term but well-paid contract, rugby league clubs in Australia sniffing round others, wealthy French teams hunting down more unstoppable wingers to burnish their already glittering line-ups. It was part of the most vicious of circles: find a player, get them fit, get them playing well, watch them get poached.

I had Ropate, I had William, I had Osea, and I had Sami Viriviri, off the fast food and on the gas, ending the campaign as the World Series' leading try-scorer, 19 more to his name than any other player. I had made other trips to far-flung villages and had more planned to more distant islands yet. There were players out there, and I would do everything to find them.

The final target remained the Olympics. The goal that came with it was a seemingly contradictory one: to make myself redundant.

A lot of coaches obsess about control. They need to be in charge because they cannot imagine any other way. One boss, one vision. I wanted my team to be self-sustaining, for me to get them working so well that they could solve their own problems and set their own destinations. I wanted players who set their own standards of behaviour and fitness and collectively made sure everyone matched them. I wanted them to unconsciously be doing their own analysis and working out how to crack other defences rather than passively accepting it all from above.

It was why I would need Osea more than anyone else. He was developing into a big brother for the squad, close enough to them to be able to put an arm around their shoulders but respected so much that he could keep them in line. Inside the group yet able to protect them from the outside, part of the family but the head of it.

I had to mine that for all I could. While I could be close to the players, I had to be a further step away. I had to be distant enough that I could break bad news to them – you're dropped, you've let us down here and here – but close enough that I could deliver it compassionately. I couldn't let emotion set the tone, be all warm to Osea when he was playing well and then walk past him word-lessly if he had a bad game. I had to be consistent so that others could take their bearings from me.

A couple of years before my arrival Osea had signed a professional contract with Agen in the French Top 14. As with so many Pacific islanders who travel to Europe with a hope of making it big and sending significant funds back home, he found the reality rather different to what he had been promised. When a new coach was appointed, bringing in his own players, Osea was left in a small flat in a foreign town with nothing to do and no one to talk to.

He had returned to Fiji disillusioned and out of love with the game. Had I not taken that punt on him at my first tournament, he might well have slipped away from rugby altogether. Now, with the way he had played over the nine legs of the World Series, it was inevitable that the big boys had come calling – a top-four team in France, a three-year contract that promised to end all his family's financial worries.

He came to see me. I don't want to go, but this is the deal. What do you think?

It was clear he was committed to me and wanted me to commit to him. If you stay on this road now, I told him, you will go to the Olympics and you will win a gold medal. You'll be my captain, and you'll be part of Fijian history for ever. And you will deserve it. I'll give you my word, we'll get you a contract, we'll get the other key players on the islands a contract too. Hang on in there. We are going to sort this mess out.

I'd have understood if he had decided not to trust the white man. While some of the agents trawling Fiji were honourable operators, others would take advantage in every way they could. Sometimes that was a contract where the headline salary would be decimated by the agent's fees, income tax and automatic deductions for dubious accommodation. Other times it was more straightforwardly nefarious: take a player out for food, get them drunk, get them to sign a terrible deal while under the influence.

Sami Viriviri, after his 52 tries across that year, was one of the players who ended up signing a poor contract for nowhere near what he was worth. Sami needed cash. He had five brothers and three sisters to support, plus a single mother, Vika, who tried to keep their noses above water by working at the Flying Fish restaurant in the Sheraton Hotel in Nadi. I was getting close to Sami and I had great admiration for Vika. When I told her what the contract meant she was wonderful. First she tore it up. Then she told the agent and club: take me to court if you want, my boy can't be bought like that.

It meant I had her son for another year but also the responsibility to look after him. Twelve months on, he would sign a proper contract with Montpellier, a clause within it that released him from club duties so he could rejoin us for the final push to Rio if we qualified. With the funds he built a house for all those brothers and sisters and Vika in their home village. Not all the big wins came on the pitch.

It had been Osea who had first told me about Sami's family. In Fiji there was what you saw on the surface and what was really going on underneath. So much of it was impossible for me to decode. I might hear a player arguing on the phone but I didn't know why or with whom, only that they had struggled in training for days afterwards. Someone else might go missing. Your instinct would be to ditch them; it took an effort to remember that I was only seeing the wreckage that washed up, not the rocks and reefs that had done all the damage.

In those shaded moments Osea would become almost a benevolent detective for me. I would give him the lead – Pio seems distracted; Viliame Mata isn't trying – and he would make subtle enquiries to divine the sub-currents and eddies. It was a narrow line to tread: I could never hang him out to dry, or let the players guess or become resentful at our relationship. All my trips across Viti Levu and beyond were giving me an increasingly expedient network of friends and allies who would also help to fill the gaps in my education. But it worked because he was absolutely committed to the cause, and the rest of the team knew it. No one pushed themselves harder than Osea. No one else had turned down a contract as big as his.

And so I learned with him. Sami might say he wasn't

coming to training at the start of the week. Too shy and private to explain why, it would take Osea to tell me that he had a family meeting, and that in Fiji family takes precedence over everything else. I might have a player I thought would eventually come good but for now was struggling. My instinct was to stick with him; Osea would say, that's not how his brain works, you need to drop him and he'll come back like a runaway train.

Ever since I had plucked Semi Kunatani from the Coral Coast sevens in my first week in Fiji, he had been outstanding for us. When he had turned up for training one morning at Uprising clearly drunk, staggering to the middle of the pitch, stinking, slurring, I didn't know what to say. That he had been taken out in Suva by an agent trying to get him signed would only come out later.

There was a crowd of a hundred or so Fijians around the pitch that day, some of them older men, respected by the young players, all of them keen to see how this new coach and his rebuilt team behaved. Osea looked around and nodded to me: 'Let us take care of this one.'

A 200m sprint, turn around, do it again. All of them together, all going flat out until Semi was on his knees retching. Then the quiet words from the skipper: you're talented, but you're lucky to still be in the team. You have potential, and you're not going to waste it, not like all those others.

We still had an issue with high tackling. That trip to Ovalau all those months before had shown me how deep-rooted a style it was across the islands, a public demonstration of your strength, an indication of how intense and aggressive you could be. In England I would have sat the boys down, shown them a video of where they were going wrong and then some clips of what the technique should look like instead.

Osea took the intention and gave it a Fijian twist: every time there's a bad tackle, make the whole team run a hard 400 metres. If you don't complete it within a specified time, you all do it again. Immediate, painful and effective, a clear consequence established for your actions. It might seem cruel to punish all for the crime of an individual. In England it would have been. In Fiji, you never single anyone out and castigate them on their own. Neither do you use the sort of expletives that every Premiership coach in England unloads without a second thought. This focus on behaviour would pay rich dividends for us, many months later, just when it mattered most.

As his team-mates came to appreciate Osea's character, so they began to utilise him too. A player worried about something would talk to him first, knowing he would listen and help. His phone would ring in the middle of the night and he would be OK with it.

Together with Ropate, we could work out what was going wrong and what we could do about it. Everyone trusted Ropate and everyone naturally confided in him. The boys liked hanging out in his room; he would give them little jobs as they chatted, helping him fold some washed kit or pump up some balls. Honest conversation would flow around those casual tasks. In the time it took to sort the laundry Ropate would have taken the pulse of the team.

All differing characters, all with varying proficiencies, the three of us developed into a curious but effective little team: the 20-stone charmer, the pale ginger constantly applying sun-cream, the minister's son who liked to stick people on their backsides with a wicked sidestep.

There was trust between us and there was growing respect, and I was happy to let them lead when that meant a better outcome. Osea might get a text late at night about a forthcoming funeral of a player's uncle. Ropate would talk to the player as they shared a coconut on the training pitch at Uprising and see how he felt about the loss. The two of them would find out that there was no money for the service, so I'd dip into my savings, pass the money on to Ropate and suggest he could earn himself even more trust by sorting it behind the scenes without anyone needing to worry about the money's origins. Osea would be part of that decision, going for a hot chocolate with the player on his return to welcome him back into the camp.

Osea wasn't perfect. Nothing in Fiji could be. A beautiful blue-sky day could be overtaken from nowhere by thunderclouds and a sudden downpour. Storms could blow in suddenly off Rovodrau Bay, turning Uprising into a mass of thrashing palm trees and flying sand, Beqa island lost as the horizon disappeared in torrential rain.

Defeat fell hard on Osea. He understood its repercussions across the villages and lonely islands. He had seen how fragile our development as a team could be. When we lost he would let it envelop him, not talking to anyone, taking himself off into a corner.

I was sympathetic but firm. You can have five minutes of that, but your team needs you to be what they should become. Share your emotions with them, and you will realise that you are not alone and that a new resolve can come out of this. I wanted to make sure that kindness was top of all our agendas and I wanted to do all I could to help the players, but I wouldn't protect them from the consequences of their actions. You can be caring and loyal as well as having strict standards. No grey areas, no blur-ring the lines.

As Osea tried to respond to those challenges it generated its own negative energy. Jealousy of his position was emerging, less within the camp than among those conscious of their standing in the Fijian community. When we got back to Nadi airport after winning in Tokyo and went to the official functions back in Suva, he was greeted with standing ovations. When the bigwigs from the board took their turn only a smattering of applause followed. Everything in Fiji is politics and alliances and currents beneath the surface. I had to warn him: the islands want success, but some people only want it for themselves.

Watching Osea growing into his role gave me as much satisfaction as anything else we achieved in that first year. When I held our regular fitness tests at Uprising in the close season it was no longer the coach winning them but the captain. When a new kid with lightning in his feet came into camp Osea would smile and then refuse to be beaten in the sprint races. There would come a seemingly meaningless match, a third-place play-off game against New Zealand in Dubai in 2014, where he tried so hard to win it for us that he passed out on my shoulder in the changing room. We had blown a big lead when we lost the semi-final to Australia, and the old attitude would have been that third no longer mattered. But if we wanted to win the World Series, those few extra points did matter, and Osea had run himself into the ground to show the team what was required. From sulking to physical collapse. In all my time coaching, in all my time pushing players around the world to new levels of speed and endurance, I had never once experienced that before.

I guess Osea might not have survived without me. I guess I would not have survived without him either. We both knew it, and neither felt the need to spell it out. I considered myself extremely fortunate.

Family first in Fiji, family second and family to the end. In England you would never take a player's problems to his parents. It would be seen as betrayal from both sides. Secrets and struggles were kept within the team. I had James Rodwell in the national side for five years and barely knew his mum and dad at all.

In Fiji you could no more try to improve a wayward talent without the involvement of his family than you could try to make him faster by doing weights on only one leg. In Wellington midway through that first year I had picked a kid called Viliame Mata as a replacement for my troubled offloading genius Pio Tuwai. He was a phenomenal talent – 6ft 5ins, 18 stone, always breaking the opposition defensive line, popping passes away when tackled that were a little less spectacular than Pio's but always found the hands of a team-mate, making so few errors that I could see him being one of the boys I would build our Olympic dream around. But for all the natural gifts, there was only minimal work ethic. He wouldn't train and he saw little reason to when his talent had already taken him into the national side.

Ropate picked me and Osea up and off we went to see Viliame's family. You couldn't get to his home village of Nauluvatau unless you specifically tried: winding across the Colo-I-Suva national park, across the Waidina River, up a dirt road that ended there and went nowhere else.

You also felt you had travelled back in time. Nauluvatau

78

was so cut off from the world that kids had to cross the river on a bamboo raft to get to school. It took half an hour to cross just 200 yards of slow water. There were 300 villagers, all subsistence farmers. When the government gave the village an eight-seater communal boat with a 15-horsepower outboard motor four years later, it made the pages of the *Fiji Sun*.

We gave Viliame's family the good news: we think your boy has the talent to go to Rio. And then the reality: he will never fulfil that talent if he carries on like this. Now it was a collective responsibility. With that visit the whole family, the whole of Nauluvatau, were making sure that he went to training and that he worked for them all when he got there.

Sometimes an invite would come the other way. Semi Kunatani, beasted by the boys for turning up drunk in training, told me in his quiet way that his family would like me to visit them. Naveyago was a day in the car from the easy charms of Uprising, hours west up the coast along Queens Road, a right-turn north deep into the forested interior, up into the mountains that divided the wet windward side of Viti Levu from the rainshadowed side. It was one dusty road and a few scattered houses, low buildings with the corrugated iron painted pale blue and the wooden frames an earthy red, a few fields of root crops running down with the streams from the hills beyond.

A woman came to meet me who I assumed was Semi's mum. And then another woman, and another. Semi's biological mother had died when he was young. These were the five women in the village who had brought him up – fed him, washed him, clothed him, sent him to school. They cried when he came back and hugged him tight when he left. When I thought about my promises to players about contracts and proper salaries, I thought about those five.

It was the women who held the family groups together and the mothers who had most influence over their sons. It was the women too who would suffer if those tight domestic bonds took a more menacing physical turn.

As we travelled through some villages you would see hand-painted signs: *This is a domestic violence-free village.* Occasionally Osea or Ropate might say, you need to drop this player, we've heard he's gone at his wife again.

Once more: the standard you walk past is the standard you become. You can't escape this. No player who behaved like that stayed with us. It was rare, but it happened. Before my time Isake Katonibau had served a two-year ban for pinning a drug-tester up against a wall after a match. I would give him another chance, but it would not end well.

Inevitably the hours spent in *talanoa* and conversation with those families turned my thoughts towards my own. On the long drive back from Naveyago and Semi's wonderful surrogates I thought about my own mother Diane and her influence on me: a teacher, just as I had been, spending many years working in pupil-referral units for troubled kids, a sport obsessive who had been taught cricket by her own dad and then played hockey for Gloucestershire.

My dad Dennis had always been a free spirit, going from job to job, for a while a mechanic with the RAF, my mum always the more reliable breadwinner. As a kid in the backstreets of Manchester he was always turning up at the family home at express pace, pursued by an irate shopkeeper or a bloke from the dairy furious that he had opened the taps and flooded Commercial Street with fresh milk. With his cousin Paul, brought up like a brother after the death of his own mother in childbirth, he would put things on the railway tracks to see them squashed by the engines, spit down the funnels of the trains as they passed under the iron bridge or crawl through the quarter-mile drainpipe that ran underneath the railway. He had once almost inadvertently sent his mother into an early grave by staggering through the door with his jaw broken and his throat split from one side to the other, having decided to cross the railway line behind the house on the outside of the bridge and lost his hold when he met a bigger kid doing the same thing from the other side.

It was 12 years since he had died. On my short trips back to London I would go down to his grave in Gunnersbury cemetery, just north of where the M4 crosses over the North Circular, where the monument stands to the Polish prisoners of war who died in the forests of Katyn. I'd wonder what he'd think about his son out on a tiny island, so far from the playing fields and streets of west London where he'd lobbed me a rugby ball and shown me how to spin-pass and box-kick.

Having Natalie come back to Fiji with me should have brought a sense of home and belonging. While she had wanted to be the one to choose the house, she loved the place in Pacific Harbour. It was rented but it felt like ours. We had a swimming pool and a social cushion to soften the landing in the staff who ran the resort – Jone, the Hagler lookalike; Mia, who reminded me of a Fijian Queen Latifah and would appear from nowhere to top up Ropate's hot chocolate whenever his tide got low.

Natalie liked having people around. She loved to plan nights out and she loved to organise, even if we had met in an untidy way. It had been a mate of mine who was supposed to be going speed-dating in the summer of 2006, but so panicked and sweat-soaked had he got on the way there that we had bailed and gone for a few pints instead. The company had sent us some matches regardless. Natalie had been one of them, and we had met for a drink a few days later. When that went well, another date followed, this time a long walk in Windsor Great Park.

I went to Australia with the England under-18s team a few days later. She went travelling round Europe with a large group. Halfway round, hating it, the two of us talking on Skype, she told me she was going to head home. I asked her where she would be on the Saturday; when she said Rome, I flew there instead of home. Oversized mojitos in the city of eternal love, boozy declarations of a future together, moving into my place in Teddington within six months.

The tournaments and trips around the islands meant I was gone for days at a time. When training was in full swing I'd be up early and back late. The informal management cartel of me, Ropate and Osea would fill many evenings with our chinwags. I thought it made sense for her to get a job of her own, to establish a sense of independence, to start building her friendships away from the subplots and schemes of rugby sevens. Natalie preferred to wait, ready for rest after falling out of love with her old job back in London, keen to travel to some tournaments with the team, to go back to her family in suburban Buckinghamshire for a couple of weeks at Christmas and throughout the summer.

I knew it was hard for her. Had her job taken us somewhere I'd never been and never expressed any interest in visiting, would I have packed in everything and moved my life away too? In Fiji you could only ever be in the shadow of your partner if they ran the national sevens side. A work visa would be hard to get hold of unless she wanted to work at the FRU, and having my wife working at the place that was already complicating everything I did would have been close to nightmarish.

And so she settled into what she could find that was familiar: other Brits at a loose end in Suva, sociable lunches that could stretch into empty afternoons, an escalating invitation list to dinners and cocktail parties.

If I was home I'd sometimes go along with her. There would be a lot of fixed smiles, nodding during conversations about people I didn't know, complaining about things I didn't mind, caught out by a sudden silence and a sea of expectant faces when I was eventually asked for an opinion on something, miles away, mulling over something Ropate had mentioned to me earlier or how I might wangle some new training bibs on the cheap from a mate of a mate.

In some jobs you clock on and then leave it all behind when you walk out the door eight hours later. You might check a few emails on your work smartphone and you might get the odd call at weekends in emergencies. As England coach the only time my mobile had rung in the evening had been over a tedious if pressing admin issue – we've got these flights on hold for this day, can you confirm? – or when a Premiership coach was unhappy with the fact I'd selected one of his players.

With Fiji it was total immersion. I was coach, I was politician, I was anthropologist, I was agony aunt. It wasn't unusual for a girlfriend that a player had broken up with to come into camp and ask to see me. I'd make them a cup of tea, ask them if anything untoward had happened to them, and ask them how they were feeling about things. As they drank the tea I'd go and see the player. If it's over, you need to explain to her why, and then, in the nicest possible way, make it clear that turning up halfway through a training session isn't going to help. Back to the girl, take her to the front desk, book her a taxi and give the driver enough money to get her home. I'd finish training and then find elders from a different player's village in reception, wanting a *talanoa* about their boy's prospects for the forthcoming season.

Respite came in unexpected places. The next place along from mine at Uprising was owned by an Aussie couple in their early 60s called Doug and Robyn, AFL obsessives who for years had spent half their time in Melbourne and half in Fiji. They had built their own house and put a similar amount of work into the local village. They also had a working espresso machine and a fridge full of chilled Fiji Gold beer. They'd invite me round for huge home-cooked meals, gluten- and sugar-free but with plenty of red wine.

On Thursday it would be curry night at the house of my landlady Natalia Larsen and her American husband Jeff, who she had met at a nightclub in Suva called Traps. The whole extended family there – her four sisters, brother, and mother Sophie, who would take me to church on spare weekends – great cauldrons of boneless chicken curry, a stack of *rotis* up to the ceiling, everyone holding hands with the kids and singing a song and sharing a little prayer of gratitude and then bang, hands in the pot. The white man would have the mickey taken out of him for not being able to handle the curries with bones in. The white man was also increasingly referred to by a Fijian name, Peni Raiyani. I hoped my delight wasn't too obvious. At the Skinny Bean café, run by Natalia's younger sister Janice, I could grab a proper espresso, fried eggs on home-made granary bread and a fruit smoothie, another oasis in an unfamiliar world.

Strolling down the little path from mine to Doug's place, his boat tied up to the small jetty that stuck out into the flat sea. Chugging out through the reef to the sandbars that stuck out at low tide, swimming off the side or sparking up a barbecue with driftwood washed up by the waves. Doug doing a little fishing, me content enough having a couple of beers while his line flicked and whizzed and the sun slunk away in the orangey-red clouds on the horizon.

About the same time, Frank Bainimarama was being appointed as the president of the Fiji Rugby Union. Blue skies and thunderclouds, storms blowing in fast.

FIVE

Noel and I always sat next to each other in class. The desks were wooden, old, battered and scratched with lids that flipped up to reveal a musty old smell and a load of old chewing gum. Ink wells on the top, not used for years. Hoping that weekend was someone's birthday, the best parties the football ones where you got to play five-a-side all afternoon at the proper indoor football places. Sean Stafford held his at his house in Wembley because his uncle had a rip-off VHS of ET, and ET was huge, and none of us minded the terrible quality or the fact that you could only hear one line in three. Suddenly into BMX because of the chase scene with Elliot and his brother and their mates, getting one for 99 francs from an hypermarché on holiday in France and riding it into the ground for the rest of the summer.

PE lessons always the best part of the day. Nothing complicated, just two of those low wooden gym benches turned on their sides at *opposite ends of the gym and off you go, two kids on each team, constant goals, non-stop running. Years later, as a PE teacher myself, using that as my go-to whenever it was wet or we were short of time.*

PE teachers were always the coolest ones. Nike trainers, younger, setting you loose when others wanted to coop you up. Mr Hopkins spotted talent in me and Noel, and taught us how to use it. High jump, long jump, 800m and 1500m for me, dropping down to 400m hurdles later on, Noel a sprinter and long jumper with all that speed. Mr Hopkins on the stopwatch for a crack at the under-11s school record for 800m: shouting out my split at the bell, legging it diagonally across the infield to give me my time with 200m to go. Relays with Noel at the end, always breath left.

No idea what troubles were coming round the bend. No idea that there would come a moment when I couldn't even remember the last time Noel and I were together.

My dad, as sport-obsessed as I would become, used to sit me down and tell tales of heroes and legends. One of his favourites was that of Herb Elliott, the Australian middle-distance great, and his eccentric coach Percy Cerutty, and how together they smashed the world record over 1500m and the mile and won Olympic gold in Rome in 1960.

Cerutty was different in every way: lots of raw vegetables at a time when most Aussies preferred raw meat, no fags or booze when many athletes celebrated big wins by reaching for a freshly lit gasper. Cerutty thought his athletes should train in beautiful surroundings, that the natural landscape inspired them to greater deeds. He set up a training camp in Portsea, 60-odd miles south of his home town of Melbourne, and worked Elliott and his training partners on the great sand dunes by the sea – bare-footed, up steep slopes, arms pumping, through the yellow gorse and clumps of grass, racing back down again with the waves breaking along the beach down below.

Summer holidays in Weston-super-Mare had offered the teenage me a chance to try that on a much-reduced scale. In south-west London, with the England sevens team, we had so many other resources that mere sand seemed a bit low-tech.

On Viti Levu we may not have had England's nutritionists, psychologists, MRI scanners, GPS tracking, and an iPad per man. We did have Sigatoka National Park, two hours west along the coastal road from Suva, an hour and a bit south-west of Nadi – a great shifting spread of vast sand mountains, some shallow and slippery, others like wind-blown walls, the river mouth opening out into the rolling Pacific on one side, thick green bush and forest stretching away inland.

The 2014–15 World Series would begin on Australia's Gold Coast in early October. Having gone there in the first year off the back of one training session and as the fittest man in the group, I needed somewhere in the weeks before to push my remodelled side to their limits. Sigatoka would be it: natural beauty and intense physical discomfort, long miles from home villages but together in effort and aim, a special piece of Fiji that we would carry with us in our lungs and legs across the world.

The province of Nadroga feels distinct from anywhere else, out on its own in the wild south-west like the Forest of Dean in England or the northern coast of Cornwall. It bakes in a drier heat than Suva, the forests thicker and the people different. Before missionaries arrived in the nineteenth century the area had been home to a cannibal king named Ratu Udre Udre, who believed that if he ate 1,000 people he would become immortal. The fact he was no longer around suggested either his belief was misplaced or he'd got his sums wrong. While we were in Fiji a Christian group called Ra Nation tried to set up an independent state within the province, at least until Frank found out, shut it down with his troops and banished the leaders. There were wild horses in the interior, and the players from there were all able to ride. So obsessed were they that when we travelled to the World Series leg in Dubai all my heavyweight forward Apisai Domolailai wanted to do was hang out at the stables. If we won prize money his would go on leather saddles, to be stashed in physio William's magic case to ensure their safe passage home.

Nadroga is obsessed with rugby. No other province across the Fijian islands has won as many domestic trophies as their main team. They were always big rivals with Suva, whom they considered to be city boys, and there was so much rugby talent in Nadroga that the French side Clermont set up an academy to pinch the best kids in their teens.

Sigatoka was perfect – 30 or 40 different dunes, hundreds of different angles and inclines for the players to run up, some of the slopes a gradual burn of 400-odd metres, others so sheer that the only way up them was to claw at them with hands as well as feet, slipping all the time you tried to move forward, sliding backwards inexorably if you ever thought about stopping for a breather. The sand was harder where the onshore winds had battered it, a thin crust on top if a sea mist had settled overnight. Shards of ancient pottery or stone tools were occasionally exposed by a big storm.

We would wake the boys hours before sunrise to get across from our usual training base in Pacific Harbour. By 5.30 a.m. we would be climbing the dunes, the players still half-asleep, dragging all their kit behind them. Silhouetted against the purple dawn clouds, smoke drifting up from little villages cut into the forest as fires were started for breakfast, the sound of kids squealing and crying carried with it if the wind was coming the right way. Standing at the top, chests going in and out like bellows. Looking one way to the South Pacific and its white breakers on the vast rolling blue, rip tides along the wide beach and sharks in the drop-off beyond. Looking north across the rolling forests and up into the hills and the mountains.

The first time we walked up I thought Ropate was going to have a heart attack. I wasn't too confident about myself. One ascent even at an easy pace, and you couldn't imagine doing anything else all day. It made no difference how fit you were. That first dune would get you every time. Then your body would get used to the sliding and the effort and the technique, and the sea breeze would dry off the sweat, and you could think about going again.

We would put plastic markers down to set a route. It was almost like a golf course: here's your first hole, 200 yards uphill; here's a horrible second, straight up that; the third, you'll have no recovery, and your hands will be shaking and your heart trying to escape your chest as you go again.

Some of the players would sprint with a rugby ball in their hands, some in pairs, competing against each other, sometimes linked arm in arm. Percy Cerutty had spoken proudly of Herb Elliott's 11-second ascent of an 80-foot sand dune in Portsea. Sigatoka had monsters compared to those tame Victorian elevations. Dark-brown trails would smear up the dunes as the players' churning feet broke the sun-baked surface, weird shapes and symbols carved into the sand like the Nazca lines. Their black shirts would turn white as sand grains stuck to sweating arms and backs, eyes popping with effort after effort, staggering from marker to marker, like sand-covered zombies somewhere between life and death.

It was wonderful training. The only way to keep moving was to drive with your knees and arms, honing a sprinter's technique that would make you fly across flat grass. There was less impact through your feet and hips and back, so fewer injuries, building instinctive proprioception because of those bare feet and constant minute adjustments to the treacherous sand, developing balance and reaction even as your lungs were burning and the lactic acid was flooding your quads and calves.

Sometimes we were two and a half hours up there. By the end the boys were strewn around like they'd been dropped from the skies, face down, limbs spread. It was the most brutal training I had ever seen.

Cerutty, breakfasting on dry oats and nuts, reading five pages each night of H. G. Wells's 1,200-page *The Outline of History*, had preached to his athletes a lifestyle of sacrifice and self-reliance that he called 'Stotan', a mix of Spartan and Stoic. I didn't need to spell it out to my team; it was there in front of them, every day of their lives. As we got closer to the dunes on those dark mornings the gallows humour would spread round the minibus – I've injured myself singing this song, no dunes for me today; I was up at 1 a.m. and did my own session by moonlight. But they all knew they had to do it and they all wanted it, understanding that it was a team thing, that to back out was to let down all those around you. The players with genuine injuries would come up anyway to carry water, or to do hundreds of sit-ups with the damaged foot or thigh cushioned in the sand.

Pushing them on was a new figure in the management team. Naca Cawanibuka had been the strength and conditioning coach for Fiji's 15-a-side team for years, a former international centre himself, someone who would read the latest academic papers and then work out how to put them to practical use. His knowledge and enthusiasm had never before been utilised properly. When the Flying Fijians went on tours to the northern hemisphere in autumn, to Australia and New Zealand in summer or to World Cups, an overseas conditioning coach would be brought in over his head. Naca would be left running the water bottles on, never asked about what sort of strength training worked best for specific players or what sort of diet could bring the best out of them. He was too nice a man to feel bitter, but he was undervalued and depowered because he had so much to give and wasn't being allowed to.

He had his eccentricities. He was fanatically religious, convinced that a second coming was just round the corner, probably borne on a flood, yet relentlessly pleasant about it.

He was always so well organised and so creative with the limited resources we had. I could take him to Sigatoka, tell him how long we had and the level I wanted the players to hit in testing in three weeks' time, and then let him go.

And it began to work. No matter how bad their legs and lungs might be feeling, there was never an exit clause. You couldn't say that you couldn't do it any more when your team-mates were still going. I was encouraging rather than dictatorial, supportive rather than abusive, and when the sessions finally ended, bodies everywhere, you could see the immense feeling of satisfaction flooding through them along with the endorphins and exhaustion.

'The main thing about Percy [Cerutty],' Herb Elliott once told a reporter, 'is that he coaches your spirit. The body itself may need only two months' training to get fit. The rest of the time you're building up your spirit – call it guts, or some inner force – so that it will go to work for you without you even thinking about it.'

When your day has begun with 200 reps up the dunes of Sigatoka you know your guts are in redoubtable shape. The reward would be waiting at the bottom. As we had walked up Ropate would have sent the driver off in the van to the butchers in town to buy a load of chicken and steak and set up a barbecue in the village. The locals would do the cooking, thrilled to have their heroes on their turf. Early on, the excitement threatened to get out of hand – elders bringing out the *kava*, village chiefs requesting *talanoa* – but with Ropate in charge the dramas diminished and the fun continued.

The Sigatoka training sessions worked so well that they became the beautiful crescendo to every week we had at home in Fiji, a Friday morning to fear and cherish. Even the climate had its own little training kick – sticky-hot once the sun climbed above the hills, water for the team before the session and then not again until the end, so that when, during tournaments, we would give them water during matches and in the short breaks between, their bodies responded in a far better way. All bound up together, it created a shield that could insulate us from the little

94

cuts and nicks that would weaken other teams. When you have Sigatoka in your legs, when you're used to training in stinking kit that hasn't been washed overnight, when you sleep in 20-man dormitories, you don't complain that the evening menu at the Las Vegas tournament only has one type of protein, or that the rooms in the athletes' village at the Olympics are a little more cramped than a hotel. In the twenty-first century sport is about big financing and perfect resources. We all think that makes the difference. On those dunes I was no longer so sure. I saw resilience, I saw togetherness, I saw the right sort of stubbornness. I saw coaches and players given the trust and control.

With England I had used ice-baths, compression tights and deep-tissue massage. At Sigatoka, after breakfast, we would go to the waterfalls on the river. Down a single-track road in the minibus, park it in a clearing and then go barefooted over the rocks to the pools, a big jump into the first one, water crashing down from a horseshoe curve, then another, steeper drop into the pool below. Each player with a green coconut with the top sliced off, down to their pants, singing songs, soaping up and washing it off under the waterfall. Players crying with laugher when Ropate stripped off and jumped in to join them. Sitting out under the trees before the steep clamber up wet stone steps back to the van, warmth between us, grateful for what we had done and that we had shared it.

Our minibus would not have passed muster on the streets of Twickenham. But our driver Bela could probably have handled himself anywhere.

It was Bela who picked up each of the players at the start of each week and dropped them all home again after we had washed down at the waterfalls on Friday. Because Viti Levu is slow to get around and our players were spread far across it, this was no easy spin. He would start at 5 a.m. with Pio Tuwai in Lautoka, right up north among the sugarcane fields beyond Koroyanitu National Park, and then wind his way south on Queens Road through Nadi and all the little villages before Sigatoka, going up side-roads and barely roads, texting players when he was 45 minutes away so they could walk down from their homes to a junction crossroads. Then it was past our training base at Uprising and on to Suva in the east, delivering a full load at Fiji Rugby House by 9 a.m. Morning tea would be waiting for them, sugar piled high in the mugs if I wasn't watching, someone else walking in with a box of doughnuts and me shaking my head and directing them to the staff offices upstairs instead.

Bela knew all the roads and all the policemen who patrolled them. Never would he be pulled over, no matter what speed he was going or which manoeuvre he pulled. The bus was his domain: a big padded seat for him at the front which he could swing round when he was parked up, Fijian music coming through the stereo via someone's phone and a frayed cable, and then into bust-up speakers that distorted it even more.

Four hours in a bus on narrow roads would not wash with elite athletes in Britain. For the boys it became a social gathering, an unofficial team meeting before the official one had convened. Kitbags everywhere, players lying all over the place, Bela bombing it around and waving at the cops as he roared past. It was a good thing he never drank. When he was done with us he'd repeat the whole journey for the women's sevens team. In total, 15 hours' driving a day for an allowance of £15. If someone needed taking to hospital, Bela would be the man to do it. If kit needed picking up, or water, Bela and his white van would hammer off.

Like Ropate, like Osea and William, Bela gradually became an unofficial conduit between team and coach. Every time he picked someone up there would be a little bit of chit-chat. Bela saw what was happening in each village he visited and understood what it meant. If a player got dropped off late on a Friday there might not be any dinner left for them when they got home, particularly if they were the youngest of several. With no cash of their own and no shops for miles around, that would be it. Bela could let me know. Next time the player went back I might hop in with him for a chat with the family, or slip him the leftovers from the Sigatoka barbecue. Part of our increasingly tight-knit group, we made sure we looked after Bela. When his house was destroyed by flooding, the whole thing swept away, he asked for £150 to get things moving again, and the thought of not giving it to him never crossed my mind.

As Bela headed west on those Friday afternoons Ropate and I would drive east to a little place in Votua village called the Eco Café. It was simple: one thatched hut on stilts, wooden benches, bamboo leaves coming through the sides so you felt like you were in the sort of den you made as a kid. The beach right outside, horses galloping past, the owners – an Italian woman called Fabi and her Fijian partner Degei – baking huge pizzas in the wood-fired oven. Even if you hadn't run the dunes or were still burping back the morning barbecue you could always justify it, a treat at the end of a tired week or a chance to chew it all over with Ropate. No booze, no sugar in the fruit juices, just natural lemon juice and mango smoothies. It could only go wrong if you found yourself in a speed-eating contest with Ropate. Watching those huge hands folding a pizza as big as the minibus tyres was both entertainment and intimidation.

It was our chance to reflect and to form strategies. Journeys back from Nadroga revealed puzzles as well as collective satisfaction. Working out how to solve the one called Apisai Domolailai would take several pizzas alone.

Apisai's fiancée was a strong-minded girl. Apisai was not the sort of bloke who backed down. She wanted them to move to her village once they were married; he wanted to stay in his, close to his family and horses. He had worked in the resorts and hotels as a porter, and with that came a certain streetwise charm. If he could sneak in a beer without me finding out, he would. When I caught him having a cigarette outside the changing room at a club match, he looked as sheepish as a 15-stone man of 6ft 3ins ever could.

At the start he was unsure about trusting me. He knew I was strict about booze and fags, but he heard me praising what he could do on the pitch too. I kept the criticism private and I tried to make it positive. Walking across the training pitch from one practice to another I might say to him, Apisai, I'm not going to say anything in front of the boys, but why didn't you mention that you would be late? I'd let him explain what had happened and discuss how he could have handled it better, trying to empower him rather than impose from above.

Trust takes time, but it does come. A fortnight later he could come to me and say, do you mind if Bela drops me off home tonight, because my girlfriend is throwing all my stuff out of the house, and she's threatening to kick me out too. Two weeks later I could say to him, I know you went round to the next village on Saturday night and didn't come back until morning. Are you going to be able to give your best to training and to the team after that?

He was lucky with his metabolism. No matter what he did his numbers in fitness testing were always impressive. But you cannot have one man in the team drinking and the next bloke banned from it. With Apisai I had to stay close and collaborative, going to his church with him sometimes, talking to the fiancée, making sure he got those saddles back from Dubai, working with him rather than against the grain.

And then you came up against the mysteries you could not solve, the problems that were bigger than your capabilities, no matter how many pizzas you put into it.

Pio Tuwai was always an enigma – 31 years old already but a siege machine of a player, 6ft 5ins tall, 17 stone, great fun to be around most of the time but with darkness always seeping in around his ankles, ringing me up late at night and asking for cash.

I wasn't suspicious at the start. He would say he needed 500 Fijian dollars to pay for a cousin's funeral. I'd sit down with Ropate and Osea, tell them what had happened and ask them what they knew. Osea would never judge, only present the facts. Yes, his cousin has passed away. No, he's been out drinking.

Pio's home village of Nabukavesi was not rich. A few red dirt roads, a Seventh Day Adventist Church, wooden bungalows with corrugated iron roofs, a fence made out of string fed through old soft-drink bottles. A hand-painted sign by the road: *God created the Earth and everything in it. Even you.*

He had been out of the side for a while when I took over,

pushed out for a lack of consistency, for being reliable only in regularly not turning up where he should. I had brought him back in as soon as I could. There was so much talent there, you had to get him involved – such soft feet and hands for a big man, so light on his feet, so much time on the ball.

There's offloading, and then there was Pio's offloading. It was so late and from so deep in a wrapped-up tackle, yet he could put the ball anywhere from absolutely nowhere, as if his wrists were double-jointed and his fingers spring-loaded. The boys knew what he could do so they would run the right support lines behind him to feed off those beautiful scraps. And he was fast, so fast for his size, always attacking defenders, and when I showed him that he could vary it too, that he could bide his time and wait for the real moment, be like a fisherman dangling his bait, drawing the fish in, drawing them in and then – *bang* – make that break with the defence stupefied, he became even more of a weapon, someone who you could nail down for one of those precious seven starting points, should we ever make the Olympics.

But he was loose on so much else. He was the principal non-mover in what I privately called the 'F.A.T.' group, the ones who would fail all the tests when it came to fitness. He wouldn't get near the minimum standards that we needed for the 40m sprint, and he wouldn't be near anyone else either. He would go off the rails at home; when he was away, he would act as if he had nothing to care about back in Fiji. I wanted to keep him and I wanted to cut him loose. He was a gift and he was a liability.

A storm without warning. After his wife gave birth to their next child, a series of strange blood tests revealed, out of nowhere, that she had the early stages of breast cancer. The doctors made plans for her to stay in the hospital. She refused. She decided instead to use the village healer. The healer, she said, could massage the tumours out.

Through all this, Pio came to training. He stopped asking for help, just when he needed it most, just when I had no idea how to offer it.

SIX

I'm 13 years old. I'm still playing rugby with Richmond on Sunday mornings. Noel has given up, although I'm not sure why. Our sporting time together is now staring into shop windows on Brentford High Street or getting the Central Line 11 stops from Ealing Broadway, the end of the line, in to Oxford Circus. Walking down Regent Street to Lillywhites off Piccadilly Circus, looking with wide eyes at the new tennis racquets with oversized heads that Boris Becker is diving around with at Wimbledon. Polo shirts and tracksuits out of our range, saving up to get a Sergio Tacchini wristband, as worn by John McEnroe, or a Fila one like Becker.

A year on and Noel isn't at school so much. One year more and he's never there. His guardian doesn't seem to intervene. Somewhere it looks as though the money has run out. Noel, left to his own devices, is hanging out with older kids, kids from further east or kids who left school behind a long time ago.

It's harder to find him. Dad drives us round to the guardian's flat and he won't answer the door. Other mates have seen him hanging round Ealing late at night.

I hang around the same places at the same sort of time. When I find him there's something different about him. He's harder. He's aloof. Our connection is there but it's weak and I can feel it straining.

I ask him if he still wants to play rugby, and give him the time and the place. He doesn't turn up. My dad, all those years watching him play sport so well and so often, manages to get him a trial at the local non-league football club. Dad rings up afterwards to see how it's gone. Noel never showed.

Finding him again, hanging out with the older kids. I'm not street-smart and I'm not being brave, but I can tell there are bad things going on. Lads with coshes down their sleeves, lads with cash and other people's wallets.

This is not my world. I am out of my depth, and the water keeps rising.

September 2014, a year on from that surprise tweet, from that late email, from the 4 a.m. Skype call and all that followed. If the 2016 Olympics had seemed distant back then, sitting in the Italian restaurant with Natalie and the emptying bottle of Valpolicella, they were now dominant in my thoughts. World Rugby and their wonderful sevens manager Beth Coalter had decided how qualification for Rio would work: the top four teams in the 2014–15 World Series would be guaranteed a spot, the seedings for the Olympic tournament would be taken from the final standings. The higher you finished in that special quartet, the easier the draw you would get.

There was a lot on my mind as I sat down with Natalie

for brunch in a local hotel one Sunday. A week travelling from London to Fiji, in constant contact with Beth, had been followed by drive after drive from Pacific Harbour to Suva, desperately trying to get the players' contracts sorted out. While my own salary was now in place, the FRU having finally found the funds 12 months late, the men I was there to coach were still playing as amateurs. I was tired and tense and sore all over.

I stood up to get some dessert. My body seemed to compress and then crunch. I fell to the ground, pain wrapped around my back and chest, unable to move. Around me suddenly a sea of panicked faces, shouting. Heart attack! He's had a heart attack! Staff appearing with the box containing a defibrillator.

My back had been bad for a long time. The night 20 years ago when I made my professional debut, scrum-half for West Hartlepool against Bath, I had bent down in the warm-up to pick up a ball and felt a sudden fizzing sensation through my spine. We had an East German doctor, Dr Ekkart Arbeit, who had been up to his white eyebrows in all that was questionable in sports medicine before the Berlin Wall came down, and whatever he had done to my spine had only made it worse. I would get an injection, play, drive home and then be unable to get out of the car, having to phone my girlfriend from the driver's seat and ask her to come down and heave me out.

Since retiring from playing I had tried to manage it and avoid an operation. Now I was being carried by four fellow diners into one of the hotel's unoccupied bedrooms. Physio William arrived at a pace that I had never seen before or since, which is what happens when someone phones you and tells you your friend has had a heart attack.

I had three prolapsed discs. I was stuck in that hotel bed while William tried to take the pressure off the nerves, unable to lift my head or arms, unable to even go to the toilet.

A doctor put me in traction. Another came over and told me that he knew an excellent healer in his village. I had seen what a healer had done to Kalepi Namoua's shattered leg a year ago, and I was in the process of trying to persuade Pio not to have his wife's breast cancer treated by a healer's massage. I put my foot down, albeit with the assistance of one person to lift me up and another to move my leg: I would go to see an orthopaedic specialist in Australia, thanks to the thoughtfulness and generosity of the Australian Rugby Union. In the meantime it would be Tramadol and pain, lifts everywhere from Ropate, and Natalie doing things that no wife ever imagines she will have to do when she's standing with you in white at the altar.

Fiji's attachment to traditional medicine could sometimes be comical. In my first month, when the players were hiding in the bushes rather than doing their fitness work, one had told me that unfortunately he was unable to move on account of his legs having been cursed. But it was serious to the players and it was a deep-rooted part of Fijian culture, that strange blend of ancient and modern, of old pagan myths and muscular Christianity. If you could simultaneously believe in the imminent second coming of Christ while not entirely ruling out the existence of a shark god named Dakuwaqa, then mending a fractured tibia with kawakawarau leaves or treating a caesarean with warusi herbs was not a huge leap of faith. My task would be to navigate through that philosophy rather than trying to belittle or dismiss it.

I had first seen Vatemo Ravouvou playing in a local sevens tournament for a team called Westfield Tokatoka Barbarians. He was raw, 20 years old but bursting with a different sort of talent – a natural play-maker at fly-half, which is every team's creative hub, able to pass off both hands and kick off both feet. He had been born in Australia, his dad playing for a club side over there, and came back to Fiji as a kid, back to his home village of Saunaka, adjacent to the international airport in Nadi.

That brought its own complications. Because the villagers owned the land under the runway, twice a year they would receive a sizeable amount in rent from the operators. Vatemo's family was one of the bigger ones in the village, so their slice of the pie was that much larger. And when it came in, because of the Fijian mentality that you spend what you have, that you enjoy a windfall while you can because you never know what lurks round the corner, that would mean a two-week party – all the booze that could be bought and drunk, all the fast food that could be eaten. Vatemo would go missing for two weeks. When the cash had been spent he would come back to camp.

We had a little traditional dividend of our own. When you were training regularly with the sevens team, your picture frequently in the *Fiji Times* and *Fiji Sun*, you would be taken to the main sports shop in Suva and bought a new pair of trainers.

It was a classic Fiji Rugby deal: free shoes for a player, free publicity for Avinash, the head of the Indian family who ran J. R. Whites, but never quite working out how it should. You would take a player in, they would have a careful peruse of the big wall of trainers, choose one and be sized up. Avinash would take the photo, shake your hands and tell you he'd send the shoes up to the union offices. When they arrived a few days later they would be a different trainer entirely. You'd phone Avinash. *Ah, we didn't have the right size in that one.* You'd look at the trainers and realise they were an old model. All the players were running around at Uprising wearing identical outmoded trainers that were nothing at all like the ones they'd asked for.

I loved J. R. Whites as a store. I liked Avinash. He was a proper businessman. It reminded me of the high-street sports shops Noel and I used to gaze into longingly in west London. Everything you could want for any sport – table-tennis bats and table-tennis bat covers, little packets of studs for screw-in boots, grips for tennis racquets. A rotating display of knick-knacks like Manchester United drinks coasters and Liverpool stickers.

I walked in with Vatemo. And then, looking up at the trainers, he collapsed into a fit.

I'd seen epilepsy before, working as a supply teacher at a school in Wembley. I knew from my training what the signs were and how to look after someone as the fit progressed.

I was still scared. It went on for half a minute, severe, William alongside me certain of what he saw too.

We were about two minutes' walk down Gordon Street from the FRU offices. Once Vatemo was conscious we walked him slowly there. The offices are in an old Grade II listed building, a reception area at the front, the CEO's office on one side and meeting rooms on the other – too busy, not enough privacy. We took him through the little garden at the back out to William's treatment room, sat him down and tried to find out what was going on.

Discreet enquiries revealed that he had suffered an earlier fit while training with the under-18 team. The coaches had no idea what it was. Deciding he was a troublemaker, they kicked him out of the team. No thought of getting him checked out, no thought of bringing him back.

I called Brett Davison, a South African sports medicine expert who had been my lead physio with England. He confirmed my initial thought that we should get a brain scan done. Something might have been causing the epilepsy. If he had been suffering from it for years he would know, wouldn't he?

Apparently not. A CT scan showed no tumour. That was the good news. The epilepsy could be controlled by medication. If Vatemo took his pills and went three months without any more seizures, he could return to play.

Sometimes the players could hide behind what they pretended was a lack of English. Vatemo appeared to have understood, once he realised that the tablets were not an instant cure, once I told him that I would pick him as soon as those three months were over. Do this and your career is still on. There is no shame in what happened, and there is no reason why it should happen again.

I found out from others first: the fits were still coming regularly. William had heard about it on the coconut wireless. It wasn't in training but when Vatemo had been travelling around the island. Family first in Fiji, family second. I got in the car with Ropate and made the two-and-a-half-hour drive round the coastal road from Pacific Harbour to Saunaka to speak to his parents.

Talanoa time. Ropate and I sat down with his mum and

dad. Ropate explained what we had witnessed, why Vatemo had his pills, why he should be taking them.

His father shook his head. The pills, they won't help.

Why?

Because Vatemo has been cursed.

Cursed?

Someone has put a curse on him. He never has these attacks in the village, only when he leaves. Someone is jealous that he is in the team. They think he is too big for his boots. And so when he leaves to play, the curse hits.

I knew enough about Fiji now that I couldn't tell him not to be ridiculous. Just in case, Ropate was giving me a look: go with this, don't fight it.

I heard Vatemo's father out, and then asked his respected opinion. How can we break this curse?

All we can do is pray.

OK. While we're praying, could he take the tablets?

If you like, but they won't do anything.

And so that was what we did. We prayed together then, and Vatemo's family and the villagers of Saunaka continued to pray, and in the meantime Vatemo took his tablets. Three months later he was back playing with us. He would stay in the team to Rio and beyond, and he hasn't had an epileptic episode since.

I tried not to think what might have happened if he had gone into another fit in the middle of a World Series match, broadcast live on television, about what it would have been like for him as a man as well as an international rugby player. Instead he went on to become absolutely crucial for us, fabulous on the pitch and loyal off it. Like Apisai, you still had to keep an eye on him, just let him know that you would find out what he got up to at weekends, that

Ropate had his uncle's phone number. But the satisfaction when it worked was immense, and the bond between you so much stronger than you could forge just by having a few beers together in the bar after a match. With England I had gone for coffee with the players on Teddington High Street to find out what was important to them and what made them tick. In Fiji the connections were becoming much deeper. It validated something I'd be thinking for a while. If you got your man-management right you could get a few technical parts of coaching wrong and still succeed, but if you failed to treat your players the right way, if you weren't consistent with them and never created a sense of trust between you, you could never be consistently successful.

I'm English. I've always been uncomfortable saying publicly what I think I'm good at. If I was being honest with myself, I would hope that I had softer skills that traditional rugby coaches maybe lacked, that I would be aware of what different players might need before others would. There was clearly a serendipity about me and Fiji, how I had heard about the job, how I had got it. Now it was about these players – both vulnerable and indomitable, instinctively gifted and naturally flawed – and the way I intuitively was too. It was less what I had learned as a teacher and more why I had wanted to be a teacher in the first place: to get the best of out of kids, no matter where they were from; to not treat players like children; to understand that every individual reacts differently to the same stimuli.

Most of my team had left school by the age of 15. There was an insecurity about their own intelligence. The white man from England is the clever one. He should be telling us what to do. I saw that early and made a point of underlining the contrasting message in training: you are the brightest rugby players I've ever come across. You see the game brilliantly. You understand seemingly impossible angles and you can predict where an irregularly bouncing ball will end up and you can work out where a tiny sliver of space might appear in five complex moves' time.

Their naivety could still shock me. As news spread around the team about Pio's wife, they all seemed relatively unconcerned. Ah, it's only cancer, she'll be fine. Even Osea, when I explained the treatment she had refused and the healer she had chosen instead, was sanguine. She'll be OK, Pio has said so. They could laugh about it with him and not seem to grasp how awful the consequences might be. I couldn't work out if there was a genuine innocence or an emotional refusal to consider the grim alternatives.

Maybe the laughter was their way of dealing with it. In professional teams elsewhere I had despised the casual form of cruelty that disguised itself as banter. It had the pretence of fun but was a more subtle form of bullying. Within this Fijian team we were building, the mickey-taking was always aimed at yourself. There was never anything negative towards the younger ones or the shyer ones or the ones who were just a little bit different to the rest. It was friendly and it was fun and it lifted us all up, coach included. Winning by being nice. I knew that would get me mocked by some other coaches and certainly some of the other organisations I had been at. I couldn't imagine Frank getting a tattoo of it. For us it was working.

Before the World Series began on the Gold Coast there was one more place I wanted to take the team. The year before, my trip to the island of Ovalau and St John's College had been the start of my real Fijian education. Now it was time to take the players with me, to reconnect us all with the grass roots and the bare mud of the nation's sevens obsession, to fulfil the promise I had made to Father John and all the kids.

The same ferry journey, this time paid for by George Patterson, another huge Fiji sevens supporter who put his money where his heart was, happy to give any of our players free travel any time they needed it. Off the wharf, the same dusty streets, we walked out along that seven-kilometre path from Ovalau's capital, Levuka, to the school, the white coral-stone church sticking up above the trees in the distance, the smell of the cannery in our nostrils.

They cleared out one of the dormitories for us. The players slept in the same small beds that the kids had, same rough old sheets, same toilets. The kid whose bed it was came in each morning with a cup of tea and a long loaf. That's my bed, this is your breakfast. The lads organised games of touch rugby with the kids and Father John watched over it all with a benevolent and slightly disbelieving smile.

At Nasau Park, back in Levuka, there was a sevens tournament with all the local teams, the pitch rock hard and the grass only occasional. I had enough with me to enter two teams, and the locals proceeded to try to knock their heads off. Players around the islands knew by now that I was a coach who would pick on ability rather than region or family, that if they played well it might be them coming back in Fiji kit the following year, and I welcomed that competition. It allowed me to blood a few new players and to season a few others before the real business of the

World Series began. At the end of each match it was all hugs and mutual respect anyway.

My back was still a mess, the Tramadol giving everything a warm glow and almost letting me forget that none of the players were contracted despite the Olympic qualification about to begin. The week before the opening World Series leg on the Gold Coast we took our young, inexperienced second team to the Oceania sevens up the road in Noosa and played a high-energy blend of rugby that was too good for everyone else – Tonga beaten 49–7 in the quarter-finals, Samoa 24–12 in the semis, a very strong New Zealand put away 21–5 in the final. We looked fit and we looked unified.

New Zealand coach Gordon Tietjens just looked worried. He was someone who hammered his players in training, a relentless slog rather than the short explosive stuff I believed made sense for sevens. His players often looked drained before they took to the field. He feared Fiji for their unpredictability but was convinced they could never have the strength and stamina of his boys. Here they were looking fitter than they had ever done before.

On the Gold Coast it kept going. It made no difference that I was totally incapacitated, unable to stand up and shout with joy at everything I was seeing in front of me. Wales beaten 31–10 in the quarter-finals, 48 points put on England in the semis. We were 28–0 up in the final against Samoa before we took our foot off the gas and let them back into it a little.

It was a wonderful way to start the Olympic charge, with a typically Fijian aftermath: seven players poached by club sides in Sri Lanka, all out of the picture for the next four months. Pio Tuwai. Setefano Cackau. Apisai Naqaliva.

Sanivalati Ramuwai. Joeli Lutumailagi. Samu Saqiwa. Leone Naikasau.

Three of them had started that Gold Coast final. It was almost half my team.

My travels round the islands had given us a strength in depth we hadn't had before. The performance of the second string in Noosa also gave us a desperately needed cushion. But what was to say these next taxis off the rank wouldn't also be hired by the overseas money men when they broke through?

I went in hard with the *Fiji Times* and the *Fiji Sun* when they asked how we were. We still have no contracts for our players. If we don't have contracts we will soon have no players. Without players there will be no repeat of the Gold Coast and no winning back the Hong Kong title and no Olympic qualification, let alone that first-ever Olympic medal.

Those two newspapers carry weight. Letters appeared in the editorial pages asking what on earth the FRU was doing, saying that the board should be sacked if they couldn't sort it out. Trying to rebuild, we then struggled a little in the next two World Series rounds, losing to Australia in the semis in Dubai and the quarter-finals in Port Elizabeth. In some ways it helped. While those new players were bedding in, the pressure was growing on the board.

The board pushed back. The newspapers could be played both ways. Full-page spreads from ex-coaches saying Ryan isn't doing this and can't do that. Board members briefing journalists behind my back, a growing sense we might not be able to make this any better.

The chairman now was a former Fijian schools fly-half named Filimoni Waqabaca. He was also the Minister of

Finance, and the knives were coming for him too. He and his chief executive Radrodro Tabualevu were trying to defend me but were about to be moved on themselves, too creative and keen on modernisation to survive.

I sat down with Natalie over dinner at Pacific Harbour. This is beyond what I've experienced before. I'm not sure we're going to hang on here much longer.

Rumblings and rumours spread. One evening I got a call on my mobile from the general manager of the Australian Rugby Union. He asked if I would be interested in going to work for them. They had seen what I had managed in a year with Fiji and thought I might be able to do even more with support from a well-run union and funding from a nation that always looked after its Olympic athletes.

The next morning Ropate was hauled into Rugby House and in front of the board. Why is Ben going to Australia? Where is the loyalty he is asking for from us?

That was the moment I feared my phone was being bugged. Everything on it: calls, voicemails, texts. Emails from my Fiji Rugby account.

I suppose I shouldn't have been shocked. Bright sunshine and black storm clouds. That lurking darkness coming into sudden view. How long had they been listening for?

I had to get a burner, a pay-as-you-go sim card in a cheap phone. One for me, one for Ropate. A new email address, a little code established between Ropate, William, Osea and me for when we had to speak on the phones we had been given by the FRU. It almost became a game. They know that you know.

Frank had certainly been busy. In September he had organised Fiji's first general election since the coup in December 2006, an election which had first been promised to take place within 12 months of the army's takeover and then by March 2009 at the latest.

In March 2010 Frank had decreed that any politician who had played a role in the country's politics since 1987 would not be allowed to stand, since Fiji needed to make a fresh start. In March 2014 he had then made a fresh start of his own, launching a new political party called Fiji First. You need 5,000 signatures to register a political party in Fiji. After a quick trip round in his campaign bus, Frank gathered 40,000.

It turned out well for him. Fiji First won more than twice as many votes as any other party. Frank was elected Prime Minister. International observers declared the process credible.

The ripples only touched me occasionally. A few months later I had a call from a friend in a high place. It was relatively succinct: we're sending a car to pick you up, there's going to be a coup tonight.

The storm blew in and the storm clouds cleared. Frank left Viti Levu on urgent government business. When he returned deals had been done and the uprising had been quelled. In Fiji you ride the bad weather out. The downpour comes but you know the sun will be out again soon.

That attitude was built into everything that happened. If there is food on the table, eat it all now because it might not be there tomorrow. Clean out the bar while you can because who knows when we'll get the chance again? Most Fijians get paid on a Friday. A really good job pays every fortnight, more of them once a week. It helps and it hinders. It spreads it across the month but so much still gets blown that first day and night.

And it works in both ways for their rugby. There is no

thought of risk, no concern about what might happen afterwards. Make the crazy offload, gamble on the supporting run. Then, if you miss a tackle, if bad luck comes your way, everything stops while your team-mates all feel sorry for you for 30 seconds. We had to put cues in place to flip that emotional response round: if something goes wrong, help them out – *cakacaka*, work even harder. Yet that lack of fear could be a wonderful weapon – he's just scored a great try, I'm going to do it as well; we're down a try with time almost up, don't worry about it, let's go and bring the sunshine out again.

We had a semi-final in Singapore against South Africa when the full-time hooter went with us four points down and in possession. If we lost the ball, if we made an error, the game was over. One play left, we had to score from it.

The boys had seen moments before that I was anxious, that I thought it had gone: Vatemo! Vatemo, you've got to come on, we've only got one forward on the field – you've got to kick it into this hole over there, Jasa's got to catch it or tuck it back to you, and then we've got to score a try, it's our only hope...

Vatemo shrugged. OK, no problem. The boys all laughing at the white English guy who thinks even for one second that it isn't going to happen.

Vatemo on. A kick into the optimum place, Jasa with the catch and pass, Vatemo slaloming through a frantic defence and passing to Alivereti Vaitokani to score the try and win us the match. The boys patting me on the back. Of course it was going to happen, he said it would.

In those impossible moments it was like having magic in your fingertips. If you could get everything else right, that holy blend was unstoppable. Get one thing wrong, leave one ingredient out or add it at the wrong time, and the whole thing would fall apart. One misjudged word to a player could see everyone affected.

It was why I worked so hard on those relationships. As often as I could I would praise people like our conditioning coach Naca to the media, stressing how impressed I was with them and how much they were helping Fiji's great dream. I would take him and William and Ropate out for dinner once a week and pay for it because I knew they couldn't afford to, and at Christmas I would put money in their bank accounts because my salary, now it had come through, was so much bigger than theirs. It was my way of backing up what I was saying to their faces: I value you, I couldn't do this without you, we are in this together. Thank you.

SEVEN

*T*here are kids at school you just know to stay clear of. Bad big brothers with a hair trigger and a terrible temper or a sense of threat and menace around them if you ever stray close.

Noel isn't like that. The kids he is hanging out with, now he's seldom in school, are. He's the youngest in that new group, and he's the one being made to do all the marginal stuff. Being tested out, being pushed on. 20-year-olds leading 16-year-olds. Noel short of money, not getting it from anywhere else any more.

I still try to spend evenings with him, even if it's out in the streets and hanging round outside Richmond Station, and these older lads are always lurking. But I'm a kid. My evenings finish at 9 p.m. Noel's go on, because no one else cares where he is or what time he's back.

The older ones unsettle me. You can't predict what they're going to do. Always the sense that they might turn on you next. They're *feeling you out all the time, little snide comments and laughs, dares that you don't have a choice about. Always uncomfortable, always scared they might suddenly force you to do something you don't want to do, or do something to you that you cannot prevent.*

Initiations. Me stepping away. Too much for me. Noel being carried along. Threatening people on their own outside the station when it's late and dark. Another step up: do this, or we'll do this to you. A mugging. Cash in hand, kudos with the leaders. Pretending it's still all a laugh when it stopped being that long ago.

And then the big one. It starts as a joke and it goes serious real soon. Noel given a replica hand gun. It's a fake, don't worry about it. Just go into the off-licence over the road from the station. See what happens. See what you can get.

Noel goes in. Noel gets caught.

February 2015. Nine legs in the World Series, nine tournaments to qualify for the Olympics. Three down, one win, one third place, one amongst the also-rans.

Going to the fourth tournament at the Westpac Stadium on Wellington's waterfront, we were in second place in the overall points standings. South Africa out on top with 54, Fiji on 52, New Zealand 47, Australia 46, England 37.

It's 22 points for winning a World Series tournament, 19 for second, 17 for third, 15 for fourth. Those top four at the end of the series in May qualifying automatically for Rio, each position decisive to who you would play in the group and how good the opposition might be in the rounds that lay ahead.

Against Australia in the group stage we had a strong team out – Osea our captain, and Save Rawaca charging on the wing; Semi Kunatani, back in the fold after that boozy training session, doing his five surrogate mothers proud; Sami Viriviri, his family pushing him on from the boondocks; Viliame Mata, working harder now, *cakacaka*.

We won, but at a cost. Osea and Semi both cited for high tackles, both banned from the quarter-final against England if found guilty. The tackles were non-events, part of a pattern I was still seeing where players from the Pacific islands were presumed to be dirtier than their big-nation counterparts, where a referee who might let things go when New Zealand were playing the USA would have his yellow or red cards out against Fiji or Samoa or Tonga. The Westpac Stadium was where *Lord of the Rings* director Peter Jackson had recorded the sound of 30,000 Kiwi fans chanting in unison to give him the sound of evil warriors going into battle. Thirteen years on, we were still the orcs.

As the coach you attend the post-match hearing with the citing officer to make your players' argument. Immediately it felt wrong: the New Zealander in charge asking if I wanted to deal with both cases at the same time, the match footage being played back on an antique VHS video player so it was not only indistinct but impossible to slow down and analyse. The whole procedure was sloppy and half-baked. I told him that Osea and Semi were discrete people involved in two different incidents, that you couldn't cite players as a job lot.

It made no difference – both were banned. We lost the quarter-final to England 26–21 in extra time when we shouldn't have done, and we wouldn't have, had those two been on the pitch as they should have been. The procedure would change the following year, after I put a campaign together, my resolve strengthened by this palpable injustice.

We were slipping. Almost halfway through the World

Series, South Africa now on 71 points, New Zealand on 69, us on 65, England and Australia closing on 58.

That was how the blend worked. Miss one or two ingredients and watch the whole thing fail. Add each tiny part of the recipe in the right amount and order, and magic could follow just as quickly.

To Vegas next for the USA sevens, the team together, the disappointments quickly in the past. We squeezed past New Zealand in the group stage with tries from Semi and winger Save Rawaca, thundering past South Africa 24–19 in the semi-finals, big expat support in clusters around the Sam Boyd Stadium, the benevolent Fiji ambassador Winston Thompson and his wife Queenie keeping it all smooth and easy behind the scenes, spinning us yarns about Fijian history and folklore over dinner. We had New Zealand and Sir Gordon Tietjens again in the final, the pitch cut into diagonal halves of sunshine and shadow, our play all blue-sky brilliance. Tries again for Save and two for Semi, all that natural power and newborn fitness sending him through weak arms and strong tackles alike.

It was Hong Kong a few weeks later, the magic still at our fingertips. Fireworks and tickertape under those two vast stands, the actual Village People performing beforehand as well as their lookalikes appearing in the fancy-dressed hordes in the capacity crowd. Drummers and dancing girls as you walked out of the tunnel from the changing-rooms to the pitch, our expat support in full effect – blue curly wigs, white team shirts, outsized Fijian flags, little groups in T-shirts with a letter on each fan's chest to spell out FIJI when they were in the right order and FJII when a few beers had gone down or IJI when those beers needed to be moved on.

I had taken England to three semis and one final at this most storied of tournaments but never won it, twice losing critical matches to Fiji. This time I could see the easy confidence in the players and feel the more cautious optimism running through me, manifested as we fought past England and their coach Simon Amor 14–12 in the quarter-finals. Simon was a former scrum-half and the inherited captain for my England team before stepping into my boots with the RFU, the two of us polite but radically different in the way we set teams up, looked after players, found and developed young talent, and believed the game should be played. When he was captain, those differences began to emerge. And it seemed to me he didn't value the foundations I had put in place when he took over as the team's coach.

World Series leaders South Africa in the semi-finals, past them 21–15. New Zealand again in the final, under the lights, the sky up above dark and the skyscrapers all around tall and bright. The players with Hong Kong memories in their blood and Serevi's sweet history in their minds. Osea in tears as the national anthem played, looking up into the night to mouth a prayer before gathering the team around him, right hands clasped together with index fingers pointing up.

Hallowed ground for Fiji sevens and a sanctified spell to follow. We came at them like holy ghosts, rampaging in pairs and slick series, cutting this way then the other, all brutal force one moment and delicate feints and guile the next.

Save Rawaca scored a try after almost everyone in the team seemed to handle the ball en route. Semi burgled the ball from his Kiwi opposite number for the second. Three

125

tries to the one from New Zealand in the first half, two more in the second, the final one created by Save's swerves and hand-offs down the left wing and the ball tossed to Apisai Domolailai once they'd crossed the try-line so he too could join in the fun, the Sigatoka kid cashing in on our collective sand-dunes stamina.

As the final whistle blew I embraced each player on the touchline. It was almost midnight in Fiji, but I knew the nation would be watching – the families, the kids being allowed to stay up late, the board members who wanted me out and the prime minister who might now want me closer.

I had loved the flair we had shown, but Fiji had always possessed that. We had also been defensively resolute and tactically astute. We had worked out when to make the big hits and when to guard space, when to dangle the bait in front of New Zealand's defenders and when to jerk the rod. Our replacements off the bench had made exactly the impact we required.

I don't like going up to collect trophies with the players. Coaches spoil the team photo, so I stayed down on the pitch as Osea led them up. They refused to accept it until I joined them; two came down and grabbed me and ushered me politely but forcefully up the steps. Serevi was there too, as he had been so often as a player. I didn't mind at that moment. We were all in this together.

That night, the celebrations going off in Suva and Nadi and Ovalau and across the archipelago, I shared a glass of wine with Beth Coalter. Before moving back to her native Ireland to work for World Rugby she had been arguably the biggest driving force in making the Hong Kong sevens what they were – starting as secretary, moving up to tournament manager, there from 1987 to 2005. In the ten years since she had done more than anyone else to make sevens an Olympic sport, but she was far more than an administrator. Beth, at ease with herself as she approached her 60th birthday, maternal to others, genuinely cared. She would send you messages asking how you were at times when everyone else had their thoughts elsewhere. She would sit down with you and listen as you got things off your chest, making you feel better about it without trying to push any trite solutions. And she would take genuine pleasure in the success of others, sending me a text when Semi Kunatani played well to eulogise about how he must be making those lovely women back in Naveyago feel, giving me an unnecessary amount of credit for his development, reminding me that in the tough times I had in Fiji this made it all worthwhile. There was no one better to celebrate quietly with.

Bright sunshine and black storm clouds. When we returned to Fiji I called Pio Tuwai to see if there was anything I could do to help with his wife's treatment. He asked if I would mind driving up to her mother's house outside Lautoka.

Pio had met his wife after the Hong Kong sevens four years before. Hungover, severely dehydrated, he had been admitted to hospital on his return to Viti Levu. She had been there too. Since then they had had three children, the last of them still tiny, her birth the point at which the doctors had first discovered the mother's cancer.

Natalie came with me. Three hours in the car from Pacific Harbour, the whole family waiting by the fence when we pulled up outside. One of the little kids ran up to me and clung on to my leg, riding it into the house as we were led in.

She was lying on a mattress on the bedroom floor. Me and Natalie and her and Pio in the dark, stuffy room and her crying to me and no hiding from it any more.

The cancer had spread fast. From her breast into her bones, diminishing her so rapidly and dramatically that she was now unable to move. Her sister had to bring the new baby to her side. Her bones were so weak she was unable to cuddle the child herself.

She knew she was dying, even though her sister refused to accept it, even as the family kept picking up the mattress and loading it into a van and taking her into the interior on the dirt roads to be massaged by the native healer. All the while her bones breaking, all of it without anything for pain relief.

I sat down on the floor next to her and asked what she needed. She thought for a while. A bed on wheels, like a hospital bed, so she could be moved around the house, so she wouldn't be just stuck on the mattress on the floor. I called Berlin Kafoa, the former acting CEO of Fiji Rugby, also a teaching doctor in Suva. Berlin, we have to do something. Two days later a bed arrived from the hospital in Nadi.

I had told Pio that he didn't need to come to training, that his place would still be there when he came back. His wife had whispered to me that she wanted him to go, to make her and the family feel proud.

She was trying to be brave. She was being far braver than she knew. I kept seeing a high tolerance of pain in Fijians; life was tough, and you got used to some of it and had to swallow the rest. But her family and her kids and Pio were all in denial. As I said goodbye to her they were still telling me she was going to be OK, that the healer would work his magic.

Natalie knew. Neither of us could hold it back when we were in the car and on our way. You saw how young she was, you saw the children. You knew there was no cure, that even if she now accepted chemotherapy her disease was far too advanced for it to make any difference. Natalie looked at me as the car turned back onto Queens Road. She's not going to last long, is she?

Third in Tokyo in April 2015, two more rounds of the World Series to go, the Olympics in our sights. I wanted us to head back to Britain early for the Scotland and London tournaments so we could get our preparations right, and went as usual for the creative and cheap approach: asking my cousin, part of the Household Cavalry at Windsor Castle, if we could stay in the barracks there for free. It was all in place until a mysterious unrelated incident bumped up the levels of security around the Queen. A last-minute request to the International Olympic Committee and their Olympic Solidarity Fund for enough money to stick us in a hotel instead, the boys heading to Glasgow rested and primed and unperturbed by the late-spring rain.

We had carried that winning Hong Kong form with us to a very different corner of the world. Scotstoun Stadium does not have the glamour of those Far Eastern tournaments. The sky was the same colour as the Glaswegian pavements and the wind was trying to blow us back to winter.

We galloped into the final. I went out to the training pitch out back with Ropate and Naca and waited for the players to arrive for their warm-up. They turned up with less than two minutes left, all track of time lost as they talked over the game in the changing room.

Gordon Tietjens and his staff were already in the main stadium. Five minutes later his team joined them. The referee and his assistants arrived. Music started playing. I looked at the clock. Where were the boys?

Osea had got carried away. The team had got carried away. Standing in a huddle, talking about how important this game was, why we had to win, how this could take us to within touching distance of Olympic qualification. By the time they came wandering out into the stadium there were 60 seconds left before kick-off. Time only for two frantic sprints, and then the referee's arm came up and the whistle was at his lips.

We were dreadful. Lucky to be just 12–5 down at half-time, Osea fortunate not to be yellow-carded. At the interval I gathered them around me and let rip.

That is a shadow of the team that has been playing for the last two days. It's an embarrassment. So you need to sort your stuff out in the next ten minutes, and decide where our fate lies. You got that right?

I walked away and left Osea to do the rest.

The response came. Osea running on to a Pio offload and a series of sharp passes to level it up. Apisai Domolailai off the bench for a shattered Pio and off his right foot for a step and acceleration inside the defender for another score. New Zealand rattled, one of their players sin-binned for trying to stop us illegally when the simply legal wasn't enough. Apisai crashing through the black shirts again like one of his wild horses. 24–17 with time up, New Zealand hammering away at us for the try to take it to extra time,

130

the boys spotting an opening with a Kiwi on the floor to counter-ruck and steal the ball away and kick it to the stands for victory.

Afterwards all the talk was of the impact of that half-time speech. Maybe it made a difference. Maybe it was more that they had warmed up properly over the ten minutes of the first half. But it meant we travelled to London with four tournament wins from eight and on top of the World Series standings. Staying there would not only mean the number-one seeding for us in Rio but the overall series title for the first time in a decade too.

Beth Coalter was there at Heathrow as we landed. With her lift into town having failed to materialise, we told her to jump on our coach instead. London would be her final tournament with World Rugby before she retired to do a little consultancy and spend more time in Ireland with her husband Bill and her pregnant daughter, a first grandchild on its way. We had brought over a *tanoa* bowl for her, inscribed with her name and a message thanking her for everything she had done for sevens and for Fiji and for so many of us as individuals. Ropate presented it to her, and for the duration of the drive into London the boys sang her songs and serenaded her, smiles and hugs and a few tears for a woman who deserved it all.

The scenario at Twickenham that weekend was a simple one. Do better than South Africa, our closest pursuers in the World Series standings, and the World Series crown was ours. After Glasgow New Zealand could no longer catch us; England were a little further adrift in fourth.

As top seeds we should have been kept apart until the final. Instead, South Africa lost to the USA in their final group game. We would meet them in the quarter-finals instead.

11 a.m. on a Sunday in west London, only a couple of miles from my old house in Teddington, from the stadium where I had worked for so many years with England, from the offices where the man who had sacked me still worked. The winner of the match takes the World Series, the loser loses it.

The night before I had gone to a favourite pub and sunk a couple of beers so I could drop off to sleep. Nerves and excitement swirling together, telling myself that if we played as we could, I would be sleeping far better the following night. Concentrating on us rather than obsessing over the South African threats, not even bothering to find out which referee would be taking charge.

The stadium filled up slowly. With a whole afternoon of action to come, the hangovers from the previous day were slowing the arrival of some spectators. London is as boozy and fancy-dressed as Hong Kong now, an end-of-term weekender for everyone in England who liked their rugby fast and loose. I could see my family, mum, two sisters, nieces. Big pockets of Fijian fans, holding out the big flags and belting out the hymns. We went through our warm-up, coaches watching carefully this time, and jogged to the supporters to applaud them as we finished. As the players went back into the Twickenham dressing rooms I told them. You're cool, you know what you have to do. You beat South Africa in the quarter-finals in Scotland a week ago and you beat them well. They are still in shock after what Semi Kunatani did to them and how he did it at will. Let's get ready and enjoy it.

In my last season with England we had shared a dressing

room with Fiji in Hong Kong. We had been knocked out; they were through to the final to play Wales. Before the big match their players had been crying their eyes out. Serevi was in there with the kids, ramping them up even more with a big speech. They would have been climbing the walls had their hands not been busy wiping the tears from their cheeks. When the national anthem was played out on the pitch they went again, total over-arousal, no longer thinking about rugby but about what this would mean to them and Serevi and the nation back home. Fijians are quite open about their emotions. There are usually no negative connotations to a man crying. But they were so highly strung in that match that it almost derailed them – three tries down in the first five minutes, heads gone, fortunate in the extreme not to have a man red-carded for a spear tackle.

I went into the changing rooms at Twickenham this time. Tears everywhere. Bad, bad news. Even Ropate was crying.

I had four or five minutes to change the mood. Into the shower area, a tight huddle, three key messages. I understand this is an important game that matters to everyone we care about, but if you go out like this, we will not perform as we should. This is what happened in Hong Kong three years ago, and it nearly went terribly wrong. A relaxed Fijian team is a ruthless one. Smile, breathe, enjoy the fact that you are with your team-mates and about to play sevens just how we want to.

You could almost hear the bubble that had surrounded them pop. From heads down to heads up. Ben's right, we're getting carried away.

Into the Twickenham tunnel, the South Africans looking

uptight, all frowns and slapping each other. I walked along the touchline with Ropate and Naca and said, let's try to make sure we're smiling and looking relaxed on the side of the field during the whole game, and it will rub off on the boys. Even if we're not enjoying it we have to look as if we are.

The boys were absolutely dominant. Osea, Pio, Semi. Save Rawaca, Vatemo Ravouvou, on his epilepsy medication and on fire. Fantastic defensively, South Africa coming at us hard in the first three minutes and the team just absorbing it all. Save scoring on the break, Amenoni Nasilasila into the team late on and stepping and ducking and setting Osea away for try number two, and then Save again, burning down the right wing.

A pale-blue sky up above the same colour as the Fijian flag, a performance down below that would have the nation on its feet. 19–7 at the end, the boys grappling each other with delight, falling to their knees to pray.

I didn't care what happened in the semi-final. What did it matter? We were World Series champions for the first time since 2006. We were going to the Olympics. Our emotional energy had been spent. Australia could have this one.

The hours afterwards were surreal ones. Seeing my mum and sisters and friends, all looking so pleased for us, Natalie all smiles, the boys singing their hymns and rocking a celebratory *lotu* deep in Twickenham's concrete bowels. A text message from Frank on my phone: congratulations to you, congratulations to the team. Ropate's phone ringing, Frank again, the phone getting passed over and his unmistakable voice coming across from the other side of the world, from my new home to my old: Peni Raiyani, the nation is proud of you.

I guessed no other head of state would have been calling the country's sevens coach had they won the World Series. The closest I had got to the Queen was that abandoned trip to the barracks at Windsor Castle. When the team flew back to Fiji the next day the madness multiplied exponentially: thousands mobbing Nadi international airport from the arrivals lounge through into the terminal, speeches and presentations organised by the FRU, dinner in a nearby village, full tides and tsunamis of *kava* everywhere you looked.

A bus ride round the coast to Suva that should have taken three hours but ended up taking closer to nine, every village on the way getting wind on the coconut wireless that the team coach was approaching and flagging it down so they could say thank you to the team, putting children in the road so it would have to slow down. They had erected temporary stands in Albert Park in Suva for the homecoming at 3 p.m. and no one moved until the team finally arrived closer to 9 p.m. Frank was there to greet them from his dais, even his bodyguards cracking a smile or two as well as fingering their hand-guns, celebrations rolling on for days across the islands.

The trophy stayed in Fiji until the start of the next World Series the following November. It did multiple tours of the islands, handled by thousands of happy hands, returned with all manner of little dents and dinks and muttered apologies.

A song came out shortly afterwards from a local artist called Babu Marley. Heavily reliant on his higher-profile Jamaican namesake, it was also built around a sample of my half-time rant in Scotland:

135

Ben is the man
He came from England
We didn't give him the pay
But the fellow still stayed
Because he's iron
Like a lion
Ben Ryan...

Ben Ryan never cry
When he shouting at half-time
'This is an embarrassment.
You need to sort your stuff out in the next ten minutes
And decide where our fate lies
You got that right?'
Because he's iron
Like a lion
Ben Ryan...

I had stayed back in London, so there was a dislocated, unreal air about it all. Ropate kept calling me from the coach as it made its way towards Suva through all the villages, the songs coming through the ether, photos pinging through from the players.

Part one of the mission was complete, but part two in my mind was already under way. In a year's time I would be selecting the final squad for Rio. We needed more strength in depth, and we needed to capture some more rogue talent. Semi Kunatani was off to Toulouse on a contract that was just too good for him to turn down, that would transform the present and future of his entire family, but we had the clause in there that would allow him to return to Fiji for the critical training camps before

Rio in addition to the Olympics themselves. The rest of the players had talked amongst themselves and made a collective commitment: we will turn down any overseas contract until after the Olympics. One year together, one big push to make history.

The team we had now was a vast improvement on the one that had started that World Series, the self-destructive mess I had inherited on arrival 18 months before. We still had weaknesses and flaws that good teams could exploit. We needed to work on our counter-rucking, when the opposition had the ball in hand on the floor, and we needed to make the defensive white wall that had swallowed South Africa a consistent feature rather than an occasional happy surprise. Sometimes our decision-making in the critical last few minutes of tight matches could go missing. And almost all of my star players were still too easily distracted and sent off course if I looked away. Demons never entirely went away. They merely went into hiding.

But we were maturing. We had failed to warm up in Glasgow but we had come back to win the game. The team had lost control of their emotions in London but got hold of themselves just in time. The hangers-on were hanging on less and the distractions and disruptions on overseas trips were being policed as they had never been before. Ropate, once a bouncer, always a bouncer.

And we were together. Sami Viriviri, outstanding all season, had been awarded World Rugby's sevens Player of the Year award for the previous year. They had tried to make a presentation on the pitch at Twickenham, but every time the microphone was put in front of him his head would drop and only silence came out of his mouth.

After six attempts he managed to mumble something but nothing that anyone could make sense of.

I took him out of the stadium. What's up? First he told me he was nervous. Then he admitted that he was thinking about his mum Vika, working at the Flying Fish restaurant in Nadi, bringing him and his five brothers and three sisters up all on her own, and that he was trying to keep it together and not burst into tears with the camera there and the whole stadium watching.

I had a chat with the television crew. They understood. We tried again in a little side room, the interviewer making it easy-going and light-hearted. Sami warmed up, slowly at first and then with a big grin. As we came out, chat done, the boys were all standing outside waiting for him. They sang to him, they genuflected in front of him. They told him: you've done a wonderful thing, and we are proud of you.

I loved that. I loved those moments that I could never have foreseen when I left London a year and a half before, the friendships that had come from our *cakacaka*, our hard work, the bonds that we had forged through the mistakes and backward steps and special days and nights of triumph.

And then the storm clouds, the ones you saw on the horizon and the ones that swept in from nowhere.

Pio's wife passed away shortly after he returned from winning the World Series. Still in London, I missed the *reguregu*, the Fijian funeral ceremony – to the house where the body lay, to kiss the corpse goodbye, a gift of *tabua* (a whale tooth) to the man of the home, presents of mats and cloth to the women. Pio let his hair grow from that point on, to show that he was in mourning, to show that he had lost someone so close to him.

A few months later, Ropate and I were in Sydney to

watch a sevens tournament when we got an email about Beth. She had collapsed at work in Belfast and been rushed into intensive care with a brain haemorrhage. She had advanced leukaemia. We were told to expect the worst.

Ropate and I were having dinner in a predominantly gay restaurant. The place was full of men, couples at every table. A short ginger-haired white man and a gigantic Fijian, all the stares and whispers about us. Before we went to bed we made a deal: whoever gets a phone call, wake the other one up.

At three in the morning Ropate knocked on my apartment door. Beth was gone. He came in and asked if I would mind saying a prayer with him. We sat there on the floor, me naked except for my underwear, Ropate in nothing but his Y-fronts. Holding hands and praying, knowing that Beth would have found the scene hilarious, not wanting to think that we would never hear that laugh again.

Beth stayed with us. In Rio I told the world that had it not been for her, we would never have been there at all. In Hong Kong they named the award for the best new player after her. One of our boys won the first iteration. The Beth Coalter award, presented by her husband, honouring a woman loved by everyone.

Natalie and I went to see Pio and his family when we returned to Fiji. We were startled by how easily he seemed to have accepted it all. Fijians don't tend to fear death. They see it as inevitable; it is around them all the time, and people die a lot. They acknowledge what has happened and they move on. Towards the next morning, towards a dawn with new sunlight and old memories and the understanding that sometimes you have no control over the things you care about more than anything else.

EIGHT

Noel goes to trial for attempted robbery. Because it involves a gun he is at the Old Bailey. When he is awaiting trial he is sent to Wormwood Scrubs.

Dad tries to help. He tries to provide Noel with a solicitor and acts as a character witness: this is a good kid who's just gone the wrong way because no one has looked after him and no one has been there for him.

I go to see Noel in the old Victorian prison, grey and austere and forbidding on Du Cane Road in White City, walls up against the Scrubs recreation ground, just a little jog up the muddy path from the athletics track where I used to train with Thames Valley Harriers. I take him cigarettes, not because he smokes but because in my naivety I think that's what you need in prison. It's what I've seen on telly. Noel takes them and there are no smiles. He tells me he would rather have the cash.

He is emotionless. There are no tears and there is no pain on the surface. For the first time in our lives I cannot imagine myself in his position. I am in a new world and I have no compass bearings. I know I am not street-wise or strong enough to be where he is.

Noel does not complain. He just seems to be blocking it all out. In the Old Bailey to receive the jury's verdict. Guilty of attempted armed robbery. A sentence from the judge of three years in jail.

He serves half of that and is let out on probation. No one knows where he goes.

I think about him all the time. I try to find him. My best mate, and still I miss him.

The first time I saw Jerry Tuwai was in the Marist sevens, the biggest annual club tournament in Fiji, 90 teams from all round the country, boats big and small coming in from all the islands, all the games live on national television. Just as Marist Brothers High School is so highly regarded, so the Marist rugby club is the one everyone aspires to play for in the capital.

His full name was Seremaia Tuwai Vunisa, Jerry being the anglicised version. I'd heard of neither. I was sitting with Osea in the little commentators' box at the National Stadium, just to get away from the crowds for a while, to make sure that we could watch the games properly rather than signing autographs all the time. There was something about this short, shy kid that made me take a second look. When he had the ball in hand he looked useful. When he didn't have it he was invisible. You'd see him in flashes, like the former Fiji sevens scrum-half William Ryder – quick, nimble, a nice sidestep – and then you wouldn't see him at all for ages. Defensively he was doing nothing. He may as well not have been in the line.

Osea liked some of what he saw. So did Ropate. I thought there was something there that was worth another look. Since Ryder had retired a few years before there had been an absence of a little killer, the sort of kid that, on form, could scare defences, who was harder to read than Confucius in the original and who could make younger kids want to do what he could do.

Jerry had footwork. He was small, around 5ft 7ins, but with serious-sized calves for a little tubby guy. His legs had punch and sudden acceleration in them. He would cock one foot and sort of hop for a second and then – *bang* – he'd be off, at least until he ran out of gas, which was pretty soon. You tried to work out where he was going to go next and thought you saw it coming and then with a sudden explosion he would be gone.

After the tournament came to an end I made some enquiries. He had been called into the national squad for training about three or four years earlier but had only lasted about one camp. In the papers the next day he read that the coach thought he was too small. No one had told him that to his face. He just went home. They never picked him again.

It wasn't an unfamiliar story. You could see why so many tender young talents disappeared; they didn't understand how to take training seriously, they were never told what to expect or given feedback afterwards and they often thought, well, that was my one chance, it's not coming back again.

And so I decided to bring him back into training, to give him a second chance, and maybe a third, if he needed it. I told him to play his normal game, not to worry about structure or set moves for now, that if he got any clean ball off the scrum just to go, don't worry about anything else, just have a crack.

He was painfully shy. For a week I don't think he uttered a word to anyone. And he was dreadfully unfit, with apparently minimal motivation to improve. He couldn't get through a single training session without breaking down exhausted. A lot of the time he wouldn't even turn up for a training session. He would stay at home in Newtown, a little shanty-town in Nasinu, about a ten-minute drive north up Kings Road from Suva, playing volleyball barefoot on the small gravel roundabout in the street outside his house.

His feet were a mess, broken toenails and infected cuts. He was full of excuses: I couldn't get to training, I missed the bus; I was ill, I couldn't move. When we did fitness drills in the sessions he did get to, his chin would always be on his chest as he ran. When he wasn't running he was hiding in the bushes. He couldn't understand the intensity of the work we were doing and he couldn't connect it with the rugby that he loved to play.

There was another kid I had brought in at the same time who had similar footwork but was even smaller. He too was woefully out of shape, but you could see within a couple of weeks that no matter how sharp we made him physically, he would eventually hit a ceiling with his skills. Jerry's potential kept going up a little more every week.

There was another problem. Like a lot of Fijians from poorer backgrounds, Jerry's teeth were rotting. You could smell the disease and infection from a pass away. I had become accustomed to seeing it with the boys; in that first year, when we had lost in the semi-finals at Hong Kong, I had been woken up in the middle of the night by a commotion in the corridor. Pio needed root-canal treatment but had done nothing about it, and was in so much pain that his team-mates were cuddling him on the corridor floor and stroking his face to help get him through it.

Within the squad there was very little brushing of teeth and a steadfast reluctance to do anything about problems when they inevitably began. Physio William would give them paracetamol. At home they might have *kava*, to try to numb it up, but you couldn't do that around a tournament.

In the first year a regular pattern would emerge. We would be on the team bus to the airport, ready to fly to a tournament, and one of the boys would quietly mention to William that he had a sore tooth. William would stop the bus in Nadi to take him to the dentist. As he stood up three or four others would put their hands up and mutter that they had a problem too. All of them would troop off the bus and come back with numb lips and glassy eyes an hour later.

It would always amaze me, the level of pain that they were happy to endure rather than go to the dentist. Sometimes it was a logistical thing. If you were not in training camp or not in the national team then there would be no one in the distant villages to help. It wasn't the cost, because dentistry in Fiji was remarkably cheap. Neither was it the level of expertise. Possibly because of the amount of practice they were getting, the dentists in Suva were extremely good. Natalie had quite a lot of work done and found it all excellent. After a while I set up regular checks for the players so that we kept missed flights to a minimum.

At the start of my second year, November 2014, seven players down after the usual post-season exodus abroad,

145

we had a gap in the squad for the second team we were taking to Noosa. I decided to take Jerry along to see how he was progressing. In the days before, I kept spotting him rubbing his jaw. The smell had grown more intense.

I hoped I had established enough of a rapport with him over the preceding weeks to make a move. Jerry, unless we get that fixed I can't take you to Australia. I tried to have a little joke about it: don't worry, it won't hurt, the injection beforehand is the worst part.

I guessed this was going to be his first time at a dentist's. I hadn't anticipated how frightened he was.

Ropate and I drove him to a practice in Suva that we knew was good. Jerry looked ready to run. We had to lock the car doors and then keep making small-talk as we drove through the streets. Parking outside, up the steps, through reception and into a small waiting-room, Jerry saying nothing now, sweat on his forehead and down his back.

The Indian dentist called us in. Jerry lying on his chair, eyes blinking furiously. The dentist had a look. There's a lot of work that needs to be done here, but we'll only do five or so fillings today. I'll get the anaesthetic ready.

The needle in hand. And then Jerry was away – rolling out of the reclined dentist's chair like a man wriggling out of a tackle, straight through the door, jumping down the stairs, gone with his wonderful acceleration into the street outside.

No one needed to spell out that I was a better chasing option than William or Ropate. Off in hot pursuit, shouting at him to come back, hearing shouts of 'I'm not coming back!' echoing back down the street, yelling back between the heaving breaths, 'Get your teeth done or you're not coming to Noosa!'

146

I caught up with him down a side-street. A complete point-blank refusal to return. I realised it was a battle I was not going to win that night, so I led him back to the car and then went to apologise to the dentist and make another appointment for the morning.

That night William and Ropate sat him down and made a deal. We will just do the minimum stuff tomorrow. We can do the rest when we get back from Australia. If you do nothing, that's your dream and this team finished.

In the end he would have ten fillings and several extractions. It almost helped that his teeth had become so painful, the alternative of the needle beginning to seem more attractive.

That was the first hurdle. There would be many more. Jerry played well in Noosa, his fitness improving incrementally, understanding that maverick attack alone would not be enough to win him a regular place slowly coming too. I took him to the Gold Coast tournament the following week as a reserve, so he could see what the big boys were doing and how they behaved. In training one of the usual starters was struggling, and that gave me an excuse to give Jerry a little taste of the first team. Against Australia, catching the ball deep in our half from a long clearing kick, he skipped forwards, cocked that leg and accelerated off the other with such an arbitrary change of direction that the defender fell over. He was literally on his backside. The stadium went nuts. I posted a clip of it on YouTube and social media followed suit.

But he struggled in the next tournament, unable to sustain that impact for more than a few days at a time. Good match, tired match. Impressive tournament, missed tournament though injury or picking up a cold. Solid week

147

of training, not enough stamina to get through the second week. His diet was poor, lots of sugars, lots of chocolate, long loaf and jam. I tried to get him thinking about the old colourful plate: fruit, greens, pale protein.

By April 2015 he had begun to travel with us regularly and had started to get his weight down and his muscle percentage up. At nine o'clock one night in Tokyo he knocked on my door. Ben, please, can we go and buy some chocolate? I need it. I haven't got energy, and I can't sleep either.

I knew the players had no Yen. Japan was expensive to an Englishman and a dead end for Fijians. There could be no buying McDonald's or beers. I wondered too if saying no to Jerry might be the wrong path to take. While it would have been consistent with the messages I had been giving him and the direction I wanted him to take, our relationship was still fragile at a point when his future was already uncertain.

My degree had been in sports science; my time in Fiji had added something less tangible. I knew in the big scheme of things a few chocolate bars that got him feeling happy would not derail him completely. He would burn the calories off the next day, as long as this was a one-off rather than a regular regime. I had let my England team enjoy a little good-quality chocolate as a pre-tournament treat and made it a fun tradition: a couple of players sent off to get it, another two measuring it out, a shirt presentation to any new faces as we shared it. All done by 5 p.m. so the caffeine and sugar would not interrupt a good night's sleep.

We walked downstairs to the small kiosk in the hotel lobby. I told him to choose what he'd liked. As we walked back to my room we talked. Jerry, this isn't usually the right thing to do, but OK, I'm going to help you out on this if you help me. I want you to show me what you can do all the time. I'll get you fit. Together we'll learn what we need to learn. But you need to give me the hard work to make it happen. Sound good?

That night, lying awake in that non-stop neon city, I thought back to west London and something that had happened to me as a kid, 11 years old, training with Thames Valley Harriers. It was after school, all of us in the group running 300m reps, Mum and Dad coming down early to watch before taking me the six miles south-west back to Brentford.

Me and one other white kid, the rest of the lads black. I hadn't noticed. I never thought about Noel being black when we were out playing football or rugby or on the table-tennis tables in the playground. I was enjoying myself, coming across the line first in each of the reps, jogging back round the bend as we got ready for the next one.

At the end of the session the coach took me to one side. Never fucking do that again. You were showing off in front of your parents, weren't you? The rich fucking white kid beating the black kids.

I had no idea what he was talking about. All I had been doing was training as hard as I could, because that's what I thought we were supposed to do. I wasn't posh. My mum and dad were working-class. He knew that I went to St Benedict's but hadn't bothered to find out about the scholarship. He thought he knew me, but he had no idea.

It was the start of the end for me at TVH. That night in the car home I felt small and I felt worried. For the next two weeks I found reasons not to go back. I was a good athlete, probably a better runner than I was a scrum-half;

149

my mum never stopped telling me that she thought I could have run internationally had I stayed with athletics. That one coach changed it all for me. Although I went back to the club for a short while, I left permanently soon after, the atmosphere at Richmond rugby club more welcoming and the memory of that furious, swearing coach rattling inside.

That man, wherever he now was, would have no idea that he was a small part of the reason why I had gone to Fiji, rugby coming before athletics, why too I had ended up in this hotel in Tokyo with a tired and worried Jerry. In that room high up in a skyscraping tower, the sense of vulnerability that had swamped me by the track that night felt fresh once again.

Too often in Fiji I had seen young men and women who felt their lives had a ceiling, who felt it was not possible for them to achieve any more. They were restricted by a stereotype, no one to help them out, to show them it could be another way. The coach calling me a fucking posh show-off, the kids from the council estate by my house that saw me in a bright-green St Benedict's blazer on the E2 bus and also thought that I was someone I wasn't. They had been part of the same deception. You are who the dominant and powerful say you are. There is no escape.

Maybe together we could find another way. Jerry's father Poasa Vunisa was originally a subsistence farmer and fisherman from Buca Bay, way out on the eastern promontory of Vanua Levu, 200 miles across the South Pacific from Suva. I had met him at Nadi airport when we had flown out for that first tournament in Noosa. Jerry had told me quietly that his dad had hitched all the way there from Newtown

Dad (middle row, third from left) gave me my love of sport, some fine athletic genes and many hours of priceless garden practice. When the final whistle went in Rio I felt him right there with me.

My best friend Noel, my two sisters, Mum and me. At the start of the 1980s these colour palettes were considered the height of good taste.

Noel and me in partnership for Richmond, me at scrum-half, him outside me at fly-half. We did everything together — it was a relationship that has defined me ever since.

Natalie and me, all excitement and hope as we arrived in Fiji. Little did we know how the next three years would change us so fundamentally.

In Fiji the nation's rugby stars are the folk heroes and warriors. Every kid grows up obsessed. Every kid plays. In their company I rediscovered a love I thought had gone for good.

The ginger-haired man's approach to sun cream in Fiji is much like that urban myth about painting the Forth Bridge: by the time you finish application at one end, it's time to start again at the other. (Zoomfiji)

Top left: Our first victory together in Dubai in 2013 brought its own pressures. I knew how much was going wrong behind the scenes and tried to keep expectations in check. (*Fiji Times*)

Top right: Our team manager Ropate became a critical part of everything we were trying to achieve. His man-hugs could transform almost any situation.

Left: Running out for a semi-final against South Africa in Hong Kong, 2015. Of all the tournaments across the world, nothing meant as much to Fijians as the Hong Kong Sevens. (Zoomfiji)

Below: Save Rawaca bursts through the New Zealand defence in Las Vegas, 2016. When we played to our peak we left images like this everywhere: defenders on their knees, covering men chasing, tacklers left empty-handed. (Zoomfiji)

I needed somewhere to push my remodelled side to their limits. Sigatoka would be it: natural beauty and intense physical discomfort; long miles from home villages but together in effort and aim; a special piece of Fiji that we would carry with us in our lungs and legs across the world. (Zoomfiji)

Alone with my thoughts on the Sigatoka sand dunes, a place to work the body like nowhere else but bring mental peace and clarity too. (Zoomfiji)

Jerry Tuwai was a talent like few others. And a conundrum: from the poorest part of a poor island, riddled with self-doubt and bad habits, but capable of moments of impossible genius. A gamble that I had to take. (Zoomfiji)

Satisfaction and smiles with my friend and assistant coach Chris Cracknell, above the waterfalls near Sigatoka, where we would wash away the sand and the sweat and the pain. (Zoomfiji)

The rag-taggle but perfectly balanced management team in Rio: Chris, William, Naca, Ropate and me. Another Ropate man-hug, this time of the one-armed variety. (Zoomfiji)

My captain Osea, the leader of our team in every sense, on the charge against New Zealand in the quarter-finals of the Olympics. Without him we could never have pulled any of it off. (Zoomfiji)

You get calf muscles like that when you train on shifting sand dunes as steep as Alpine mountains. Josua Tuisova beats his man for pace and then readies a hand-off just to be sure. (Zoomfiji)

I had planned a grand speech to make to the players before the Olympic final. I ditched it all. I looked around me, and they were singing and dancing. They looked like a bunch of kids going out to play touch rugby on the beach. (Zoomfiji)

No one had told the Princess Royal how the team would respond to having medals placed around their necks, but she understood from previous tours of duty — two cupped claps in return, her smile mirroring that of the players. (Zoomfiji)

I wasn't quite sure how to celebrate when the big moment came. I went for a very English self-conscious, half-arsed thing. I didn't know at that point that the image would end up on Fijian currency. (Zoomfiji)

With Osea and his dad back in Suva. His father, former special forces, now a minister, spoke about how it had all been fated: the new coach trusting his son, his son the single-most important player for the coach, a journey to gold that was scripted from above.

The bus ride from airport to Grand Pacific hotel normally took 25 minutes. In our open-top victory chariot we were lucky to do it in two hours, and that was with full road closures and police escort.

An ocean of pale blue flags, a sea of hugs and kisses and garlands of flowers. How could we feel pressure on our shoulders when we were being carried on the shoulders of every Fijian? (Zoomfiji)

to say goodbye, sleeping on the airport floor to make sure he hadn't missed him.

Buses aren't expensive in Fiji. From Suva you can get the Airport Express, which takes about three hours, and you can get the Sunbeam bus, which stops everywhere and takes for ever but would only cost £1.50 or so.

You only hitched for a reason. Four other kids to support plus Jerry's mum Seruwaia Vualiku, his only income from the fish he might sell by the roadside, having gone out into the bay with his nets early each morning. It was a cruel and competitive way to make a living – a couple of locals using explosives to blast fish to the surface, others dropping a little poison. You would see kids on the pavement with dead fish going off fast in the sunshine, shouting to the passing cars that theirs were the clean ones, that theirs definitely weren't the poisoned ones that had made everyone ill the week before.

Ropate and Osea sat next to Jerry during mealtimes and on the coach. Growing up he had been one of those kids, hawking his dad's fish on the roadside, out digging cassava from the plot they had cleared up in the bush when the sun first came up and the pot was calling. To say he was lacking the hard-work gene was only to showcase your own ignorance. At the same age that I had been getting up early only to play table-tennis, Jerry had been working to help feed his family. When I had been on a pristine athletics track racing my evenings away he had been gutting fish. Jerry's button was there to be pressed. I just had to find it.

One morning in the summer of 2014, when we were deep in pre-season fitness work, the players doing four sessions a week, we totted up each man's attendance record and noticed that Jerry had been missing gym sessions. That week he had only done half of what he was supposed to. A few hours later I spotted him waiting at the bus stop outside the National Stadium in Suva. Jerry, I'll give you a lift home, jump in.

On that short drive to Newtown I realised again how little I really knew. A contract for Jerry wasn't about the career security and challenge of being a professional rugby player, it was about being able to afford the bus fare to the gym. It was having sufficient money not only to be able to eat after training but to buy the sort of food that his body needed that night to recover and get him back again with sufficient energy the next morning. Forget the contracts so we had players to get us to Rio. He needed money to get to the pitch.

You don't go to Newtown unless you have to. A grey shale road becoming a track, puddles and then mud, a drop-off to the left to slums and weeds and half-arsed trees. There is crime and there are seldom police, for there are easier places to spend a shift and more important people to keep content. Turning right up the hill, the road worsening, a roundabout or just a circle of gravel and broken tarmac, a place for occasional cars to stop and turn round fast rather than a traffic feature. A couple of kids playing touch rugby with an empty plastic water bottle, another pair spin-passing a T-shirt rolled and tied up into a makeshift ball.

Jerry's family house, a one-room shack with corrugated-iron walls and the same for a roof. No fridge and no television because there was no electricity. No running water, no gas. Similar shacks clinging on to the hill on either side and down the valley, a grassy space out the back where the fire was burning and the washing hung on a line strung between the trees. His mum and a sister sitting out and washing clothes in a tub and cleaning up fish. A track beyond that would lead eventually to the coast and the sea, cassava crops further up the hill in the dark-green brush.

Jerry had never been to my house. No coach had ever come to his. He was embarrassed. I realised too late that he just wanted to be dropped off as quickly as possible, without me seeing inside or noticing too much of what was around.

My car was not a flash one, but as one of the few ginger white men in Fiji it never took me long to be recognised. The kids on the roundabout ran over to say hello, others coming out of the houses to stare, a camera coming out from somewhere to take photos of the coach's visit.

Out came his mum Seruwaia. We went inside and sat down on the floor. Jerry is doing really well. He's got to come to training every day, and if he does and he gets in the team, we will look after him, we will give him a contract.

Jerry with his head down, staring at the floor, his mum nodding. I'll make sure he's there.

A week later, Ropate went back up. Jerry, I'll give you a lift down to training. That was how it had to work: make the initial connection, go back a second time to reinforce it. Just as we did for Viliame Mata, another talented but lethargic youngster who would become an increasingly important part of our squad. Viliame's father was away in Iraq, trying to make money for the family by working security gigs. The influence had to be worked through his mother and his two enormous twin brothers.

Before I headed back to London at Christmas 2014, contracts for the players finally coming through, I drove back to Newtown to see Jerry's family again. I wanted it all to be transparent with each of the families: this is what your son is being paid, this is when the money will arrive each week in his bank account. The proof of the salary came with a gentle reminder that it also came with consequences. I need Jerry to rest as well as play. I don't want him up at five in the morning selling fish or raking the cassava plot. He earns this money when he is recovering and when he is training as well as when he is playing matches.

The Fiji Rugby board wanted the final say on which players would get a contract, who might get cut and how quickly the money would stop if they failed to make a squad. I needed to have full discretion. Control had to come at both ends. Jerry would never have made the initial cut if his contract had been dependent on getting up to level 18 on our yoyo fitness test, as the chairman would have liked. I wanted Pio to keep getting paid even if he took two months off to cope with the death of his wife. I needed the players and their families to understand that the responsibilities were more specific than that. If they were consistently late for training without explanation or were caught drinking in camp, there would be consequences to what they got paid on the Friday.

It was such a small amount of money. Jerry's first contract paid him £5,000 for the whole year. But when I told his mother what he was getting she broke down in tears. The family had never come close to earning that, not for all the fish that his father Poasa could haul in or Jerry and his siblings could sell on the streets. It took them from the breadline to the bread-and-jam line.

His mum told me a story on that second visit. When Jerry was 15, dropped out of school, he had gone to see

Seruwaia and told her he wanted to be a rugby player. 'I'm small so I can't run straight, because it would be too easy for the big boys, but I can get round them and through them.'

On the roundabout outside the house he played in bare feet. Even now his toes were splayed and the soles nicked and scarred. In tournaments you need boots. His mother gave him a hug: 'Don't be so silly, we can't afford a pair of those.'

Three days later she took him aside and gave him a pair. Both she and her husband had gone without food to get the money together.

'Jerry, from this day on, these are your knife and your fork. This is how you will feed yourself. You are going to use these to put food on the table for us.'

And Jerry went away and wrote 'knife' on the bottom of the left boot, and 'fork' on the bottom of the right boot. Those were the boots that he was wearing to training when I had been wondering if he was capable of working hard enough.

He thought nothing of his family looking after his salary and handing him a little back for himself. It's how you grow up in Fiji; your family and your extended relations and your village look after you when you are young, and as soon as you start earning money it goes back into the collective pot. It's not a case of getting to a certain salary, or deciding how much you might share. It all goes in. When we gave the players their living allowance at Nadi airport for an overseas tournament, it would be handed straight to the parents, who would then hand a small fraction back, and no one argued about it for a moment.

If that wouldn't have worked with my England players,

neither would the *kerekere*, the tradition in Fiji that if someone you knew asked to borrow something of yours they liked, you had to hand it over, even if you knew full well you were never getting it back. In Vegas the Fijian expats would sometimes club together to give the boys a little spending money, a little *banou* or gift. The players would then go to a sports discount shop of the sort that the England lads would never have been seen dead in, pick up a discontinued T-shirt for a couple of dollars or some fake sunglasses or cheap flip-flops, one of them inevitably trying to pay with Fijian dollars. They would wear them all week and throughout the flight home – right to the point when the plane was about to touch down at Nadi again, when all the old clothes would come out and the new stuff would get hidden right at the bottom of their bags. They wouldn't dare wear the new gear until they came back to the training camp at Uprising, because as soon as someone in the village would *kerekere* they'd have to give it away. Breakfast at Uprising thus became a secret cut-price fashion show. Remember this top? Remember these shades? I'm going to wear them to every meal for a week, and then not again for a month.

I knew that Jerry was no angel. He told me in one moment of shy confidence that he had done bad things, things that could have put him in jail. I was tougher on him than anyone else when it came to training. We both understood why. The trust between us was growing, and the dividends were becoming obvious. In Dubai Jerry was named player of the tournament. Stories started appearing in the *Sun* and *Times*: is this kid the new Serevi? He was being recognised at the bus stop and he was no longer having to buy his own boots. With a team around him of

Osea as the benchmark, Ropate as the warm uncle, William to keep his battered body mending, Naca to push him in the gym and me to let him know that none of us were going to give up, he was becoming a regular starter and a constant menace to the opposition. I had searched all those faraway islands for the missing X-factor that could take a very good team to the heavens. Maybe we had found him just up the forested hills from Suva.

You absorb behaviour from those around you. What can feel like instinct is probably more the accretion of what you have seen as a kid from parents and siblings and friends, day after day. My mum and dad were never big on public affection. I wouldn't see them hand in hand or snuggled up on the sofa. But they would always do a little bit more around the edges than some others. My mates always loved Dad; they called him Denson, even though he was Dennis and so Den's son was logically me. He was never a shouter, always a man for the quiet thoughtful gesture. He would make sure my friends were all dropped off at home properly after rugby matches. Aged 14 I did a week's athletics camp at Borough Road with my mate Danny Carroll, track and field all day and then us playing football during the lunchbreak. By the Friday we were completely broken. Dad not only dropped Danny off at Osterley Station, he saw that he was struggling to walk down the stairs. He stopped the car, physically carried him down to the platform and then rang his mum to make sure that she would be there to help him at the other end.

You see a lot of the world growing up in London. Council estate at the end of my road, scholarship to St Benedict's, then out of there at 13 years old and into one of the biggest state comprehensives in the country: 180 kids in a year, run by the flinty-eyed discipline-obsessed Jesuits, kids from across south and west London. Rough kids and cool kids and kids who needed a hand and kids something told you to stay away from. From school to Loughborough and then Cambridge, feeling inside that you understood a little more about different characters and how to get on with them than the ones who had gone prep school–boarding school–internship–university. It prepared me for dealing with Frank on his dais by Domain, or heading into the slums to sit down with Jerry and his mum.

Wherever you travel in life, you carry with you the experiences of the past and the examples you have been set. From what I had been through, I knew you can't just tell someone that they can trust you. It needs to be established gradually and on solid foundations.

With Jerry, what began with two bars of chocolate in Tokyo continued with what, on their own, were trivial little gestures: sitting down next to him as the team had dinner after training, taking his plate up afterwards to clear the scraps into the food bin. Walking back towards the hotel when we were away and asking him if he fancied a hot chocolate, not talking about his tackling technique or the South African scrum-half he was coming up against the next day but just chatting, listening to how his mum was, to his plans with his girlfriend for when their first child arrived in a few months. Keeping the bond between us soft and flexible. Sometimes walking past J. R. White's in Suva with him and saying, I need to pick up a new T-shirt, do you fancy one? Paying for both, not to be patronising, not as bribery, but just so we could talk a little more, find out what brands he liked and why, and so then who his sporting heroes were, and why he loved them, and so now understanding why he did that sidestep like he did and why his tackling might be going in high, and what sort of player he wanted to be and what he would need to get there.

I would do it with all of them. As often as possible we would do it as a team: ask Bela to stop the bus at the Eco Café as we rattled along Queens Road through Votua, order up the big pizzas and fresh smoothies. A treat at the end of a brutal day, a way to ensure flat batteries were recharged for the next day, an undemonstrative contentment in your belly as the warm food settled and the waves washed the beach and you looked around at the smiles and Ropate's bright patterned shirt and Jerry sat there with Viliame towering over Ropate and all of them talking away.

Jerry had worked out that I wanted to see the best version of him. Whether that was sometimes going to be a painful experience for him or an enjoyable one was less significant than where we were going. He realised I cared about him and he knew I would help him. When we won Hong Kong in March 2015 he was the first one to hug me on the touchline. A pure smile, a pure connection.

I appreciated that he would be helping me just as much. If he became the player he could be, the happy ripples would touch everyone in my team. For now it was important for me to understand that there were things he had been through that I could not relate to. I got a lot of it but I had so much to learn too. You are not always who the dominant and powerful say you are. There can be an escape.

NINE

When Noel gets out of Wormwood Scrubs he goes back in pretty soon. I am in my gap year between school and college, working out of Twickenham, and it is hard to keep track of where he is and what has happened now, only that because we have turned 18, it is adults' prisons all the way.

Midway through the year I manage to track him down. I am more mature now, more able to express myself, more confident in a wider range of situations. I try to tell him that there are still people who care about him. There are still people who are willing to help out if he needs it.

There is no remorse from him for what has happened and there is no emotional reaction. It is like trying to talk to an automaton. I still recognise him physically but the kid I used to hang around with is gone, or hiding somewhere I can't reach. We separate and the connection feels weaker than ever before.

News comes through from a mate of a mate. Noel's back in trouble again. He's in Wandsworth Prison this time for aggravated burglary.

All the time a hidden memory of my own trying to come back to life. The two of us are 12. We are in the school playground, and we are fighting.

I can't remember what triggered it or who started it or how it ended. I just know that whatever happened that day changed everything.

August 2015. Exactly a year to go until the Olympics. This pre-season would be my last with Fiji. I had decided that whatever happened in Rio, my time there would come to an end the following summer. It had always been the natural crescendo to the gamble, to the adventure, and whether we made it to the summit or not, the exertion and stress would be too intense to replicate.

I loved being immersed in the team and the players' lives, the tactics and the politics. I loved our little rented house in Pacific Harbour, the way I no longer instinctively reached for my smart-phone in the morning but wandered outside to the cool damp dawn, the big beanbag on the patio, the outside shower round the side of the house with the sky turning from dark blue to pale. Every day I looked forward to strolling over to the big 20-man dorm at Uprising for *lotu* with the boys. Singing harmonies rather than scanning Twitter, giving Ropate a morning hug rather than staring angrily at my phone wondering why a video clip was taking so long to load.

Immersed in the grand project, detached from every-thing else. In the first year, the isolation and loneliness had tightened the bond between Natalie and me. We had jumped off that cliff holding hands. Getting back to the house to tell her about the dunes at Sigatoka or what the team could be like if we got Semi Kunatani and Sami Viriviri playing together had been to share my own pleasure and see it reflected back at me. When she returned to the UK to spend time with her parents it allowed us to get some balance back, her with friends and home comforts and her father's Friday nights in Gerrards Cross curry houses, me no longer trying to juggle the incessant demands of the team with the need to be at home in time for dinner or to fulfil invites with her new friends among the Aussie and Kiwi expats.

That scene around the embassies and banks and big companies in Suva held minimal attraction to me. It was like being cooped up with all the people I had tried to avoid at university. While the staff at the British High Commission were excellent, sensitive to all around them, others appeared to have little interest in their adopted homeland. Drinking heavily at lunchtime was fine for rugby tours and Christmas Day. Doing it every weekend at the house of someone with whom you have nothing in common except the colour of your passport would have been dull enough in London. Doing it in a country that was a puzzle and a charm and was there to be explored seemed as pointless as getting drunk in a windowless room. So rude would some of them be to staff in restaurants and bars that I would sometimes go back afterwards to apologise on their behalf.

But I was engrossed. Natalie was on her own most of the day and was referred to as the wife of the sevens team coach when she did meet people. When she came to overseas tournaments she would feel more tangential still. You could shop in Singapore or Dubai but when your husband was out all day and awake for maybe half an hour when he got back, there were a lot of hours to fill staring at window displays. Those afternoon teas and evening drinks in Suva were always there. She was welcomed and she was asked about herself, rather than having to listen to stories about a player she had never met or a family she could only imagine.

In our early days her love of nights out had been good for me. She had a fun outlook on life; when I got too serious with England, she could always lighten the mood. Hanging out with her showed me new corners of the world. She knew nothing about rugby, which was exactly what I needed. People liked her, and I bobbed along in her wake.

I understood that some couples would look at the way our relationship worked now and call me selfish. I thought of it in a benign way. I wasn't doing it for me but the team. If it was for the team, it was also for their families and villages. There could be no other way, for if I tried to make it a nine-to-five gig then it would all fall apart around me. Natalie could sometimes blend in beautifully with what we were trying to do. With Pio's wife and her sister she was able to comfort them in a way I couldn't, to be physically intimate with people she had just met when I was all handshakes and awkward pats on the shoulder. In rare moments on my own, driving back from the Eco Café or going for a swim in the lagoon off the beach at Uprising, I knew I was being selfish in a different way: not wanting to confront anything else in my life until the Olympics were over. Everything else on pause, nothing to get in the way of what I was trying to do.

The same house that I loved to wake up in could be a lonely place in the day for Natalie and a mess of tension in the evening. It worked for everyone when Chris Cracknell, the first player I had ever contracted with the England sevens team, came over to help out with coaching the *Fijiana*, the national women's sevens team. Chris was still young enough to be playing but two knee injuries weren't going away. Without rugby he was feeling lost, taking it out in the wrong way back in London, lacking direction or a sense of purpose. Fiji got him away from that and got him looking forward. Natalie knew him well; she enjoyed having him staying at the house, someone else to cook for rather than just herself, someone to watch TV with and talk about London. I felt slightly better about being away so much knowing that Chris was there to keep her company. Chris, up at 4 a.m. several times a week to surf the break down the coast at Frigates, getting on well with the boys when he helped out in training, great for our work on the breakdown, tackle and set-piece, started to emerge from the fog that had surrounded him in London and become increasingly integral to what we were doing on and off the field. When I was home his easy-going presence would help defuse the tension that might otherwise easily build up.

Over in England the 15-a-side rugby World Cup was about to begin. New Zealand were favourites as always, England tight behind after three and a half years under coach Stuart Lancaster, a man I knew well. Both teams had been praised for the integrity of their internal culture. Lancaster was a disciple of the Super Bowl-winning San Francisco

49ers coach Bill Walsh and his management book *The Score Takes Care of Itself*. The All Blacks talked about enhancing the reputation of their famous jersey, about how their superstar players still swept out the changing rooms after matches.

There was an established paradigm for the way that a successful head coach should behave. Work relentlessly hard. Lead by example. Don't be particularly nice to other people, because being nice is being soft and when you're soft people take advantage. Rugby is a hard sport, so act hard. Weakness is there to be exploited. Who respects a man who is known for being nice?

We were nice. Ropate was the most personable man in Fiji. William's best friends were all old ladies, the same old dears his regular drinking partners. None of the management group screamed or shouted at the players.

We were really nice. In the baggage hall at airports the players would take their own bags off the carousel and then start fetching the suitcases of anyone near them. On one flight home two other passengers were suffering with such severe sunburn that they both passed out, those on either side screaming that they were having heart attacks, the stewardesses panicking and ditching their meal trolleys in the aisle as they tried to revive them. Our boys just stood up and said, you need to focus on that, we'll serve lunch and drinks for you. Down the aeroplane, these huge men, politely handing out napkins and cups, asking each passenger in turn, chicken or fish?

It had all been quite instinctive, but the goodwill followed us for weeks. An Australian journalist on the flight had seen it all happen, taken photos and published a story about it, which went viral. That was the strange thing about being nice: it worked. When we arrived in foreign cities skint and with no gym access, William could always wangle us into somewhere or find a load of medical strapping, because people liked him. Ropate got upgrades where none had officially existed because he made the airline crew laugh and spent time getting to know them.

It's easy to establish high standards of behaviour for your team. It's much harder maintaining them when you are tired or under pressure or it appears to be only a small incident that doesn't really matter in the greater scheme. I wanted ours to be a collective responsibility. If you see one of the players being rude to a cleaner in the hotel and you don't do anything about it because you're tired and you want to go to your room, then you're that person being rude to the cleaner. You've had a long day and you think you'll deal with it in the morning. Then the morning comes and it's too late. It seeps into your demeanour. The standard you walk past is the standard you become.

As a younger coach with England, I probably had more grey areas. I let my players go out after tournaments and drink a little bit and let their hair down. If one got away with something later that night, I thought the escape rather than the act was what mattered. With Fiji I learned a different perspective. I had seen other teams that talked at length about their culture but had players getting into fights or shagging around or drinking. I was better now at not overprotecting players from the consequences of their own mistakes. We all like you, you're a good bloke and a great player, but you've stuffed up and let us all down, and this is what will happen as a result. The grey went and it stayed gone.

It became our little private mantra: if we don't win Olympic gold, it will not be down to one bad pass or one missed tackle, but because we let it slip six months before. Everything we did in this final year would have an effect in Rio.

I travelled to London for the opening match of the 2015 Rugby World Cup. England against Fiji at jam-packed Twickenham on a warm Friday night, no official duties for me but to keep a keen eye on what the biggest tournaments did to coaches and teams and their best-laid plans.

What it mainly seemed to do was cloud thinking and crowd touchlines. Both teams had more than 20 staff on the pitch beforehand or around the team benches. Even with the Fiji team there were people whom I'd never seen before. Coaches, assistant coaches, multiple analysts, liaison officers, commercial staff. No one appeared to be thinking about simplicity or about chains of command. It seemed instead to be an arms race: they've got that many, so we need to have one more.

Stuart Lancaster, a well-intentioned, hard-working man, and an excellent coach, seemed to have got himself lost. A rugby obsessive who loved the training ground, he was instead mired in everything else – managing, organising, keeping commercial partners happy. His team selection was uncertain and driven by his assistants. At the tournament launch at the O2 Arena his team had taken to the stage for a gala send-off, almost as if they'd already won something, a scene that could not have been more perfectly arranged to fire up their two group opponents, Wales and Australia. The whole campaign seemed over-thought and over-hyped. Stuart, getting up at a time when only milkmen and insomniacs were awake so he could start work, pulling radically long days, looked like time was accelerating for him just when he wanted it to slow down.

England beat Fiji that night, albeit unconvincingly. A week later they were beaten by Wales at the death, having led by 10 points with half an hour left to play. When Australia thumped them by 20 points the Friday after, they were out – the first World Cup hosts to be gone in the group stage, the first time an England side had ever failed to make the knock-out stages. Watching Stuart get torn apart, seeing how the same man who had sacked me was not there at a difficult post-tournament press conference. I was overwhelmingly relieved to be outside it all.

I had made mistakes with the England sevens team. I assumed I had to let the culture take care of itself, that I should trust bosses to do what they were supposed to. I had an amazing team operations manager, Nadine Cooke, who tried to help, but she could see that I was lost in pointless protocol and needless power struggles. With Fiji, sitting back and letting it happen wasn't an option because the stakes were so much higher.

Everyone knew Francis Kean in Fiji. A commander in the Navy, he ran Suva rugby and the Navy rugby team. He was also Frank's brother-in-law and a man with an even darker past.

In December 2006 Kean had attacked salesman John Whippy at the wedding reception of Whippy's nephew and Frank's daughter Ateca at the Royal Suva Yacht Club.

Having punched him three times in the face, he then kicked him in the chest before being pulled away, coming back moments later to kick him in the head. At his trial he was tried for murder. A lack of witnesses saw him instead plead guilty to manslaughter. He was released from prison after a week.

One morning Kean came into the gym in Suva where I was training the boys. An old-school place, like a hangar, similar to the one Mr Hopkins had Noel and me playing non-stop two-a-side football back in Ealing all those years ago. A soldier on either side of him, both in uniform. Ben, these two men are in your next training squad.

I knew I could not face him down but that I could not step back either. OK, they can train with us today. Then I will send them home, knowing that the feedback would then arrive via Ropate that they were not good enough, that their skills and fitness were short of what the Fijian people expected, that they should not come back.

It was a shot across the bows from Kean: I have this power. A few months later, it was announced that he was going to be made chairman of the Fiji Rugby Union. At the AGM, a loophole had been discovered – you can only vote for the chairman if you have brought your region's full accounts for the year, and, hey! only Suva have theirs, so only Suva can vote, and Suva seem to have voted for their own chairman.

A shot back from me. An email to World Rugby: one of your national unions is about to appoint a chairman who has served time for manslaughter. This is the man who you'll be paying to fly over for the England vs Fiji match, where he'll have the best seats at Twickenham and a five-star hotel that you will also be paying for. He'll be the man you deal with for the next four years whenever you deal with rugby in Fiji. The reply from World Rugby: this is an internal matter.

Kean couldn't go in the end, a travel ban still in place from his conviction. He sent two board members instead.

That was Fiji. Frank the president of the FRU, Francis Kean the chairman. Frank's son-in-law Sale Sorovaki head of development, nephew Inoke Bainimarama working in the media department. His daughter Litiana Loabuka head of the Sports Council. Litiana, Sale and Inoke were all very good at their jobs; they all helped me a great deal. That was Fiji. White shirts, black shorts, grey everywhere else.

The Prime Minister for a boss, your shareholders 900,000 Fijian sevens obsessives. Rumours and plots and deals and compromises. Repercussions to everything you say. Nothing slipping away forgotten.

London felt increasingly strange to me. Not just the noise, and the pace of everything, and the number of cranes and new buildings that were fighting for space along the river every time I returned, but the sense of what was now important to me and what direction I wanted to travel in.

With the old house in Teddington long sold, I was staying at my mum's in Brentford, Natalie at her parents' 20 miles out along the M4 and M25 in Buckinghamshire. It just seemed easier that way. I had always struggled on our stays in Gerrards Cross, and each month in Fiji served to underline why a little more. A pastiche house, a strange stage-managed facade of a life – little England made big.

With the clock ticking down to the end of my time in

Fiji, it was suddenly clear what one version of the future looked like. Natalie and I had been talking for months about kids. We were the right age, rapidly approaching the wrong age. I looked at her father and I looked at his preoccupations and I realised: I don't want to bring kids up in this environment. That was no longer my world.

I loved having time on my own. A day when I worked, watched rugby, cooked, went to the gym and went to bed early would be fine for me. For Natalie that was hell. Her favourite day of the year was the fancy-dress party she would throw for her birthday. Fancy dress to me was as enjoyable as wearing a beard of bees.

I was on the train up to Cambridge and a 20-year anniversary of our Varsity rugby team when Natalie called and told me she was going to stay on with her parents at Gerrards Cross. Not for that weekend, but for the next three months.

I knew deep down she was probably right. I was so wrapped up in the team and the final push for the Olympics that I would carry on being half a husband until we won or failed. I also felt consumed by anxiety. Shit, I need to hang on to her. What if I get back to Fiji and I'm a mess? It wouldn't be a break-up that we could keep between the two of us and close family. The coconut wireless would be humming day and night, the story across the *Fiji Sun* and *Fiji Times*. What if I get back and I can't focus on the team because I'm thinking about Natalie all the time?

The benign selfishness of the rugby coach. The fear of the kid who lost his best mate. Now that she had initiated what I had been thinking for a while, it flipped my thinking around. I want to be liked. I like to feel needed. Anxiety and rejection. Let's stay together. Come back with me.

I knew it was the wrong thing for me to be doing. Even at the airport departures lounge a week later she almost walked out. I was telling her the future was ours but blocking every route she was plotting through it – I'm not sure about kids, I can't live in Gerrards Cross, I'm not sure I can settle down into a Monday to Friday.

When there is doubt everywhere and the old intimacy has gone and the trust is leaching away, being together can perversely be the loneliest place you can be. You don't want to share anything because you fear what the response might be. You don't want to spend time together because you know every conversation will come back round to all the stuff you're running away from – what happens next, whether you should be doing it together. And yet you're married, so you have to push it to the breaking point. You have to try everything. 'Til death us do part, or until we play six games of rugby in a well-heeled suburb of an edgy South American city, one of the two.

It felt strange to see my old Cambridge team-mates again. After the phone call with Natalie I was ready to lose myself in amnesia and neglected friendships, but reunions are always as much about taking stock of where you are now as what you had all been doing back then. There was sweet collective pride in what we had achieved and an understanding of what we had missed out on. Men in their 40s recognisable as the young lads in their late teens or early 20s, the loose ones a little tighter, a few dinks in the bodywork and bumps and bruises that you could ignore in the bar's low lighting.

We watched the current Cambridge first XV play at

Grange Road and then watched them celebrating in the Hawks' Club on Portugal Place. Almost 150 years of tradition, or what was thought to be tradition, mixed in with strange standards and a collective culture that spoke proudly of what it was but seemed to be something quite else. The players drinking and taking their clothes off in front of the girls and doing some sort of naked catwalk, and then coming up to us old lags and saying, this is what you used to do, isn't it, this goes back years and years, and isn't it great?

One of the senior players sat down near me. No, this isn't great. You were poor on the pitch and you are worse now, and the two things are causally connected. You think you have a standard of behaviour but you're walking past it every day, quite often with your shirt off and your backside hanging out. My old team-mates on the leather sofas all around, the ones whose own standards I had absorbed 20 years before, quietly nodding. From Fijian kids in villages with nothing but dirt roads and cassava crops I would never have accepted this. From kids with the world wide open in front of them it was a form of collective blindness. I was glad to be flying back, even if I was unsure that Natalie should really be coming with me. I was ready for my house on the inlet and the training pitch at Uprising and Ropate with his hot chocolate.

And it seemed simple back in Pacific Harbour. Back in training with the boys, my marital relationship in tangled disarray but the team and our routines settled. Contracts in place, players committed, Semi Kunatani to Toulouse but with clauses in his contract to bring him back when we needed him, Sami Viriviri in Montpellier but on the same sort of deal. Jerry bouncing around like a rubber ball,

174

Osea with his paternal eye on it all. Pio... Pio seemed to be heading deeper into the darkness. We left the door open and put Osea on man-marking duties.

Ovalau had been our pre-season destination the year before. This time it would be Labasa, in between the mangroves and the coconut plantations on the north coast of Vanua Levu, the second-biggest island in the archipelago, up in *babasiga*, the burning north. It takes time on the boat from Suva, a long slog on the decking unless you get in the VIP area, which is a tiny cabin with piles of the Fijian version of *Woman's Own* from ten years ago, a plate of those cakes with fluorescent icing, a big pot of tea and some coconut matting to sit on.

Coming ashore at Nabouwalu Landing or Savusavu, taking the only sealed road on the island up north to Labasa, you soon realise it's not a pretty place. It's not a spot for tourists. A great belching sugar mill on the edge of town, dusty streets, a lot of very reasonably priced coconuts for sale. I had been there at the end of the previous season with Ropate for a look around, having been sent by the government to speak at what I was told was a youth rally for struggling kids. We stayed in a hotel that had no windows in the bedrooms, just up the road from a club where you ordered your beer through a grille and were offered it in two serving sizes, half-crate and full crate.

The youth rally turned out to be an army base with ten ageing officers who wanted to get smashed on *kava*. As a guest you always took some of the root, or some money to pay for a few high tides: $5 was enough to sort everyone out; I gave them $20, spent two hours answering all their questions and then told Ropate he would have to take one for the team for me. I was at my *kava* limit.

175

A few hours later he arrived back at the windowless hotel, grinning sleepily, almost horizontal, working his way through a huge tray of chicken thighs. Ropate didn't bother with alcohol. He'd discovered while working as a bouncer in Wellington that it made him angry, and angry wasn't Ropate. He had got through tsunami after tsunami and desperately needed something to soak it all up, unable to leave until the hosts gave him the green light, his roots on the island of Koro out in the Lomaiviti chain meaning he had got mired in a long sequence of formal mickey-taking. Ropate was the Big Bear. It took a lot of *kava* to get him in that state. I pointlessly drew the curtains and tucked him up with his chicken and a beatific smile. Shouting *kava, kava, kava . . .*

No coach from Fiji Rugby had ever been to Labasa. No Fijian national side had ever played there. When Ropate and I had taken the World Series trophy to the town's stadium, Subrail Park, we had signed autographs and watched the locals have their photos taken with the silverware for almost seven hours, plates of luminous cakes being put down in front of us, plates of chopped-up banana, cups of sugary tea, the pick of the local coconut harvest. All of them kept telling me I would have to bring the team back with me.

And so here we were, back in Subrail Park to play in a tournament with loads of local sides, the burnt-caramel stench of the sugar factory drifting across the pitch, rainforest clambering all over the hills and mountains to the south, looks of happy amazement on the faces of the locals packed in to watch.

Ovalau had worked out brilliantly. Labasa brought a kick in the tail. Against the prison wardens' team in the group stages Amenoni Nasilasila got clobbered after scoring a try, sparked clean out. It looked for a while as if he had broken his jaw. Then things got worse.

Donasio Ratubuli had played impressively for me in our first year after making his debut in my very first tournament on the Gold Coast. He had then been tied into a terrible contract in the lower reaches of French club rugby, getting homesick, fat and drunk at an accelerating rate. I brought him back, got him fit again and was excited by how well he was playing.

And they smashed him. One player pulling his leg away from underneath, his mate stamping on it. Twisted and snapped, both his tibia and fibula shattered, bone sticking out through the skin. Medical facilities are basic in Labasa. William looked at me in horror as he ran back to the sideline. Forget Donasio's Olympics. He could lose that leg. We had to do something.

Doing something in Labasa was making a splint out of an old sheet and trying to lift Donasio on to a stretcher and then on to the flatbed of a truck. He must have been in extraordinary pain. Frantic calls back to Suva, the promise of a helicopter flight back as early as they could, which wouldn't be until the following day, but at least that gave us hope that we might save the leg.

I took the prison wardens' team and their stand-in coach into the corner of the pitch and tore them apart. Why have you done this? We're coming here as the national team. These are the players who will be trying to win an Olympic medal for Fiji. I understand you're trying to get into the team, but do you really think you're going to impress me by doing this?

Their heads were down, their eyes on the rough grass.

177

We were due to play them again in the final. I told them that they could forget it. You lot are a disgrace. You, even as a temporary coach, should be ashamed.

Nine months to go until Rio but that was Donasio's dream over. The FRU shrugged their collective shoulders. He's not playing now, we're not paying him. I refused to accept that. This wasn't his fault. We needed to keep him on the books.

The whirlpools sucked him down again. He lived in a village not far from my house. When I popped into the petrol station up the road I would hear that he had been into the shop there to buy alcohol. A taxi driver I knew who lived next door to him told me the drinking had accelerated. He would spend his days at the petrol station, limping on his crutches, getting stuck into the booze.

I would drive down there to pick him up and take him home again. Osea would go to talk to him. You can come back from this. Wherever you go from here, this is not the place to start.

I gave his family some money to keep their noses above water and to help get him off the sauce, but he was off the rails for a long time. He's playing again now, and fighting his way into the team, but it was a long way back.

We returned from Labasa fit and hard, travelling to Dubai in early December for the first World Series tournament, all that pre-season work and Sigatoka and togetherness combining in a way that only Fiji could do. Past Australia in the quarter-finals and New Zealand in the semis, up against England in the final.

We went 7–0 down early on. No one blinked. Four tries from us in four minutes – first Save Rawaca, crashing down the wing with a look of total determination on his face, feeding off Osea's pass; then Jasa Veremalua, taking a pass from Vatemo; another try straight from the restart, our players leaping like Michael Jordan to win the ball back. And then Jerry Tuwai, taking the ball with four navy-shirted defenders in front of him, a hop and a wiggle, scorching round the outside of the first two, then a step inside the outside man, then running straight at the last covering man and ricocheting past him like a ball-bearing in a bagatelle, smashed into the post by a desperate last-ditch tackle as he made for the line, sitting up slightly stunned and plopping the ball down across the line.

From 7–0 down to 28–7 up. A hot sticky night, a nation watching, a beautiful chaos.

It was Jerry's fifth try of the tournament. He was named player of the final, making 17 tackles across the weekend. Not bad for a kid who was too small to make it, notorious for turning invisible when the ball wasn't in his hand, a kid they said didn't have the hard-work gene.

Vatemo Ravouvou, our cursed epileptic, made 18 tackles. He also kicked 17 consecutive successful conversions. Pio made ten offloads, more than any other player in the tournament. When Osea lifted the trophy he did so for a team that was ours and could not have come from anywhere else.

I would need 13 men for my final squad for Rio. Barring cruel injury like Donasio's or emotional sabotage of the sort I hoped Pio was going to survive, I had maybe seven of them. There might be a few more jokers I could play. The former All Blacks star winger Joe Rokocoko – now 32 but still with much of the speed and power that brought him 46 tries in 68 matches for New Zealand – was born and raised in Nadi before his family moved to

179

south Auckland to look for work. Having last played Test rugby for the All Blacks in 2010, he might be able to re-qualify for us. Then there was Jarryd Hayne, the brilliant Australian-born rugby league and American football back who had a Fijian father and a gap in his diary after leaving the San Francisco 49ers and before going back to the NRL. The two of us were ambassadors for Fiji Airways, and a conversation in Sydney was left intriguingly open-ended for both of us. Maybe a couple of older, wiser heads was what we needed.

One other piece in the jigsaw. Jeremy Manning was a young Kiwi goal-kicking coach who, as a player, had won the Heineken Cup with Munster. I had met him in Abu Dhabi when we had run those sessions with the local Harlequins club. Hey Jeremy, the boys are out on the pitch doing some kicking – these are the drills that I've got them doing and this is the outcome we want, why don't you have a look?

Immediately there was a rapport with him. Technically he was excellent. He knew things about kicking that I didn't. He was conscientious and planned each session perfectly; the boys loved him. His day job as a personal trainer wasn't giving him much satisfaction.

Look Jeremy, if you're ever allowed an opportunity to come to any other tournaments, we'll put you in our management group and you can be our kicking king. And he managed to wangle it – when he needed to go to Hong Kong to recce gyms he could time it to join us, his flights paid for so that our bijou budget would not need to be stretched any further.

An easy win, a big impact. Those tries in Dubai from the restarts, set up with perfectly placed high swirling kicks, all those conversions of Vatemo, piling up the points, piling up the pressure on the weary opposition. Christmas did indeed feel like a time to celebrate.

TEN

*T*hirteen years old, captain of athletics, football and rugby, head boy. And then one day I get home to my mum and dad and tell them I want to leave. I don't care about the scholarship, I want to go to another school.

They don't tell me to be quiet, or that I'm being weird, or that I can't. We go to look at two state schools. One has an impressive computer room with loads of BBC computers. Wimbledon College has a Slush Puppy machine. The Slush Puppy machine wins it. Noel stays at St Benedict's.

Thirty years on, 43 years old. I am in New York, visiting the Knicks. One of the friends of the people I am with in New York is a hypnotist. She says she works with regression therapy. A few days later I go to her clinic and begin.

Straight away I am back in the playground by the table-tennis tables. Something has happened between me and Noel. The tables *are folded up. Noel is grabbing me by my blazer. There is shouting and arms and fists everywhere. The rest of the school all around me, watching and yelling and pushing.*

I wake up. The therapist asks me: what sort of thoughts does this bring back to you?

Well, he was my first and best friend, and immediately something's happened that has broken it, and someone has let us down on a pretty huge scale, and this in front of the whole school. I don't know why it has started or what has happened but I feel I've got to go home and say, that's it, I'm leaving, because for me, it's all gone, everything has just blown up.

The therapist takes me back under. An hour later we talk again. Ben, this is hugely significant for you. Your best mate, all your trust, a loss of control over the friendship that's most important to you. Noel suddenly changing, suddenly taking out on me his anger and fear and rage that had never been there before, attacking the only one who might have been able to help. Staying away from what should have been home. Looking for a sense of belonging somewhere else, to feel part of something, for a new identity and validation.

In December there is a heavy humidity in Fiji. Getting ready to return to London for Christmas, ready to start the year that would peak with the Olympics.

I would wake up each morning into silence, energy fizzing through me. A pure darkness in my adopted world, no light pollution, no white glare from a phone left beside the bed and turned on with the first movement of the day. Stepping out into air that was so clean you could smell the individual plants and trees, and the salt from the ocean settled on your tongue.

When it got dark at the other end of the day it all dropped down. A silence that in London would have been unsettling because it was so unexpected. The sounds of something skating over the lagoon by the house, a coconut dropping onto the sand. A dog bark in the distance and then nothing else.

In those untroubled evenings I would sit out on the beanbag with my eyes open but not focused, no lights on or music, just letting my thoughts fall. Seeing what came up, not sticking notes in my phone or sending emails with every conundrum but letting my mind turn it over and drop it back down. Breathing that night air and feeling thousands of miles from the anxieties of old and a lifetime away from England and Twickenham and everything on frantic fast-forward.

Simplicity ran through all of it. When you open your fridge and it's not packed full of everything and you can't get every cuisine on the planet with one call or delivery, you have to think about what you're going to eat. Cooking becomes a ritual and a shared experience. Going round to see friends with no music on, no televisions on in the background, none of the kids on any gadgets. Preparing food together and letting the conversation ease this way and that, eating slowly and putting your fingers into bowls and not caring about the mess around your mouth because there's more on its way.

Always laughter, at daft things, at stories about a man someone saw in Suva who walked into a lamp post looking at his mobile. Singing a Milli Vanilli song to Ropate because he was a huge fan as a kid, posters on his bedroom wall, and was yet to get over the heartbreak of finding out that they had mimed the hits. Hysterical laughter coming out of his massive frame, shaking and wiping his eyes.

And then back to London with Natalie alongside me on

the plane and the awareness that complications were just around the corner. The plan had been the usual sort of relationship deal: we would spend Christmas Eve at my big sister Lizzy's down in Alresford in Hampshire, and then drive up the M3 and round the M25 to Gerrards Cross for Christmas Day.

Christmas Eve was the sort of soft landing I needed. Lizzy is a drama teacher who works with autistic kids. My nieces were in the nativity play at the village school. Carols and angels and donkeys, then mulled wine at my sister's house. After a glass or two it began to come out. Natalie, I'm going to stay here tomorrow. You go to your mum and dad's. I'll come up on Boxing Day.

I tried to soften it. Lizzy's been having a tough year. I need to catch up with her properly. And yet I knew that this was the first physical manifestation of our gradual emotional pulling away. Inertia and fear can keep something together for a while. You need more to sustain it. You can't grow fresh blossom on a tree with withered roots.

There were weeks when we would still have good times together in Fiji, just me and her on the beach or a day when we strolled over to my landlady's with her four sisters, brother and mother Sophie and all the kids for one of their curry nights. At those times we were back to being the two people who had stepped out on this illogical adventure all those months before, everything just stripped away, no space for arguments about where we were going to live when we got back to England, how often we were going to see her parents, how quickly we should start trying for kids. When all of that didn't come up on the radar then it was lovely and it was peaceful and it was like going back to the start.

We would stroll down the beach from Uprising, head west along the sand to the Pearl Resort a couple of kilometres down, a place run by an Aussie couple also named Ben and Nat. At theirs they were referred to as Ben & Nat One, us Ben & Nat Two. At Uprising we reversed it.

Walking slowly, only the most apologetic waves on that flat lagoon, breakers out there on the reef. Maybe stopping at the restaurant at the resort, or something planned in advance – mates with the butchers who supplied the local hotels, Yangara Meats, Woody coming over in his van once a week with the best steaks he had left. I'd get the barbecue going outside the house and it would just be the two of us and the view and the sunset. And then even if it was just one bottle of wine between us, the conversation would change and the radar would start bleeping and flashing again.

We didn't scream and shout. Maybe the connection was already too frayed to sustain that sort of energy. Natalie would have weeks when Fiji seduced her, when she talked about coming back for good, setting up a charity at the hospital in Suva where she was volunteering during the week. Then a phone call would come from home and it would all be about getting a house in Gerrards Cross and a job that would keep me there and kids and grandparents heavily involved in everything the kids did. Sometimes I would try to confront it. Natalie, that's not me. We both know it. After I while I tried to avoid it. I know where this is going, I know where it ends. All the time feeling the old anxiety rising and looking around and not knowing how to escape.

It had taken me a while to understand that her father and I saw the world differently. He had owned a factory that made platform boots. When the Spice Girls wore them in a video and then on stage and then in every public appearance for months, suddenly the money was pouring in and his house got bigger and the cars on the drive were going forth and multiplying. He would watch our Fiji games on his flatscreen and tell me what I was doing wrong. Ben, you're never going to win the Olympics with this lot, they keep lobbing it around like they don't want the ball. They should be hanging on to it, trying to slow it down.

And so Boxing Day came with me trudging up the drive and thinking: I'm not sure I was ever comfortable with this lifestyle, and all I have seen and done over the last two years has pushed me even further away. Into the big room at the front of the house that you were only allowed to use once a year, the one with the grand piano in, walking round with the white wine, smiling and nodding and wondering how quickly I could drop in the excuse about being jetlagged and needing to go out for some fresh air or upstairs for a lie-down.

Leaving through their electronic gates felt like the Great Escape, albeit one done in a reasonably priced hire car with the compass set for Costa Coffee on the High Street rather than the Swiss border. I would sit there ordering espresso after espresso and wait until I got the phone call asking where the hell I was. It was terrible behaviour to deal with a horrible situation. I would make things up: the Fiji Rugby Union have called, I've got to have a long Skype meeting. Lizzy's been on the phone, I'm going to have to go back. The inevitable argument with Natalie – why have you left, you've only been here a few hours – was preferable to sitting it out and hating myself for letting all the good stuff I'd found in Fiji slowly leach away.

My mum had always liked Natalie. They both made a big effort with each other; Natalie was great with the nieces and would go round to see Mum when I was away with England.

Everything else, Mum was characteristically blunt about. At our engagement party she had given me a funny look in the kitchen. I don't think I've met a single woman here who has a job. This was a woman whose career began in a hospital school for kids with polio, who had gone to London University to get qualifications in child development and psychology, the first man or woman from her family to go to college, who spent 18 years training teachers in west London, and then in retirement worked with children who had special educational needs and alongside the Metropolitan Police with young offenders.

Before our wedding the numbers had spiralled. I had 40 friends and family, Natalie's parents closer to 80. It was then that her mother said to me, we're getting a bit heavy on guests now, can we stick yours in another room off to the side? They can have their dinner in there and then come in later. They won't mind. It might be why in all the photos there wasn't a single one of my mum smiling.

I drove back to Hampshire as soon as I could, counting down the days to my return flight to Suva. It was hard to find time to talk to my sisters – lots of people around, food to cook, everyone together in the same room. Over the washing-up in the kitchen some of it came out, on walks round the village and its pond and stately home a little more.

They knew what I was like when I was happy and they could see what I was like now. If you have a dog and it keeps getting kicked, it goes quiet and stops bounding up to greet you when you come in the door. We like Natalie but think about what's best for you. I talked about wanting to get through the Olympics and seeing if that might somehow change things. Ben, what's going to change?

Some people couldn't change. Pio Tuwai was starting to miss training. He would tell us he had to be somewhere else in the country, and then we would find out he was somewhere completely different, doing something he shouldn't have been doing.

We were ready to give him leeway after all he had tried to deal with. Osea considered him his best friend in the squad. We sat down with him. Come on, we've been through a lot together, and this isn't how the story ends.

For Osea it was hard not to take it personally. A teammate who he had shared so much with, a friend whose wife he had seen die, whose funeral he had attended as team captain, now lying to him, self-sabotaging with the Olympics only months away. Pio on form and in control of his own limbs would have been one of my guaranteed picks for any squad. But he wasn't on form, and he wasn't in control of anything, and so he was moving from the centre of the squad to its margins.

The stress of those Olympics was starting to seep in throughout the team. In Cape Town for the second of the ten legs of the 2015–16 World Series, it had been Isake Katonibau who cracked.

I had never been entirely sure that what Isake produced on the pitch was worth what he would do off it. I had brought him back into the set-up after his ban hoping he might be chastened or reformed. For a while he tiptoed along the straight and narrow. Then came a sizzling night out in London. Deciding to enjoy a late-night cigarette in his hotel room, he left it on the floor and came out of the bathroom to see the curtains on fire.

Isake seemed to find it genuinely funny. He didn't rush to put the curtains out and he didn't apologise in the morning. It was the only time I had ever had to pay for damage to a hotel room in my entire coaching career. I thought, right, get him back to Fiji and then I'll get rid of him. I'll deal with him there.

Isake had come through the army. He had travelled extensively with them and considered himself quite worldly wise. He was adept at manipulating the younger lads by playing the experienced old lag. Follow me, boys, I know how this works. He was like the kid at the back of the class who is always testing out what he can get away with from the teacher: a good tournament here, and then two average ones because he thinks he has done enough and can loosen off a bit. I was having to breath-test him in training. At one tournament I caught him having a fag in a downstairs corridor at the stadium.

I liked him as company but he was hard to trust – telling me in front of the other players who to bring on, messing about on the bench in the middle of a match, asking a New Zealand player to step outside for a fight after another close contest. Waiting for him before a team meal at a steak restaurant, I found him in his room smoking.

In Cape Town we were up against France in the quarter-finals, our good form from Dubai still in our legs. The only real danger in the opposition ranks was the Fijian-born winger Virimi Vakatawa.

Fijians play hard against one of their own who has left the islands to take money and citizenship elsewhere. It

191

turns into one of those games I had seen in the club tournaments in Ovalau and Labasa: let's see who's bigger and stronger and tougher and more skilful.

Isake wanted to take down Vakatawa. Instead he lost control – thundering through two tackles to cross the try-line, only to lose the ball trying to showboat, and failing to touch it down for the try. He tried to smash Vakatawa in defence, went in far too high and got fended off twice. With us deep in French territory and acres of space all around, he then threw away a ridiculous offload from a tackle that went straight to Vakatawa again, who ran away and scored. A 17–14 defeat, stuffed up by a man who had lost his head. If he was like this now, in a quarter-final seven months before we left for Brazil, what would he be like when we got there?

Back in Fiji, Isake and Jerry were on a trip to Labasa on behalf of Fiji Airways to publicise a new flight link the airline was opening up. Isake turned up drunk. He shouted abuse at one of the cabin crew and started to abuse a high-ranking government official.

I got a call from one of the official's bodyguards. Isake has been running his mouth off. It's a bad scene, you need to know. I thanked him and made two calls of my own: one to Isake, one of apology to the government. Leave this one to me, I'll deal with it.

Isake had been hammered in the newspapers for his display in Cape Town. The letters page in the *Fiji Sun* had been dominated by calls for his suspension. This man let the nation down. He let Vakatawa show us all up. There could be no happy ending for this story, no matter that Isake was making plans to take his wife and kids to the next couple of tournaments to help keep him out of trouble.

The coconut wireless was humming again. Get rid of him. No more chances.

The pressure was bearing down on all of us. We went to the Wellington sevens in January and got third place but were thrashed 31–0 by South Africa in the semi-final. In Sydney a week later we could do no better than third again, beaten 14–12 by New Zealand, their coach Gordon Tietjens all smiles on the sunlit pitch of the Allianz Stadium, the floodlights of the Sydney Cricket Ground high above us. Save Rawaca was the one to lose it that time, going in for late hits on their star centre Sonny Bill Williams, wound up by their player Kurt Baker patting one of our boys condescendingly on his head after he missed a tackle to let in a try.

I was back in Pacific Harbour when the first threatening phone call came through. No number on the screen, an anonymous voice with a distinct message: you'd better start winning, or else things will happen.

A few hours later another one. The next day another.

I would ask them who they were and what they wanted. What do you mean, or else? I tried to work out who they might be. I knew there were a couple of coaches who appeared jealous of the success we had enjoyed and the attention it had brought us, and I had a feeling they were also behind some of the approaches our players were getting from agents offering overseas contracts that were all bait and no substance. They would ring the papers and offer to write columns on where I was going wrong and why the tactics we were using were going to end in disaster.

I told Ropate what was happening. He stayed by my side until the next call came in. Taking the phone out of my hand, letting rip in Fijian, blasting whoever it was on the other end. We changed my number later that day and hoped it would take a while for the new one to get into the same errant hands.

Pressure everywhere. One of the reasons Gordon Tietjens had celebrated in Sydney was that it had been New Zealand's first tournament win in the World Series for almost a year. We had won four across the same period; we were the team that had given them their heaviest-ever defeat. Kiwi national sides are expected to win at their historical average of around 90 per cent. They are supposed to take the little Pacific brothers to school and show them what happens when the big boys spend big money. Gordon had an ego buttressed by the long run of success he had enjoyed over the previous two decades: twelve World Series titles, four Commonwealth gold medals, two sevens World Cup trophies. He hated losing as much as the coin toss.

I respected Gordon as a coach, but he seemed to have one way of doing things. His way. No matter which player he was dealing with nor how tired they might be, it was always the same: long sessions, punishing routines, flogging them into the turf. Forwards and backs treated the same. Players with full seasons in their legs pushed through the same drills as ones coming back from injury. An old-school discipline with them all. Cross me and you're gone.

One of his star men told me that he had been made to run 20km in training, for a sport where each match lasts 14 minutes. They played a game in training called 'Death' which was constant sevens for what seemed like for ever, the ball never allowed out of play. The theory was that they would become used to making good decisions when exhausted. Instead I thought it produced players who could keep trundling along at a certain level without the explosive edge a sevens player needs. It was like training a 60m sprinter with mile-long jogs. They never seemed to have the real electric edge to win a game from nowhere, the absolute top-end speed that could break even the most organised and resolute defensive line.

In coaching you can get stuck in patterns that no longer match up to the world around you. It can be hard to abandon something that for a long time gave you the critical edge. Gordon's drills had worked 15 years before when no other sevens teams were taking their fitness so seriously. He also had access to players from the very highest echelon: Christian Cullen, Jonah Lomu, Joe Rokocoko, Mils Muliaina, Rico Gear, Julian and Ardie Savea, Charles Piatau, Ben Smith, both Ioane brothers, Liam Messam – players other teams could only dream of. As rival nations began developing their own programmes and signing talented players to sevens contracts, the gap narrowed. Titch refused to bend.

Pressure comes and pressure tells. When some teams lost a game, their coaches would sit down with the referee for an hour afterwards, going through every decision, questioning all the big calls, looking to find blame anywhere but at home. I thought that approach was counter-productive; it changed nothing, it used up precious time when you only had a couple of hours before your next match, and it sidetracked you into meetings and furious emails when you needed to be with your players and keep your emotional energies in reserve for the contest itself. I could also see it seeping into referees' minds: this team, this coach, are bad losers. Sympathy in big matches does not go from officials to bad losers. We decided after Sydney that there would be no more conversations about rugby with the referees. We would ask them how they were and stay friendly but we would complain about nothing and never confront them about anything that had gone before. It would force us, too, to be honest with each other about our own failings. No blaming it on anyone else. If we failed, it would be on us.

I could see the Olympic effect on all the national coaches. Travelling the same circuit, standing on the same touchline, eating in the same dining tents, you watched how men twitched under duress and gave away their hands with nervous tics and tells.

The South African head coaches, first Paul Treu and then Neil Powell, would be fired up when you played them, shouting at their players, giving you the daggers. I liked that – it showed that they cared, that they were up for it. Mike Friday, my predecessor as England coach, at this point in charge of the USA, liked to dominate, always pushing for little changes to the benefit of his team rather than the collective. Simon Amor of England was a very good politician, working those above him, autocratic with those below him, but socially awkward. I had seen him throw tables in dressing rooms after we had lost, be approached by a dad with his lad saying my son's your biggest fan, could we get an autograph, and Simon staring at them and striding off. He would sometimes blank other coaches and players when England lost.

In the coaches' meetings before tournaments it would all come out, part rutting stags, part Machiavellian deal-making, a certain amount of chest-beating. Gordon might start by complaining about the travel plans and how the schedule was leading to injuries amongst his players. I might point out that it was only his players who were struggling, and that they were soft-tissue injuries and so down to training workload and management, and hadn't he run a bleep test on them the day after they got off the plane, when no other team was doing anything but a light jog or splash about in the hotel pool?

I had been in meetings with England when it had played out like something from the nineteenth century. When the home nations were trying to work out how they could best come together to form a Great Britain team for the Olympics – who should coach it, how many players should be picked from each country – the English officials would tell everyone what to do; Scotland and Wales would then get together and vote against them because they were English.

Fiji were considered the bottom of the barrel. We were sitting with Samoa and Kenya and having the same issues with kit that hadn't turned up or been paid for in the first place, coming in on the same budget flights routed in zigzags across the world's airports to save money, not having enough funds to fly in early for proper preparation. And then the meeting would begin and Gordon would be incandescent about something that to us seemed inconsequential.

Before the Las Vegas sevens, Simon Amor objected to the size of the gap between the edge of the pitch and the grandstands. This isn't safe, players are going to injure themselves. World Rugby repainted the pitch to make it a few metres narrower, which had been Simon's aim all along; a tighter pitch is easier to defend on, with less space for the opposition's wingers to run into. Not good enough, we want it narrower still. They repainted it a second time.

England failed to win a single match. Beaten by Scotland and Australia in the group stages, beaten again by

France on the second day and then comprehensively by the minnows, Canada. The artificial pitch could not be watered because the paint had not dried, and so most of the teams suffered friction burns on their legs and arms. Our boys were fine – they spotted the problem and kept the ball alive rather than taking it into rucks or battling at the breakdown. Meanwhile England were sending official complaints and documents from HR, threatening to pull the team out of the competition.

For Gordon the outrage came in the form of cupcakes. A tray had been left out in the dining hall, nutritional information on a card next to it. He spotted it and let rip. This is a disgrace. Do you think this is what athletes should be eating? The cook standing there in the blast zone, wearing a chastened expression, hauled in by his intimidated superiors for another reprimand later on before World Rugby gave Gordon a warning of his own. I wondered how Gordon and his team would cope in the athletes' village at the Olympics, where all food is free and the McDonald's never closes. Wouldn't it be better to have players who consciously chose the right options rather than having the decisions made for them from above? When we finished a tournament I would let my players have fast food as a treat and to keep them off the booze. As we were sitting down in the food court, other teams' players would slowly come in to eat too, plenty of Kiwis among them. Our lads were doing it in front of me, others behind their own coach's back.

Men under pressure fall back on what they know. They don't take risks because the stakes seem too high, and they stop searching for the little innovations that might yet pay off in handsome fashion.

Two hours before tournaments you could find those teams hammering themselves in any available space – running up hills, doing repeated sprints in the hotel car-park. There had been a theory that these sorts of blowouts would trigger a second wind by the time the game began.

I had organised a PhD with Bath University to look into the theory's efficacy when I had been with England. There was no evidence at all that it helped. I never did it again; we ended up as the only team in sevens history to have a perfect run of opening matches: 10 tournaments, 30 group match wins out of 30.

Instead we did hot and cold baths. A hot one on one side of the corridor, a cold one on the other, a couple of plastic gauges in there bought from a local garden centre to get the temperatures where the statistics told us they should be. Moving from one to the other and back again helped flush the lactic acid from our legs, getting the blood flowing, waking up weary limbs and heads. Breakfast, baths, a look out of the hotel-room window at the other teams thrashing themselves in the car-park or diving around on the ornamental lawn.

Even as an adult you can learn and you can change. Keep being brave. Don't let the past dictate your future.

ELEVEN

What happens to you in your childhood stays with you as an adult. I lost Noel and I struggle to stay anchored when relationships come to an end. A girlfriend at college I haven't known for long and haven't done much with says she wants to break up, and suddenly all I want to do is stay with her. A year on, I'm with a girl who isn't right for me, and we both know it, and when we sensibly start thinking about letting it go, all I want to do is hold on.

I'm a new teacher out of university, a young coach at Newbury. I find it hard to open up with people because I don't want to risk losing it again. I go for handshakes rather than embraces, even though I know hugging would work and feel good, because it is intimacy and that feels unfamiliar now.

It's there in the family too. Mum loves us and we know it, but in 1970s and '80s England it all goes unsaid. It takes until my older *sister has kids and they run to their nan when they get to her house and she has to hug them, for it to happen. I don't see Mum for six months and I knock on the door and she smiles and then she'll just walk off back down the corridor towards the kitchen. The love is there. It's shown in more subtle ways: she has gone to the kitchen to make me bacon sandwiches, because she's a mum and she remembers her boy can eat a plateful of them. Her the hard worker who made sure there was enough money when we were kids to feed us all. Dad more of a dabbler, no pension for him but one carefully put away by her.*

She missed out on a lot of that maternal love too. Her own father was a smoker and a talker, the loquacious Welsh gift of the gab, but I find out late that her mother was a heavy drinker, shadows stretching over her. Childhood stays with you. I can't deal with rejection. Maybe knowing this helps. When you know what you are missing you can try to fill in the gaps. Even as an adult you can learn and you can change. It's why forgetting is not the way to deal with it. Remember and attempt to make it right.

Fijians talk about the weather all the time. Suva is the second-rainiest capital city in the world, the wind coming in from the west and picking up all that moisture over the warm South Pacific, intense thunderstorms blowing in, tropical winds coming through behind to dry it all before the next front rolls onto the coast.

There had been cyclone warnings before, broadcast on state radio and television. It all seemed very theoretical: yes, this one's coming for Fiji, it could be hitting us or it might not, is it coming, yes it's coming, no it's not. One had come close, tailing off and clattering Vanuatu and Port Vila, 1,200 kilometres out west.

None of us thought much of it when a tropical

disturbance was first reported to be developing over the same part of the Pacific in early February. Four days later, travelling south-west towards the Lau islands in the south, the system was bringing with it gale-force winds. Mentions on state media, and then the usual pattern – winds building up to 110 miles an hour, but still way out at sea, and then turning north-east towards Tonga on 17 February. We got some high winds in Pacific Harbour but nothing that did more than loosen a few already wobbling coconuts. It wasn't going to affect anyone. A collective Fijian shrug. That was that, and it wasn't up to much, was it?

And then the storm began to drift west again, accelerating, intensifying. In our training camp Ropate took me aside. Let's maybe release the players for 12 hours so they can all get home. I'm sure nothing will happen, but they can tell that to their families. We can ask Bela to drop them all off.

All of the players now had places to stay on the main island, even the ones from further afield. OK, let's send them off. More government bulletins, on social media as well as television and radio, every hour a slightly different scenario, models online showing what routes the storm might now take.

People out in the streets, talking about it relentlessly and doing as much about it as they could. Queuing up outside the supermarkets, shelves emptying, buying as much water as could be carried home and anything tinned, and then containers they could put water in. The cyclone now with a name, Winston, intensifying again, up to category five by Friday the 19th, heading straight for Vanua Balavu, the third-biggest island in the Fijian archipelago.

And then it stopped, and turned, and came straight for

us. Six hours' warning: this is going to hit. Get to shelter, get inside.

Back to the house, Natalie there already. We had stashed everything in the kitchen – candles, yes, place them in piles around the house, make sure each room has a box of matches. Bottles of drinking water all around the house, and then the preparations for a safe area, for us the little box room as you came in the main door, the room with the smallest window that could be shuttered tight – a mattress on the floor to sleep on, another shoved against the door, your phone fully charged and a solar charger with back-up power in it by your makeshift bed. Tins and food that you could eat without having to heat it up. Getting ready to turn off the gas pipes that led from the tanks in the garden to the house. All the time that six-hour warning disappearing, the countdown coming, the winds stinging the palm trees and whipping up the water on the usually plate-glass lagoon.

The latest prediction came through on the radio. The eye of the storm was going to pass close to the north coast of Viti Levu, right over Ropate's home island of Koro. That left us about 70 miles south. Gusts were being recorded of 190mph.

News came that a curfew was going to be imposed by Frank from 6 p.m. Families ran around helping each other out, my landlady sending over hers to help board up our windows and slash off the branches on nearby trees that looked most likely to come down. Chris Cracknell was away with the Fiji women's team in Brazil, so every minute of additional assistance was making a difference. The sky a churned-up grey, the wind so strong that holding the wooden boards in place over the window frames to hammer them down took three people.

In a surreal way it was almost exciting. You knew something enormous was coming, something that you could do nothing about. Nature seemed to have disappeared – no birds in the trees, no dogs in the road, a great emptiness where usually there was teeming life. But there was fear and there was the realisation of what could happen when the storm made landfall. If it swung any closer to Suva it would be a disaster on an unimaginable scale, so many people there in houses that couldn't stand up to this, thousands of buildings right on the waterfront where the storm surges might come in, Jerry and his family in the settlement slums high up on the hills.

The curfew came. Trying to get onto the internet while there was still power to see what was happening. No wind-up radio in the house so running outside to the car to try to use that one until the winds became so strong that it was no longer an option. Sending a text message back to my mum – we're here, safe, we're boarded up, just waiting for it now.

Night dropped in and the darkness was made more intense by the boards across the windows. Our house was a strong one, but I had no idea what would be strong enough. As we lay there I could hear branches crashing onto the plastic corrugated roof of the car-port. I began to wonder how the world outside would look when daylight came again. What would be left?

Our neighbours from Melbourne were back in Australia. The big hedge in between the two properties was being torn by the wind, the noise growing more intense, the trees bending and swaying to ludicrous angles. We lay there in the darkness and watched the hours tick by as gusts thumped the house.

Midnight. 1 a.m. A change in the wind from a heavy battering to a constant ear-splitting scream, like a jet plane's engine blasting or the feedback from an electric guitar over a bank of speakers in a stadium rock concert. A sudden lurch – had I disconnected the gas tanks?

Shit. I'd forgotten the gas. Natalie, I've got to go out there. Ben, don't be insane. Natalie, what if it goes?

The tanks weren't far away. Just across from the car-port, around the side by the trees and some bushes, maybe six or seven metres in total.

I got the door open. The car-port was shaking, the air full of debris – twigs, leaves, sand. Absolutely pitch black, not a light anywhere, my one feeble torch almost making it worse by exaggerating the darkness all around. Through its yellow beam you could see fragments of tree and soil flashing past.

It was like leaning against the side of a bouncy castle – a constant vibrating press against your face, chest and legs, a solid soft wall in front of you that you could no more push through than you could fly. All the time that horrible whistling in your ears, the premonition that something bigger was whipping through the air towards you, a branch, a wooden board, a sheet of corrugated iron. Beaten, I fell back to the door, heaved it shut behind me and wedged the mattress back into place.

I think we must have fallen asleep at some point. Waking up around dawn, the wind still going but no longer screaming, peering out past the boarded-up windows to see what had happened.

The first thing you saw was the hedges around the

house, or rather what the hedges now were. They had been stripped of everything as effectively as if they had been fed through a giant threshing machine. Just skeletons left, black and bare. Around them the grass was under a random dump of anything that had come to land. Palm leaves, coconuts, branches, chunks of plastic and splintered wood.

We were still off grid and under curfew. No power, no one out in the streets. No phone network for our mobiles. No idea at all what had happened in Suva or across the islands, or how the players were.

I went out to the car to get the radio working. The most powerful cyclone the southern hemisphere had ever seen, said one report. News coming through of hundreds of villages destroyed, of the north of Viti Levu around Rakiraki being ripped apart. Storm surges in Ovalau of seven metres above the usual high-tide line. No contact made at all with Vanua Balavu and the islands around – Lakeba, Cicia, Nayau, Taveuni, Qamea.

A complete blackout from Koro and the entire Lomaiviti archipelago. I tried to call Ropate but there was no signal. I picked my way through the debris and across to the training pitch at Uprising. The Spanish sevens team had been staying there and had put out almost a thousand sandbags between the beach and the resort. It had saved it; with great tidal waves coming across the reef, the lodges and the dorm and the pitch would have been washed away had that wall not been put in place.

The phone network began to come back in patches. I got a text through to my mum and then one through to Ropate. He had been trying to contact the players. The ones in Suva seemed OK. The ones in the west, around Nadi and Lautoka, no news.

Over the next few hours the text messages pinged through in clumps. Pio's home had been destroyed. Jerry's house had lost its roof. Alifereti Veitokani, maybe the luckiest of all, had been hiding with his family in the kitchen in their house when the walls had started shaking; they had run into the adjoining room and then watched as the ceiling and walls collapsed behind them.

Newscasters were grave on the radio: 44 people killed; more than 40 per cent of the population affected; 40,000 homes damaged or destroyed.

News from Koro, coming back from satellite images and army helicopters. A thousand homes destroyed, more than 3,000 people homeless, the main jetties gone and so no way for emergency help to get ashore.

Ropate was always someone who kept it all inside. If he was really quiet one morning you might ask him what was up, and he'd give you a smile and say that his wife had just given birth to another son. There would have been no mention that she was even pregnant and no request for time off to attend the birth.

Somehow he was still calm. Half his home island was underwater. His house had been flattened, his mother was waiting for a tent to be dropped by the army. He had kilns on his property where they dried out *kava* roots and land where he grew cassava. It was all gone – kilns destroyed, land flooded, soil poisoned with sea water. No insurance, because ordinary families in Fiji couldn't afford insurance, his financial security all gone – his savings, his future income. And nothing he could do about it, because there was no way of going back.

208

Ropate being Ropate, he threw all his energy into the team. Let's try to bring the boys in, Ben. I'll send messages out. Let's see how they are and how we can all help.

Together we went out on the road. There were trees down across it every hundred metres, locals standing there in the puddles and the rain hacking away with their machetes. As we headed west the telegraph poles that ran alongside the road had been skittled, bowled over as though a great ball had come rolling through. High on the hillsides houses looked imploded, or as if they had been shot out from the inside. Girders that had formed the frames of family homes were halfway down the slopes, embedded at crazy angles in mud and leaning drunkenly against each other.

Coconut trees are very robust. They flex. Driving slowly along that coast they looked instead like toothpicks, stripped of all their fronds and nuts, lying white and shattered on the ground. You could see where one distinct part of the cyclone had just ploughed through a village, carving a wide trench through buildings, trees and fields, cleaning up anything in its path.

Meeting points were being set up where you could leave clothes and provisions to be sent to the most devastated areas. People were walking down from villages that had themselves been badly hit to bring bin-bags full of spare clothes. Natalie and I did the same.

Slowly the players began to arrive at Uprising, first the ones from Suva, then the ones from Nadroga, then the ones who I had never expected to see at all. Alifereti Veitokani walked six hours just to get on to the road where he could thumb a lift onwards.

All of them were in pieces, hungry, exhausted,

emotionally shattered. Some carried stories of villagers trying to run between houses during the night of the storm, some people being hit by something, dying in front of their own families. It was like they were coming back from war. A fierce heat had come in the cyclone's aftermath. There was not enough water – streams and springs had been contaminated by mudslides and floods. Most of the players had barely slept for three days, none had eaten hot food.

I gave them meals from what Uprising had in the stores and I tried to get them to sleep. Instead they wanted to help – let's go together to the villages, let's use our strength and numbers however we can.

And so we went around as heavy movers, as waterboys, as mobile wardrobes. Getting into villages and helping with whatever needed doing, moving branches, trying to rebuild houses and huts, taking bottled water and clothes from our own supplies and leaving them with the locals.

The players possessed an ability to process tragedy and deal with its aftermath that continued to astonish me. They had left their own families to be with the team, not as a selfish act but because their families wanted them to. Already the saying and hashtag was developing: *Stronger Than Winston*. Fiji's sevens team were the epitome of every-thing the nation wanted to be. By travelling the island, doing what we could here and there, we could play a small but significant role in the start of a vast rebuilding process.

There were no complaints and there were few tears. Fijians are emotional people but only when there is celebrating to do. When darkness came they would phlegmatically push on until dawn. Pio's wife dying, a devastating cyclone; to me these were disasters that could take a lifetime to recover from. To my players there was an acceptance of what the day had brought. Death happens. Storms come through. We had little to start with so we'll rebuild and go again.

Ropate had made his plans without fuss or requesting assistance. We had a masseur who was also a builder. Ropate sent him over to Koro on a boat carrying emergency supplies with whatever money he could find, to attempt to reconstruct one corner of the homestead so there was at least one room for his mother to sleep in. All the time there was no sudden outburst of grief nor any sign of self-pity.

A week after the cyclone had made landfall we were supposed to be heading to Nevada for the Las Vegas leg of the 2016 World Series. After our inconsistent first few months we were battling New Zealand and South Africa at the top of the standings, but I assumed the boys would not want to travel. Rugby seemed so inconsequential compared to what was happening all around us. As the cyclone had tracked closer, Fiji Airways had flown all their planes off Viti Levu. We had no visas, because there was no electricity to get online and check how the applications were progressing. As waterborne diseases spread in the aftermath of the storm, as players had been forced to wash in dirty water and drink what they could, so sickness was breaking out across the islands. Several of the team had contracted the Zika virus, and with it conjunctivitis. Their eyes were red and sticky, with gloopy tears forming in the corners, their vision compromised. They tried to train in sunglasses. Four of the boys had gastroenteritis and were unable to hold any food down.

I had it wrong. There was never a thought about not going to Vegas. Osea made it quite clear to me: this is our way of showing that we're resilient. This is not about us, this is about Fiji. Rugby is how we will put smiles back on the faces, rugby is how we will bounce back. Stronger than you, stronger than Winston.

I made a personal trip to the US embassy in Suva to beg for assistance. Sunglasses on all the players as we tried to board the plane at Nadi, three of them sent back for being infectious. Four of them still vomiting as discreetly as men of 6ft 2ins and 15 stone could. Discussions as we flew out about what level of government funding we were going to get for the Olympics, and me saying publicly, despite all the battles for financial support over the previous two and a half years, we understand as a team if we get nothing now, because the nation has other priorities.

I wasn't worried that we were going to be landing late in the US and fighting jetlag on top of everything else. It was more a case of whether we could get there before the tournament began at all, and with enough fit players to get a team out on the pitch.

As it turned out, two of them would never leave the hotel. All Vatemo Ravouvou would manage to eat across those three days was a tube of Pringles. At the coaches' meeting on the eve of the tournament I was thrilled just to be there. That was when England coach Simon Amor began his complaint about the width of the pitch, and New Zealand's Gordon Tietjens decided to lose it over a cupcake.

It was difficult to keep the disdain off my face, to not stand up and say, you don't get it, do you? You just don't understand what's actually important. We had nine fit players rather than the usual thirteen. We had done no training. I had to go to World Rugby and admit that we were rife with conjunctivitis, which in a contact sport like rugby could barely have been more transferable, and that these players probably couldn't go on the pitch as a result.

I was also giving a debut to a 22-year-old forward called Masivesi Dakuwaqa, from the Tokatoka Westfield Dragons team over in Saunaka, a little village a few miles inland from Nadi. I had spotted him in the Coral Coast sevens two months before. He had no passport, although the more significant issue was that he was almost blind in one eye. As a kid in primary school he had been messing around with a rubber band and a stick when the band had flown backwards into his eye. He could no longer focus with it, as if it was full of sleep, just a hazy light coming through. If he had wanted a cupcake someone would have had to hand it to him.

Our opening group match was due to be against Samoa on Friday, 4 March. Exhausted, the players woke up late for *lotu*. That made them late for our hot and cold baths, which meant no one checked what time had been given by the team liaison officer for breakfast, so breakfast was missed. Already down on fuel from the previous ten days, several then fell asleep on the bus from the hotel to the Sam Boyd Stadium. Late for the warm-up, late out on to the pitch, beaten 28–24.

Osea could not believe it. Our plane has crashed, Ben, hasn't it? All the little things that on their own don't matter, we have got wrong. The plane crashed because one bolt was loose and no one checked it, and the pilot was late for his pre-flight checks, and everyone assumed everything was going to be all right.

You're right, Osea. Have a *talanoa* with the boys tonight.

213

And they talked about it, about how the things that had gone wrong were all things they could control. About what their families and friends were going through at home, and what they would think if they found out we had lost a match because we had an extra hour in bed.

The next morning they were up on time and *lotu* was rich and fierce. Ropate was at the heart of it all. No one needed to be told what had happened on Koro, or what it meant that he was with us. Hymns sung with arms around each other, in spiritual and physical harmony, white strapping from William around wrists and forearms, Bible verses on some, *Stronger Than Winston* on them all.

Across the next two days we were fantastic, beating Argentina to top our group, all over Japan with 43 points in the quarter-finals, easing past a noisy and fast-improving host nation in the semi-finals.

And then, before the final against Australia, the most curious thing. On a calm afternoon, in the sunshine, in the Nevadan desert, a wind began to blow. First gently, and then with increasing intensity, until it was howling through the stadium, bending the goalposts, blowing bags and litter and leaves along the length of the pitch.

We couldn't cope with it. With the gale at our backs in the first half, every pass we threw went forward. Every kick sailed out of touch or over the dead-ball line. Australia scored one try, and then another, and then a third. We were 15–0 down, lucky that they had missed all three conversions, the attempted kicks stalling in the wind and falling short.

I gathered the boys around me at half-time. My cap blew off my head and landed 30m away. Ropate was laughing himself to tears. Smiles on all of us, something with us that day, something bigger than the team. I had to yell at them just to be heard, words snatched away off my lips. Boys, just keep the ball. We'll score tries. Find the energy. When we do, make sure you score under the posts. We need the conversions, and we'll land them from nowhere else.

The gale was so strong as we kicked off the second half that the ball stopped and blew back over Osea's head. The floodlight towers were swaying dangerously.

Australia came at us again, forcing us back deep into our own half. With our usual more experienced options back in Fiji or retching back at the hotel, I threw on a pair of kids as our substitutes: 22-year-old Kitione Taliga, from a village in the west of Viti Levu called Dratabu, one of the ones hit most badly by Winston, a winger I had seen playing for the wardens' side, fresh off a debut in Dubai a few months before; and 22-year-old Masivesi Dakuwaqa, his first World Series tournament, the biggest match he had ever played in.

With his first touch Kitione took the ball behind our own try-line and accelerated away, past two green-and-gold shirts, out of our own 22, across halfway and away. One try back, the conversion over for 15–7.

A minute later, a turnover off Australian possession. Jerry Tuwai with the ball in his hands and two defenders closing in like a yellow vice, a flicked pass to his right and Kitione there again to race away under the posts once more. Try converted, 15–14, Ropate jumping up and down and laughing, the Fijian supporters in the red stands trying to punch the air and hang on to the flags being pulled out of their hands by the wind at the same time.

Australia stayed calm. With Quade Cooper at fly-half, a man who had starred many times for the Wallabies in the

15-a-side game, played in World Cups, beaten England at Twickenham, they drove up to our line. Cooper took the ball five metres out, dropped his shoulder and went for the line, and was stopped dead by a shuddering tackle from Vatemo Ravouvou, powered on by his enforced diet of 30 Pringles a day.

The ball went loose, Osea there to dive on it, Vatemo back to his feet to take it from between Osea's legs and spin it out to his right. Kitione waiting, Save Rawaca on his outside, still five metres behind our own line.

You shouldn't have been able to run into that gale. The Australian defenders could not, as they turned on their heels and gave chase to the disappearing Save.

We had Sigatoka in our legs. We had run up sand mountains. We had a nation behind us.

Save away down the right wing, away with defenders tumbling in his slipstream, away untouched to the full length of the field.

21–15. In the aftermath, back in the dressing room after the trophy presentation and taking it to our supporters, hats and coats on in the teeth of that wind, flags still snapping and flicking wildly, the emotion came out. Tears from all of us, tears from me. *Lotu* together, phones pinging with messages from back home, Frank calling me and sending emails of congratulation from the nation, forearms being held in the air with their strapping and message scrawled on in black ink: *Stronger Than Winston*.

We fell apart a little the following week at the Canada sevens in Vancouver. Beaten by 12 points by South Africa in the semis, again by Australia in the third-place match. I didn't mind. You couldn't go that deep without struggling to get up again so soon. And what did it matter? We had done what I knew no one else could do. We had won for ourselves and we had won for a nation on its knees.

You worry about cupcakes. You complain about the width of the pitch. Only the island teams just get on with things. Only Fiji has so much less but so much more, too.

TWELVE

There is no sign of Noel through my university years. From Loughborough to Cambridge, playing scrum-half in two Varsity matches, not knowing where my old half-back partner is any more.

Going back to Brentford and discovering all your old mates now have mobiles. Going down to the High Street to get my first, an authentic brick, and finding out that communication is now easier, that people you had left behind are only a text message away. Putting the word out that I am looking for Noel, asking if anyone has seen him or heard where he might be.

Word coming through from a friend: I think I saw him down Tooting railway station. Another one: spotted him in Tooting on Friday nights.

So I go down there. A bus across from Brentford, hanging around the station on Friday evening, hours standing there and searching the faces as commuters come and go, and it gets cold and then it's the pub crowd.

No Noel. Going back again the following Friday, doing the same again. No Noel.

Other mates wanting to find him too. Another lead. Asking a mate in the Met Police to run a background search for him. All that comes back: last known sentence, Wormwood Scrubs; no forwarding address.

I have thought about what I will do if I find him, about how much he will have changed. When I picture it we meet and something clicks and the intervening years drop away and we're back where we were, or where we are now and ready to carry on. It doesn't feel too late. It doesn't feel like we're too old to get our friendship back up and running.

No more news. Teaching now at St Edward's in Oxford, getting the rugby team working like Mr Hopkins did ours. Talented kids like me and Noel, getting some into England age-group sides and teams into the final stages of big nationwide competitions. Coaching Newbury in the evenings, steering them from the third tier of English rugby into the second.

I meet Natalie. In the first rush of talk and who are you, I tell her how special Noel was to me. I want her to meet him. I want her to see what I do and I want Noel to see what I see in her.

I do wonder if he is still alive. Multiple custodial sentences, nowhere to go, no one to go back to. But if he is dead there would be records – something in the prison system, a notification to the police. There is nothing.

Maybe he's gone abroad, except he's been here since he was nine years old, and he never went back before. They wouldn't be deporting him, not after 20 years in the country.

He's there somewhere. I just need to find him. It's not over, not yet.

April in Hong Kong, four months until the three days in Brazil that would define us. I decided to run the tournament as a dress rehearsal for what we would find in Rio. The same number of matches, the biggest crowds on the World Series circuit, the pressure of a tournament that mattered more back home than any other.

I had a curious feeling throughout. We needed a last-minute try to beat Canada in the group stage and another to squeak past Kenya in the quarter-finals; we lost our leading try-scorer Save Rawaca to a hamstring injury in the first minute of our semi-final against Australia. In the final against New Zealand warm tropical rain was hammering down, making it harder to play our liberated, adventurous passing game.

I didn't stress about any of it. There's a saying in Fiji – *seqa na leqa*, no worries. Why should it matter whether we scored with ten minutes left on the clock or ten seconds? Tries could come from a metre out or the length of the field; they were still all worth five points. We had lost Save but we had Kitione Taliga and his late-breaking speed and power.

I felt no concern when New Zealand went 7–0 up, or when Jerry Tuwai kicked ahead into the biggest, emptiest space not built on in Hong Kong, only to be blocked off on his chase. A penalty in front of the posts, the defenders still arguing with the referee, Jerry taking it quickly to step and snipe under the posts. Stretching that same defence from side to side in the second half, runners teasing with angles and moves that disappeared as quickly as they threatened to materialise, Kitione waiting out wide on the right to run on to two flat fizzing passes and between the last two Kiwis to make it 14–7.

New Zealand pressing, our own defence relentless. Mud and grass turning our white shirts grey, supporters in the stands with pale-blue translucent plastic capes over their own shirts leaping around in the rain. Pio Tuwai playing like a man possessed, the irony of which would only become apparent later. Going through an opposition ruck like a wrecking-ball to clear out two defenders, us snatching the ball and breaking upfield, the ball flicking from man to man, Semi Kunatani blazing on to the final pass for the try to seal it all.

We gathered in a tight circle at the end with arms around each other and sang hymns and songs of celebration. I had my head bowed, reflecting that if we could hold this form and mood to Rio we would scare anyone, thinking too that on this holy ground for Fijian rugby they could probably have won without a coach. That thought didn't upset me; it had always been the theoretical end goal, and no other stadium brought the same guarantees. A week later we would lose to Kenya in the final in Singapore, walloped by 23 points, their first-ever tournament victory. But we would go into the final two rounds of the World Series holding a narrow lead in the overall standings, on course, if we could hold it, to win back-to-back World Series titles, something no Fijian side had ever done.

I knew better now than to take any of it for granted. We had brought in a masseur to help the boys recover from the increasingly challenging fitness sessions we were planning as the Olympics drew closer. As part of the deal I had given him some money to set up a massage practice in Suva. One morning he rang me: my wife has taken the cash out of the bank to pay the rent, and she's had her purse stolen. Could you give me some more until we're up and running? News from the team via Osea: he has been asking us for money too. I had to let him go, no matter how he good he was at his job or what a difference it made to the players' stressed-out physiques.

That second Hong Kong win had set off ecstatic celebrations in Fiji. Soon afterwards I was at an event in Suva with Frank. He was there with his wife as well as the usual bodyguards, and yet all the attention seemed to be directed at me – requests for autographs, for selfies, for interviews. It was obvious that he wasn't particularly happy about it. When an invite came to attend another event he would be at a few days later, I turned it down, apologising that unfortunately I was snowed under with the team and so wouldn't be around. I realised what Frank was like and I understood what angered him. As the team had become more successful he had become an increasingly dependable and expedient ally. That could not be jeopardised, not for me, not for the team.

In Paris, the penultimate leg of the World Series, came further disturbing evidence of old issues and flaws. Having beaten Samoa 42–5 in the group stages, we suffered a collective brain freeze against them in the final to lose from 26–7 up at half time. That night Vatemo Ravouvou's cousin took him out drinking when I had told the players to stay off the booze. Mindful of how quickly standards could fall, of Osea's plane-crash analogy a few months earlier in Las Vegas, I told him he would not be considered for selection in London the following week. He could carry the water on for the boys but no more.

It no longer felt as if this team could stay afloat without

a coach. The World Series title was on the line, yet we were down to 11 men rather than 13, Pio Tuwai having failed a fitness test. We couldn't fly a replacement in from Fiji. We didn't have the money.

Time to be creative. I had stayed in contact with Jarryd Hayne after our initial chat at the Fiji Airways event. He had come to watch us once and hung out with the team, and we'd talked on email as his time with the San Francisco 49ers had come to end. Hayne could play anywhere in the back line – centre, wing, full-back – and could do things with ball in hand that had made him one of the biggest stars in Australian sport. In his time playing rugby league for the Parramatta Eels he had twice been voted the National Rugby League's player of the year.

A couple of the other wildcards I had been keeping an eye on had fallen through. A tweak to the international eligibility regulations meant that the former All Black wing Joe Rokocoko was no longer an option. Neither was Radike Samo, another Fijian-born star playing for a bigger, wealthier nation. Samo was a forward with the pace of a back and hair like a member of the Jackson Five; he had once scored a try for Australia against New Zealand that was voted World Rugby's score of the season.

I had always been open to these sorts of curveballs. With England I was often emailed by a parent of a young player, and I always followed up the leads. It was how I had found Jeff Williams, who had been playing for the tiny Chateaurenard side in Provence when his dad got in contact, and Jeff had gone on to play in the Premiership for Bath. Greg Barden was another, playing for the Royal Navy and a local club at the same time under a different name. He ended up as England's sevens captain.

There had been plenty of duds too, pushy parents blind to the flaws in their sons that were obvious to everyone else. In Fiji it was always worth the effort. A buzz on the coconut wireless about a big kid playing in a tiny village. A guy who picks up your bags at a hotel and tells you about his brother who is so quick it's like trying to catch a lizard by its tail.

There was a good chance it might backfire with Jarryd. I had a tight group that had trained together and suffered together. We played flat-out in seven-minute and ten-minute bursts; he had been enjoying a sit on the sideline and a cool drink after every truncated punt return for San Francisco. I had burned my fingers a couple of times dropping 15-a-side players into the England sevens team – the outstanding Tom Varndell, the all-time leading try-scorer in the top flight of English rugby, unable to adjust to the rapid-fire chaos of sevens after a long time away.

I had seen Jarryd playing rugby league. At 6ft 3ins and 16 stone he had power and a swerve, but he had never played rugby union. He needed to learn the rules, let alone how to implement them when he had three vengeful Australians trying to trample him. But he seemed genuinely committed – in touch with his Fijian parentage, a Fijian tattoo from his spell playing with the national rugby league team at the 2008 World Cup, a kid who had grown up with nothing in a tough part of south Sydney, got a fair few things wrong and then tried to put some right. He had found God, which with his speed and vision made sense, and it was real to him: he loved the sound of our *lotus*, chose stories from the Bible that he wanted to bring into them. We made a plan. He would pay for his own flight from the US to London, train with the team for the week before the tournament and see how it felt.

There was a risk that he would come with an entourage. Such was his status in Australia that his first day in the team hotel saw us besieged by television crews and reporters. Jarryd, what do you want to do? Mate, I know this lot, they won't go away until we give them an interview.

They were waiting in the road outside. As we stepped onto the pavement they swarmed all over us, onto the hotel lawn, onto the steps. A security guard came out apologetically. I'm really sorry, but you aren't allowed to film here, would you mind moving back onto the pavement?

The TV people came straight back at him: Fuck off, you jobsworth, we'll film where we like. Fuck you, mate, what's it got to do with you?

The standard you walk past is the standard you become. When you let someone be rude to hotel staff or liaison officers or supporters because you are too tired to care, it is you being rude to them too. So I stood up: Sorry, I'm not going to answer any of your questions. You're being rude to a man who is only trying to do his job, who has only asked you to move six feet.

Another rant: You fucking English prick, we're not here for your shitty little sport, we're only here because he plays rugby league.

The next day a big piece from the reporter in his newspaper: Ben Ryan has cracked, he can't handle the pressure, he stormed off in the middle of an interview.

All that came with Jarryd, though none of it was his fault. The boys too were star-struck in training, letting him glide untouched through welcoming gaps left in our defence. Lads, this isn't helping him or you. Sort yourselves out.

We gave him what we thought was a light week of training, but his legs were gone after a couple of days. I thought, this is going nowhere, but what else do we have? At least he was hanging out with the boys, trying to get to know them. He was the only player in his room at the hotel rather than sharing, but only because he had arrived early and booked it himself. And he had gone for a single rather than a double, a superstar off the pitch, but so far no ego in the way.

We played OK. Jarryd came on for a minute here and there as a substitute; we beat France heavily in the quarter-finals and then lost a tight match to South Africa in the semis. In the third-place play-off we lost again to the USA, one of the three teams we had been drawn to play in the group stages of the Olympics.

It was enough. After that quarter-final win no one could catch us at the top of the standings. A second World Series title in two years, in my old home city, amongst my old friends, celebrated with the new breed.

At times that season I had been filled with an unmatched confidence. Walking out of the dressing room for some matches, I had felt like Frankie Dettori at Ascot on that famous September afternoon in 1996, six wins behind him and bursting out of the stalls just knowing he was going to win again. I thought I had the best players prepared better than any others, that I was exactly where I wanted to be as a coach. In those serene moments you felt as if you had 360-degree vision. You could spot the tiny things, like the slight shift in angle of a shoulder in defence, and the big patterns, like intensifying fitness targets across the next three months. I could read the players' body language and

I could steer their moods. I had Osea and Ropate, William and Naca. Frank was with us. The nation trusted us.

And I understood how fragile it all could be. We needed to be fitter than we were, and we needed to eat better. We had critical tactics to put into place – if we wanted to beat South Africa, who would stand in our way in Rio if seedings went to plan, if we were to avoid another upset against the USA or the dangerous Argentinian team. We were still losing matches that we shouldn't, and we had never started a game with the seven men I thought most likely to be at their peak in Rio.

Together we could produce the perfect storm. We could also blow ourselves out. Now was the time to put all those special ingredients together. No more time for mistakes, no next year, no more second chances.

Our final training camp began in the middle of June. A familiar set-up for an unprecedented challenge – the pitch at Uprising that we had first used more than two long years ago, with drainage channels that we had cut ourselves. There was bottled water on hand from Fiji Water where before we had none, piles of coconuts cut by the locals for when we wanted more. No players hiding in the bushes any more, a sense of purpose where there had once been laziness and mistrust.

We ate in a room at the resort. The players slept in the long wooden dormitory, up on stilts to keep it free of the mud and rainwater, threading their way through a little vegetable patch growing chillies for the evening meals to get to the pitch. Up with the sun, *lotu* together, walking barefoot to breakfast, back to the pitch. Playing with smiles on our faces as well as sweat down the back and bruises on arms and foreheads, down to the beach and into the sea to cool off and recover before lunch. A little lucky triangle, every morning, from dorm to pitch to sea.

Our rivals would be training in private. No England supporter was allowed close to the pitches at the Lensbury Hotel in west London when we had prepped for tournaments. Gordon Tietjens would no more let strangers watch his team's Olympic preparations than he would email me his video analysis. We had every car that passed pulling over to watch, every bus full of kids screaming out of the windows. Public buses would turn off Queens Road and park under the trees, the passengers climbing out and asking for photos. Cars stopping and even more people running over onto the pitch in the middle of sessions. We've travelled especially for this, would you mind? And Ropate would say, could we just wait and let them do it?

I loved it. They were our supporters. They were why we were doing it. I'd get the kids to run water on for the players when they had their short breaks and ask older lads to machete the tops off the coconuts when we were ready for those. We put up a short net around the pitch to keep balls from disappearing into the crowds and to protect the players from unexpected tackles or support runs from the wildly enthusiastic, but it was still public access from start to finish. There was no point trying to bring an English mentality to a South Pacific island. This was a community coming to be with their own.

Osea was the elder brother watching over it all, his minister father coming in to take *lotu*, the *Fijiana* women's team and their coach Chris Cracknell joining us too. Bela the bus driver would pick the players up on Monday mornings, driving his long loop from Nadi and further on in the north-west all the way round the coastal road to Suva and back. Vatemo Ravouvou the first man waiting by the side of the road, then Pio Tuwai, the text messages fizzing on – get ready, we'll be at the crossroads in 40 minutes – and then the next man passing it on again. Training all week, all sleeping in the dorm, and then up at 5 a.m. on Fridays to head west again to the dunes at Sigatoka and sunrise over that beautiful, cruel testing ground. Prayers and song before, the barbecues and waterfalls afterwards, and then home for the weekend, one bus going west, another east. On Sundays no one would play, everyone would go to church. Saturdays they needed to rest too, Sigatoka in their legs and lungs and the next week of training and its step-up in intensity rattling round the corner.

I had made up my mind what to do about Jarryd. It was going to be too big a jump in too short a space of time, and so I rang him to be honest: you're obviously a fine player, but the runway isn't long enough for you this time. If you want to go back to Australia I'll understand.

He surprised me: You know what Ben, I felt the same. I don't think I'm going to make it. But I'd love to stay, even if it's only for a week. I might be able to contribute something, I might be able to share a few things with the boys.

I was happy with that. He came and he trained and he was bottom of everything – fitness, passing, tackling – and he was OK about it. I'm coming into the best team in the world, I can see why these guys are so good, I will try to improve. He began to finish sessions, which he hadn't managed to do at the start, and he got through the week. He stayed in the dorms, a millionaire among the paupers, and he washed his kit by hand in the sinks, just as they did.

I asked him if he would like to stay for another week. He nodded. And he kept hanging on, for a second week, and a third, and then a fourth. We still had no masseur, having lost ours to temptation, but then found a Kiwi who happened to be travelling through the country but soon had other places to go, and so the boys were trying to massage themselves. Jarryd flew his personal guy over from Australia. Paid the plane fare, paid for his accommodation, paid his salary.

You could see Jarryd's talent as his sevens fitness came. He had time in possession, slow motion around him as he cut through at pace, able to hold the ball on the run as defenders came on to him, skilled at putting team-mates into little gaps and spaces, and seeing opportunities before they became obvious. You saw all of that and yet he was still way behind the curve set by Vatemo Ravouvou and Josua Tuisova, Pio's younger brother. Pio had brought Josh into the Westfield Barbarians team and captained him as a youngster; a lot of the good stuff had clearly rubbed off.

The coconut wireless could not keep still. All about selection, all about the prodigal son and his lengthening stay. Will Ben pick him? Ben can't pick him. Why is he still in camp, have you been to see him, have you seen my photo with him? For us it was rather like an unexpected, unannounced audit. Someone coming in who expected the highest standards, a good kick up the backside for anyone thinking they could cruise, a validation of all we were doing well.

Two weeks before I was due to make the final selection, Jarryd was up to third best in his position. He still wasn't going to make it, because someone third in another position would have got into his position as well. He knew before I told him, but I took him aside all the same: Jarryd, this is a big thing for everyone when we pick the team and with the media so crazy about you. If we name the team and you're still in the mix in the week before and you're still in the camp, then you'll get all the headlines for not making it. So let's get those headlines out of the way a week or two before. OK, Ben, I'll help out in training, I'll be the water boy for the players who are staying.

On his last day he bought every man in the rest of the squad new kit. He took something away too; when he signed a record-breaking deal with NRL team the Gold Coast Titans shortly afterwards, their coaches said that it was the fittest they'd ever seen him. When the Olympics were over, his personal recommendation got Masivesi Dakuwaqa (he of the near-total blindness in one eye) a long-term contract with the NRL's Canberra Raiders. Karma flows and karma pays back.

Now to decide what to do about Pio Tuwai. He had already started to see another woman, which came as a shock to my English mentality but not to Osea and Ropate. This was the Fijian way once again. Ride out the storm, accept the damage that has been left behind, move on. Don't dwell in the darkness, walk forward into the dawn.

With it, however, had come an increase in his drinking. He had never been the hardest worker in training, sometimes doing the tough stuff almost by accident when he was so wrapped up in the ball-work or a match scenario we were playing out, and now he was dropping further behind. I didn't want to use the same collective punishment that had succeeded with others in the past, because there was already so much negativity in his head. So we kept giving him little boosts – changing his diet, getting him extra medical assistance, taking him to the dentist, getting him orthotics made for his rugby boots to keep him moving smoothly and the aches down. When he rang up and asked for money I generally gave it to him, all to get the best out of him, because his best was so good.

If you make an exception to the general rule you have to do so with honesty. We couldn't pretend to the players that Pio was hitting his fitness targets. It was obvious that he couldn't. So too was what he could do on the pitch. I talked to them all: this is where we are with Pio. He's getting fitter and he's breaking his personal best. It's not the standard you guys are hitting but he creates so much for us in attack, and that is what we need, and this is why I'm picking him.

We still had to establish minimum targets for him. If the boys were reaching level 20 and 21 on our regular yoyo fitness tests, he would have to make 16. That would still be superior to anything his counterparts in Fiji's 15-a-side team were capable of hitting, and it was enough to get him through three days of Olympic competition without breaking down. The sprint test didn't really matter because he was never really going to finish try-scoring moves off by getting on the end of an 80m burst. He was the one who would be creating the spark that led to the fire.

I had to be honest with the local media too. During tournaments both the *Fiji Sun* and the *Fiji Times* would have something like 12 pages a day to fill with sevens stories. That's a lot of space, a vacuum that could suck in a lot of bad stuff if we let it. That meant letting reporters into far more sessions than would happen anywhere else. If we didn't, stories would be made up; when we did, boundaries still needed to be set. Don't call me at midnight on a Sunday because you haven't got a story for the paper on Monday morning. Come to training Thursday and we can have a chat then. If I see stories that are clearly made up I won't be able to invite you again.

Those newspapers became another useful little tool in those final weeks. Sami Viriviri had come back from his contract with Montpellier lacking specific sevens fitness. A line about that to the reporters, a mention in the papers, Sami out early the following morning doing extra work on his own. You could play games but you had to establish the rules.

We had done our homework on our opponents in Rio and began to test out different tactics that might surprise them. Against the USA, we were focused on the breakdown, when an opposition player was tackled and on the ground. They had dangerous runners; the best way to stop them was not with a tackle when they were in full flight but to cut off the source of possession long before. You could send a player of your own in to compete for the ball at the breakdown, but the laws around his body position and timing were tight and open to interpretation. Get it wrong and the referee would give a penalty against you. Keep giving penalties and you would be giving away possession and control and risk having a player sent to the sin-bin. Our plan was to counter-ruck instead – get our first player to go past the ball and clear the opposition out of the way. For South Africa we planned a different defensive system – two men back sweeping behind the main line to deal with the threat of their long-range kicking game – and to mix up our line-outs when the ball went out of play. Usually teams set up with three men in the line. We worked on throwing to two and to four. Squeeze some space, create some elsewhere. Make the opposition uncomfortable and keep them guessing.

I had 21 players in camp, because that was the optimum number to work with, but I could only take 13 to Rio, one of whom would be a non-playing reserve. More than 21 and the extra players were not going to give me anything that I didn't already have; fewer, and I wouldn't have given myself sufficient options.

I kept it simple. Three deep in every position. The stellar talents, like Osea Kolinisau, like Jerry Tuwai, like Semi Kunatani. The guys coming back from overseas contracts: Leone Nakarawa from Glasgow Warriors, Josua Tuisova from Toulon. The young bolters – Kitione Taliga, Masivesi Dakuwaqa. Kids who were coming fast from nowhere, like Alivereti Veitokani, a fly-half who could kick, run and keep going at the sort of flat-out pace that would leave others in bits. Alivereti had come into camp tired and slow. When he started eating three meals a day with us, and not all white carbohydrates and processed sugar, when he slept all night in the dorm rather than waking up every couple of hours with the rest of his family, his energy levels were astonishing. No one could recover from an intense sprint and go again as readily.

The third choices knew who they were. It might have caused friction, knowing how unlikely they were to get the nod. Instead those bottom seven drove the competition beautifully, desperate not to get the chop, to stay in the story for as long as possible. We had given no set deadline when the numbers would be culled. It could happen after a training session or at the end of the week. If it sounds cruel, it was the only way it could be. You earned your place and you were given everything we had to help push you on.

The problem came instead at the top. Save Rawaca had been arguably our most impressive player of the past two years, with a big contract in place to play for Saracens in London when the Olympics were over. Faced with a challenge from Josua Tuisova, rather than front up and take it on, he became increasingly jealous. With that came a selfishness on the pitch. He began to play for himself and his place rather than the team. Even the best players can fall fast when they are heading in the wrong direction. Guaranteed selection, he was letting his ego push him towards the margins.

The discussions among the management group were constant. Ropate, Naca, Osea, William, kicking coach Jeremy Manning. Never in an office or round a whiteboard with me standing at the front, always around a meal, over coffee, sitting on the grass by the side of the pitch. We tried never to let a player hang. If he wasn't going to make it, we made the cut a quick one, to keep expectations in check and disappointment as constrained as possible. The message to all was simple: eat well, work hard, be nice.

And yet there were victims. Pio could sense that his own journey with us was in danger of coming to an end. His offloads had inspired us for years, but we now had players with the same abilities who were fitter and in better form.

The realisation was too much for him. Ben, you need to go and see Pio, he's in the dorm. Running over there and finding him shaking in his bed, his eyes rolling back in his head, shouting that he'd been possessed. Calling an ambulance, the ability to speak deserting him now too, being taken off to hospital in Suva and kept in for two nights.

I went in to see him, wondering if it had been made harder for him that his kid brother Josua Tuisova was doing so well for us. Pio told me he was unable to sleep. When I went outside and spoke to the nurses, they told me that when they checked on him every two hours he was always fast asleep. I asked them to run every test that made sense: all were clear. A suggestion from the doctor instead: we think perhaps a psychiatrist is the next port of call.

A few days later Pio came back into camp. I took him for a stroll on the beach. What's done is done. Whatever happened back there, we're not judging you on it. Get back to training and show us what you can do.

He lasted five days. And then another call to the dorm, and the same sight awaiting me. The body shaking, the eyes rolling.

I had seen enough and so had he. He had worked out that he was probably going to be chopped because of the quality of the alternatives, and he was finding an excuse. Self-sabotage on the eve of the biggest sporting challenge Fiji would ever face, the chance to be a national hero, to go down in island fable. Of course I had sympathy for him. I wasn't sure I could have dealt with what he had been through. I loved him as a rugby player – there were matches when he was unplayable, when other coaches would come up to me on the sideline and say, this guy is on another level to anyone else here. When I looked back I thought, wow, we actually got him on the field for about 20 tournaments, and that might have been 20 more than we should have been able to. He was an unforgettable part of our story but not the final chapter. Not every tale would have a happy ending.

*

It was intense for the players and it was relentless for me as a coach. I would barely notice the working day stretching out to 16 or 17 hours, in part because it so seldom felt like work, often because the absorption came naturally and with such rewards. When I did get back to the house I would sometimes be glad that Natalie had made arrangements with some expats up in Suva; it let me crash in peace, it made her happy. I barely noticed the aggregation of those evenings, the way we were ships on different timetables and contrasting courses.

Natalie was busier now. She ran the hospital trolley service over in Suva, a mobile system to make up for the lack of resources on the wards. When there was no toilet paper provided and you were bed-bound, the visit of a trolley with tissues, little bottles of shampoo, parcels of *rotis* and small bags of cakes brought gratitude from the patients and a sense of reward for her. She became friends with the English wife of a retired Fijian soldier who had been part of the first 200-strong intake into the British Army, way back in 1961. I liked Johnny too – a proud member of what they called the Union Jack 212 Club, all of them teenagers who had signed up for the full 22 years' service in order to get the maximum pension, his money sent home to Viti Levu and invested in a house in Pacific Harbour. I would play a few holes of golf with him and enjoyed sitting back with a beer and listening to his tales of wide-eyed adventures past, but it was another outlet that ended with Natalie and me in different houses at different times. My sources of happiness and relaxation were with my retired Aussie friends Doug and Robyn in the house next door and their gentle fishing trips out to the sandbar, or the curry night on Thursdays with the landlady's family, who were now far more friends than proprietors. The sadness at the slow loss of what had been love, the loneliness that came with it, I kept at arm's length as I brought the team and its challenges even closer to me.

Pacific Harbour, Uprising, Sigatoka. Another week gone by, another player sent home. The crescendo to it all was a three-day tournament within the camp, 17 matches, rival against rival: Tuisova vs Rawaca, Kunatani vs Nakarawa.

Six matches on the first day, a ferocity there in keeping with what was at stake. Proper referees, Ropate and me rotating the teams, giving every single player a chance. Six more on the second day, the speed of the rugby and the intensity of the tackles mesmerising, five more on the last day.

By the end I knew 12 of my final 13. The question was Save. We had got him fit again, but was he going to be a team player again? There was still something not quite right, not quite firing. All the time Ropate and William's inside knowledge was essential. This player isn't quite right today, Ben, but this is what's going on in his home village. Osea acted as a conscience. When I had made the decision to finally cut Isake Katonibau, his maverick skills outweighed by his adverse impact on the younger players, Osea came to see me with Jasa and Jerry. You sure you want to do this, Ben? We know how good a player he is. I explained my reasons: he does all that, but he does all this too, he could implode at any point, I'm not prepared to drop our collective standards. All three of them accepted it; I was glad they had come.

Everyone you met on the street had an opinion on selection. Everyone had their personal favourites and their region's darling and their dark horses. A couple of journalists were insistent that William Ryder, scrum-half a decade before, scorer of 105 tries for the national sevens side, should be recalled. I had to point out that he was 34 years old and hadn't been in serious training for years.

I made the announcement to the team one warm July evening. Ropate, William and me in a room at Uprising, the players told to come in one by one whenever they were ready. I had been on the end of selection decisions as a player and I knew a few things: that as soon as you tell someone they're out, they won't remember anything else after that; you had to give them the reason afterwards, and you had to be absolutely honest, because if you just plucked something from thin air, they would know, and it would fester; that you could praise without being mendacious – you've done brilliantly but this guy is better than you. I knew how to keep my body language neutral.

The surprise came in their surprise. Osea walked in and admitted he wasn't sure if he was in, as if he had ever been anything but the first name written down. Sami Viriviri, full of doubt after witnessing the impact that Josua Tuisova had made. A giant winger we had brought in late from a contract with Stade Francais called Waisea Nayacalevu, a star in France's Top 14, convinced he would make it, but I had seen him outworked and outplayed by the men I already had. Villiame Mata, picked by none of the punters who assailed me in the street, and without the pirouetting skills of Pio or the raw pace of Nemani Nagusa, so not a typically Fijian player but with offloads that always worked and a refusal to give away penalties and bang on form. Bill, you're coming to Brazil. Pio, poor old Pio, trudging in slowly and somehow still hopeful, nodding, walking out with the world heavy on his shoulders.

240

The ones who hadn't made the cut could leave whenever they wanted. A few went out and got drunk, Nayacalevu among them. I didn't blame them one bit. They had given up a lot to try to get in the side, especially the overseas-based players. Ropate had a quiet word: that's fine, but don't come back to sleep here if you're smashed, dry out in the village.

I felt OK about delivering that bad news to men who I liked. As much as I cared for all those players, I was ruthless about making the right decisions on selection. I couldn't let in any of my feelings about them being good blokes or knowing what they'd gone through or how far they'd come. It all had to be based on what they were doing now. I hadn't always found that part easy. There were times with England when I had been over-sensitive, shown too much loyalty to players who had performed for me in the past. It had come back to bite me in critical matches in big tournaments. Anyway, all my Fijians had their bad-luck stories. They all had their nicks and dents. Half had been on the scrapheap, half were playing so their village could eat.

The official announcement was made by Frank at a big ceremony in Suva and carried live on national television. It was supposed to be secret until that point but the coconut wireless and the very obvious presence of all the parents blew that one.

I had to tell a few lies. To protect Pio I said that he was injured. Isake asked me to say that he was crocked too. I didn't mind. A little cushioning might help the hard landing.

THIRTEEN

*T*here are echoes of Noel everywhere I look.

In Fiji now, a grown man, 30 years on from the two of us at our tightest. I saw how quickly Noel fell away and I can see the same happening to some of my players – the same traps in their path, the same steep descent once they start to slip.

Noel could have been whatever he chose. A footballer, a rugby player, a coach. I have become what I wanted to be, in the end. Sitting out on the beanbag watching the sun come up, plans in my head for today's training and what little tactical tweak I can work on, asking myself other questions too.

Could I have done more for Noel? Why did reaching out not bring him back? Where might he be as I sit in this moment of the Fijian dawn?

I was too immature and too scared when he first began to fall, too worried that those kids might turn on me when they were *holding lads against the wall down the High Street and taking money off them. I didn't feel like I had the muscles or bravery to step in and stop them.*

When I tried again at 17 and 18 maybe I'd left it too late. I was wiser then, those years in a big state school exposing me to more, the head boy killed in a fight, other kids going off the rails after losing relatives in the Zeebrugge ferry disaster. Football hooliganism, shoplifting, time in Feltham Young Offenders' Institute. I was wiser and I had tried to persuade him but I failed. I knew I could have stepped further into his world but that would have taken me down too. I put myself first.

And adult friendships could never be as deep. You can't spend all that intense time together. You can't have the same adventures. You can't spend an hour and a half playing table-tennis like we did before school.

You are older and you are more cautious. You are more complicated. It is harder to fit together three-dimensional shapes than ones that are still being formed. I am with the players as I was with Noel. I see him in them, and I treat them accordingly.

Echoes down the years, echoes ringing on.

Standing on the stage next to Frank, I watched the players get announced and called forward. Looking forward and looking back too, at where we had come from, at what we had done. Sunshine on our faces, Frank with that *dakuwaqa* shark god's grin, television cameras and supporters waving the pale-blue flag.

Osea Kolinisau, our captain, the big brother to them all. The mainframe of our team, a man who always ran hard, who never cared about what it did to his body, the preacher's son who had been out in the wilderness and come back home. Kitione Taliga, the late charger, a try scorer, always cackling off the pitch, a kid who could produce an opening where all others saw only closed doors. Save Rawaca, so much ability and raw power, the *Bua turaga*, the big man from Bua, on his way to London with Saracens and just about clinging on for Rio.

Josua Tuisova, finally with us after two years of badgering his club side Toulon for his release, brooding, intimidating, putting pressure on Save. Sami Viriviri, smooth by contrast, slicing through defences like a sharp machete, doing it for his single mum at the Flying Fish restaurant and all those hungry siblings. Vatemo Ravouvou, epileptic and undervalued, the glue in our attacking patterns, our *kai wai*, the fisherman who threw out the bait and waited for defenders to take it. Jerry Tuwai, from bare feet on a muddy roundabout and selling fish by the roadside and a mouthful of rotten teeth to the genius who linked our big forwards and our rushing backs, a shapeshifter, a rubber ball bouncing where no one could follow.

The forwards. Apisai Domolailai, obsessed with his horses, so awkward to haul down on the pitch, a rascal sometimes with his sneaky cigarettes but with a spark and smile even at the bottom of a Sigatoka dune. Jasa Veremalua, the master of The Cut, the rampaging diagonal run with the ball under one arm and the other one out like a lance to fend off any tackler. Leone Nakarawa, lord of the skies, attracting defenders and then bouncing them off, the target for every kick-off. Viliame Mata, the precision and the power, the hands of a centre and the height of a coconut tree, able to step and accelerate like no forward should be able to. Semi Kunatani, our Lebron James, able to do it all, raised in the wild interior by those five surrogate mothers, as laid back as a hippy camper at Woodstock and as explosive as a depth charge. Masivesi Dakuwaqa, arms and legs everywhere, the one-eyed wonder, a kid who cares only about now.

I welcomed them onto the final leg on the Olympic journey by taking them off all sugars and carbohydrates. It was a gamble. The long fitness drive had worked; you could see it in their energy levels, in their body composition, their robustness. Naca had done an outstanding job, been everything I hoped he would develop into. But I had noticed how sugar led to slumps and midday sleeps and drops in concentration, and when the players put on fat – and Fijians can get either fit or fat quickly – it was because of bread and sugar. It was a mindset too, a signal to the players that we were willing to do anything we had to, a sign to opposition teams when they saw us in the dining hall checking all the plates, taking stuff away, that we were different to previous Fiji teams. It added to their fear: this Fiji team have got their shit together.

I expected a little drop-off from the players before a bigger bounce-back later. Instead, for the first two days I just got miserable players. Then I got reports from my spy at the petrol station up the road, the nearest place to our training camp to get chocolate and sweets.

I had gradually built up a mutually beneficial relationship with the staff there. It was where I went to stock up on bottled water or to swap the big gas canisters around, or to pick up a taxi to get out to the airport. Sometimes you'd just hang out in the little café and chew the fat. I'd given them all rugby balls and the odd bit of kit over the years too.

It was them who had told me about Donasio Ratabuli getting drunk there after having his leg broken by the

Wardens' team in Labasa. It made sense to keep them in the loop. Lads, I've banned them from bad food. So if they come in for crisps and chocolate and other crap, no insult intended to your product range, would you mind giving me a quick call? It was the coconut wireless at its very best. Not only did I find out who had cracked and how badly, but the players learned that I had eyes on them everywhere.

It was a benign sort of dictatorship. Osea rang me on the first night: I really need to eat something. OK, this is your joker, you get to play it once. Lads at the pumps, avert your gaze. Because he was so fit it was easy to miss that Osea had one of the highest-carb diets, not realising how much white bread he was eating to fill the gaps. But he would still have the peaks and crashes of glucose flying round his system. We needed players with energy on tap, not random spikes that they could not control.

Managing down, managing up. Frank now trusted me and was letting me do what I needed, his version of carefully controlled delegation. In return I had to ensure that he felt involved. Inviting him to Uprising to say a few stirring words to the boys worked for everyone. A warm-up to show him how fit they were, the chance for him to spin a few passes about and show that those daily games of touch rugby had kept him sharp, that he could still cut it. And then into a huddle, Frank leading a *lotu* of the most muscular sort of Christianity, his status underlined, the newspapers with an excellent photo opportunity of the prime minister with the nation's favourite players. Everyone happy, everyone aligned.

Each day on the training field I saw progression, all based around the Pareto principle, that 80 per cent of our success would be based on 20 per cent of what we did.

Lots of practice of one-on-one tackling, of our line-outs, of our kick-offs and our catches. We had wonderful natural height in 6ft 7ins Leone Nakarawa, 6ft 6ins Viliame Mata and 6ft 5ins Semi Kunatani. If every player could combine with another to form a lifting pod wherever the ball went, we would be well placed to cope with the kicking games of the USA, Argentina and South Africa. We had luck; the players were smashing into each other in training, but the injuries were minimal. I wanted them ready for the brutal contact that was coming their way in Rio, not placed in cotton wool to make the coach sleep easier at night.

With every session we sharpened things up a little more, the pace quicker, the tempo higher. By the time we arrived in Rio we would have time for just two training sessions. By then I wanted each one to last no more than 40 minutes. All the big stuff done, only a little flick to keep all the plates spinning.

I had to manage my own energy too. Staying off the easy hits of fizzy drinks and chocolates as always, cutting back on the carbs, dropping the stress levels when I could. Not spending the few spare hours staring at my laptop and poring through statistics, not going on a Google-led wander on my phone. I'd watch an episode of a box-set that had nothing to do with rugby, jump in the swimming pool at 9 p.m. and float around on my back, looking up at the bats swooping in from the mangroves, keeping the mosquitoes on the move. If I finished in daylight I might walk up to the Pacific Harbour Golf Club behind the house. I would be recognised and waylaid for advice on our best starting line-up but I could also climb in a buggy and get away on my own, a couple of the holes right out the back totally isolated, the fairways and green encased by forest. Stick a load of balls down, play a few shots, walk up to collect them and go again, an hour wasted in a worthwhile fashion.

I should have been cracking up. Everything I had tried to do over the past three years coming down to three days in a month's time. Everything I hoped to do subsequently would either be enhanced or destroyed by it. Instead the fact that there was a definite end date to it all brought a sense of liberation. It would all come to a climax on 11 August. Do everything I could and let the rest drift away like empty coconut shells on the tide.

We could have gone straight to Rio, as the Kenyan team did. We could have gone first to a holding-camp in Belo Horizonte, an hour's flight north, where Team GB were staying. I wanted to do something different. Being in the athletes' village in Rio for 12 days would send us stir-crazy, what with all the hype and medals being won and free McDonald's in the vast dining barn. Being out with the British team and all their resources, the stuff I would have been controlling had I taken the other sliding door and stuck with the job offer from UK Sport all those months ago, would have felt like walking across my own grave.

I looked at Argentina, Chile and Peru, and chose Chile. A direct flight from Auckland to Santiago, an easy hop on to Brazil when we needed it. A little bit of altitude, no Olympic fever. There was an English coach named Nick Hill who worked at the Grange School in the La Reina district. He had emailed me for advice when I had been with England and we had kept in touch since. A chat with him and he was straight into action – letting us train on the school's pitches, finding us a good gym, contacting the Chilean Rugby Union to see what additional help they could offer. More of that serendipity, that sweet sporting karma, the affection that existed around the world for Fiji and its sevens side.

Off the Olympic treadmill. Off the coconut wireless. Our own room at the hotel with our own sugar- and carb-free menu, intense hour-long blasts on the training pitch, all at match pace, teetering along the line with New Zealand and their two-and-a-half-hour slogfests on one side and South Africa with their players in bubble-wrap on the other. Just the 13 players, no distractions, the bond tightening. A trip into the Andes to stand knee-deep in snow, half the team touching it for the first time. Snowball fights and fistfuls of it shoved down each other's backs. I was pretty sure no other team was doing it the same way.

We were so relaxed that we landed in Rio about two hours before the athletes' village went into lockdown for the opening ceremony. The last team in, the least stressed on arrival. The village was a series of new tower blocks a couple of miles west of the main Olympic Park in the Barra district. The Australian team had most of one block, with the rag-tag remnants of the Oceania nations on the top four floors – us, Samoa, Tonga, Nauru, the Cook Islands.

The Fiji Olympic Association had been there for a week, ostensibly to get everything ready for the arrival of their athletes. Instead, because none of them had any prior experience of elite sport, it was more like a school trip. Things were chaotic: no water for us when we came through arrivals at Galeão Airport; insufficient tickets to get the team to the opening ceremony; going to the office of the chef de mission and finding an enormous box of *kava* stashed under the desk. I was told it was purely for ceremonial purposes. There was enough to ceremoniously floor a herd of elephants.

It wasn't just because we were a tiny island that Fiji had never won a single Olympic medal. The officials were nice people but there was no sense of how to prepare athletes and how to look after them should they get there. We watched the Germans, the Austrians and the Belgians getting around the vast village on bikes they had brought with them, saving their legs for when they were most needed. We had kit that was arriving at the last minute and beyond, sticky-tape being used to cover up the wrong logos from the wrong companies. Some of our bedrooms had yet to be finished. There were no curtains, or the toilets would block if anyone used toilet paper. If someone on the storey upstairs had a nervous morning, everyone near a bathroom down below would know about it too. The well-run teams had all that sorted out weeks ago – checks done, improvements made. Fiji were congratulating themselves on successfully importing 20kg of *kava*.

I was relieved we had only a couple of days after the opening ceremony before our tournament began. Everything we did now would be about togetherness. Mobile phones to be handed in before our first match and put away until it was all done, walking in one group to breakfast, lunch and dinner, sitting at one table right at the back of the vast dining hall. A *talanoa*, chewing it all over, watching the USA team come down in full Ralph Lauren team blazers, Rafa Nadal wandering over with a grin for a chat with the boys and a few photos.

It's so easy to get distracted in an Olympic athletes' village. Free food, free Coke, the tallest women you've ever seen, the heaviest men, weird mish-mash builds taking

251

body shapes to their wild extremes, men with huge shoulders, chests and arms and tiny skinny legs – OK, they must be canoeists – and then the opposite, powerful legs and the leanest upper bodies – right, road cyclists. The boys, so used to keeping it simple, enjoyed it without getting swept away.

The day of the opening ceremony. The Fijian Olympic Association had now found seven tickets for the team. I told them that we were together, not two discrete parts. Suddenly they had tickets for all the players but none for management. Right, boys, off you go. I'll watch it on television and try to hide my disappointment.

Some teams banned their athletes from the ceremony. Too much time on your feet, standing around without food and water in the bowels of the Maracana Stadium and the heat and the risk of all those perky new germs. We knew our players would come home later than we thought and that they wouldn't have eaten properly, but we built it into the plan. The experience was a one-off: Osea carrying the flag into the stadium at the head of the entire Fijian team, ceremonial white and black robes around his bare chest, Serena Williams coming up to him afterwards and asking for a photo.

Frank arrived in style. His motorcade was bigger than that of the Chinese premier. He had brought his own water from Fiji, so concerned about the risk of being poisoned that he advised me to do the same. I thought he was joking. He was deadly serious.

Two days later the competition began. Argentina were the biggest danger in our group. They would bring a big support north across the border, they had a great kicking game, and they were hard men – never a backward step, always scrapping, unlikely to implode. We would have to overpower them. The USA were going to be all about their English coach Mike Friday – always a perceived injustice against them, Mike screaming at the players and constantly in the ear of the referee and touch-judges. Brazil... well, Brazil would come at us like maniacs for the first few minutes. We would have to take the sting out of that one.

I was still sure I was the most relaxed coach in town. Keeping it simple, keeping it calm. Days of competition in sevens are long and tiring. Up early, intense physical exertion, home late. When you get the players home you need them to rest and to switch off. You don't want them in a classroom after breakfast or post-dinner being lectured for an hour or staring at PowerPoint presentations. That was what the US were doing, what Great Britain and New Zealand and South Africa were doing.

I thought it was all for the coaches rather than their players. It made you feel like you were doing something, even if that something was wrong, and it gave you a false sort of defence if the team did fail – ah well, I had them in for hours of analysis, I left no stone unturned. If there wasn't enough physical and mental recuperation, then none of the other stuff mattered anyway; you would be in no state to put any of it into practice.

Players need to feel they have some level of autonomy, and they need to feel as if they're in a safe environment. That means feeling valued, having a sense of belonging and a purpose. Being able to say what you feel, to act normally, to be true to yourself. If you've got a coach who's telling you how to do things all the time, who behaves differently with you when he is stressed, all of that goes out of the window. If the coach is throwing too much technology at the players, employing a specialist coach for every aspect of the game, telling you in minute detail what you should be doing in every moment, you might feel you don't control very much.

We should have been the ones under pressure. It was gold or nothing for us, after all we had come through, having won the last two World Series, for all the hundreds of thousands of Fijians back home still picking through the wreckage of Cyclone Winston.

Trust and simplicity. We would go back to our rooms, the boys in twins and me with a single bed and an en suite and nothing more, a little break-out area with a washing machine and a TV and a couple of beanbags. Phones tucked away in a box under a bed, chats amongst us, *lotu* and warmth and hugs and affection and smiles. Doing very little else, letting our thoughts fall, as relaxed in this concrete tower block on the other side of the world as we were on the beach at Uprising with green coconuts in our hands. Lying there full of contentment thinking, I bet all the other teams are on their laptops doing an hour of analysis.

Belonging: that connection to their families, to their villages. A purpose, to do something for their nation that had never been done before. Security, now they were no longer finding out about selection from a newspaper, now they had contracts.

And belief. The feeling had been growing stronger in me during the last few weeks in Fiji and then through Santiago into Rio: we were going to win.

I had never had that sort of certainty before. I had felt confident going into individual matches with the team in the past, but this was the greatest challenge we would ever face. I had never been one for blind faith; forget rugby, there had never been anything else in my life where I felt, yes, this is definitely going to happen.

I wasn't sure if it was intuition or logic or somewhere in between, a fanciful notion that it was all meant to be. I didn't believe in fate. I believed in taking control of your life and aiming it where you wanted to go. It hadn't felt like fate when I had been sacked by England. Maybe it was simply that I wanted us to win, or that I was surrounded by men like Ropate and William and Osea who believed in a higher power who would reward you when he chose.

But it was there: the ingrained sense that there was a reason I had ended up in this strange part of Rio with this particular set of men, a reason why I had reacted to that initial tweet about the coaching vacancy, why I had set off without knowing the country or my salary or the fact that there wouldn't be one for six months.

And it was powerful. It relaxed me. If I had thought about the fact that, should we fail to win the tournament, it would have such a vast bearing on my future and on men and women I cared so much about, it could have scared me sleepless. But it didn't worry me because I didn't think that was going to be the case. We were going to win a gold medal. The first thing in my life I had never had any doubt about.

It was wonderfully potent for the team too. No one was thinking about the what ifs. It was all about the when. *Seqa na leqa*, no worries. It seeped into everyone around us, the officials, the referees. The tournament office up at Deodoro where the temporary stadium had been built could be a stressful place – other coaches storming in there to complain about the food or the changing rooms or the practice pitches, us wandering in because their espresso machine was so superior to the one in the village, sitting down and chatting about everything except rugby. One woman in there, Marjorie, was dating a player in the Brazilian women's team, Isadora Cerullo. Midway through the tournament Marjorie proposed on the pitch and Isadora accepted. We celebrated that and we complained about nothing. A waste of energy, a little disease that can start with the coach and spread fast to his players: no wonder we're not winning, look at the food they've given us; we've got no chance here, everything is against us. World Rugby's head of referees, Paddy O'Brien, chilled out with us because we were pushing nothing and he'd had half a dozen coaches yelling at him; and referees talk to each other, so they might all be thinking subconsciously that they could trust Fiji, and maybe that would affect some of their decisions quite inadvertently when we got out on the field.

We were close to the holy grail for sporting teams: to be in that state of relaxation, to be in that form and to have that level of relaxed confidence. It doesn't happen very often in your career, maybe once or twice if you're lucky, not at all for many.

Not arrogance, but confidence rooted in evidence. Relaxed but ruthless. We were ready.

FOURTEEN

Thursday, 9 August. The first day of the three that would culminate in the Olympic final. Two group games in our sights: local darlings but rank outsiders Brazil at 1.30 in the afternoon, the dangerous Argentinians at 6.30 p.m.

We had been to the temporary stadium in Deodoro, with its banks of yellow and green seats and its long line of flagpoles and its blue hoardings, to watch the *Fijiana* women's team two days before. There was nothing to shock us except a result earlier in the day. Walking into the complex, I spotted one of the Japanese players I knew, Lomano Lemeki, and asked how they had got on against New Zealand in their own opening match. He told me they had beaten them, a shock almost to compare with Japan's 15-a-side defeat of South Africa in the 2015 World Cup in England. I gave him a spontaneous hug. Wow, that's awesome! At that moment Gordon Tietjens walked by. A killer look, and on he stalked. I didn't mind. He would have celebrated a defeat for us in exactly the same way. It meant they would have to beat Great Britain to avoid meeting us in the quarter-finals, should we win all three of our games. Revenge was in the humid air.

The team selection felt straightforward. Not our hardest game but our best side. Jasa Veremalua, Semi Kunatani and Leone Nakarawa the forwards, Jerry Tuwai scrum-half, Osea Kolinisau, Vatemo Ravouvou and Save Rawaca outside him. Height and power up front, multiple creative sources in the backs, three good kickers on the pitch, two more on the substitutes' bench. Players who could slot into almost any position, multi-skilled, born with ball in hand and raised barefoot and balanced on those mud pitches and beaches.

So much noise from the stands for Brazil, a fierce tranquillity in our ranks. Their threat would come from a little kick or chip over the top of the first line of our defence, so our man sweeping behind would have to watch his depth to cover that. I was more worried about Save Rawaca, an unstoppable try-scoring machine for two and a half years and yet now stuck in the self-destructive tailspin that had begun in the final training camp in Pacific Harbour. Standing offside in the first minute, failing to make a simple pass a few moments later.

You look for a flow through your team in the early stages of a match – what we called *soli-a* – to give the ball to the next man, pass, pass, let it go. It takes time to come and it can sometimes look messy – a pass bouncing before it reaches its target, another falling behind a player – but that's fine, waiting for the flow to go through one man to the next and then one more, the electricity starting to crackle through the circuits. Looking for The Cut – the *koti*, one player running diagonally across the field, sliding across the noses of defenders at pace, trying to get one of the opposition to over-chase just a little so he turns his body too far one way, and then when his shoulders are facing up and down the pitch rather than across it, dropping a little pass to an attacker coming at speed in the other direction so he can run right at that weak shoulder and bust through it. Don't take the ball into a tackle and get wrapped up on the ground, because it slows everything up and you can lose possession if they're quick on to you, or you can give away a penalty if you hang on too long. Fishing all the time, dangling that bait in front of the opposition, keeping it swinging on the line always just out of reach, waiting for the impatient lunge and bite and then flicking the rod back and charging through the kink in the defensive wall and away.

There was adrenalin there, of course. Vatemo was a little impetuous, hitting a tackle a stride too late or a few inches too high. Us fishing but not waiting quite long enough for the bite. And then they scored, flying down the left wing, a crisp pass to take the last defender out of play, sliding into the corner, the whole place going ripe bananas.

Panic did not engulf me. The team were not rattled. The way we played meant we could score three tries in a minute and a half and suddenly the game would be ours. Then we'd take our foot off the gas and cruise back into the slow lane.

And so we kept looking for the flow, and the flow came. Running the *koti*, Leone coming on the reverse angle but marked, Jasa coming again, so good at running those acute lines, gliding through the shadows of the defenders, and the team spotting the cues and body language and pop-ping the pass for him to canter away for one try and then another.

Watching from the sidelines, I stayed in the moment. I made my notes mentally rather than jotting them down in a book, because seven-minute halves fly by and you need to stay immersed rather than distanced. Save made another mistake, Osea in his ear as they came together, me signal-ling for a substitute to take his place.

Half-times in sevens are like few other sports. We gather in a huddle on the pitch and a television camera and long sound boom join us. Everyone at home can hear what the coach is saying to his players. If they cut away from us, or the sound isn't working, there will be outrage from high government offices back in Fiji. Emails fired off: why aren't the cameras in, the people of Fiji want to hear what's hap-pening...

So I always keep it simple and I keep it courteous. Two or three simple tactical points, making sure I make eye contact with each of the players, that I stand and move so everyone can see me and take confidence from my body language. I am aware, too, that against New Zealand and South Africa, they will have an assistant listening in to the TV feed and relaying my tactics straight back to their own coach and team, and so I take Osea aside for a few mo-ments to give him the detail and then get him to repeat it to the boys in Fijian. Even New Zealand haven't got round to employing a Pacific Islander linguist just to translate our team-talks.

Against Brazil I stayed casual because I could see the flow coming. And it kept coming – two tries for Josua Tuisova, one for Save, another for Sami Viriviri, one for captain

Osea. Five conversions from Vatemo, 40–12, crowd silenced, on our way.

You work through a timetable between games. You get fluid and food inside the players, you warm them down, you warm them up again. A decision made with Ropate. Save Rawaca is not where he should be, let's start Josua in his place. A captain's exhortation to the rest of the team: this is not like other tournaments where you can cruise through day one, all these teams except Brazil have had to qualify to be here. We have to be at them from the start.

Darkness coming to the Rio sky, the floodlights beginning to burn bright. In the afternoon Argentina had beaten the USA. That meant if we beat them to go two from two, then we would effectively be into the quarter-finals, with the USA to come the day after to decide where in the table we would finish and so who we would meet next.

Jerry had picked up a knock against Brazil. William's advice was to go easy on him, to let him rest on the bench unless he was desperately needed. Vatemo in at half-back in his place, a word to the replacements telling them that it wasn't about who started, that they were more likely to have a bigger impact if they were on the field at the end of the game. The boys into a huddle with arms and fingers pointing to the heavens, dedicating what was to come to the greater glory of God.

Josua had played just one World Series tournament for us. As much as Osea's return from excommunication, or Jerry's isolation in the slums, or Vatemo and his fits, Josua's story was one of reincarnation. As a teenager he had been picked by the previous sevens coach to play for Fiji in Wellington, had a difficult game against Tonga and then faked an injury so he could come off – something which

Fijians sometimes did, part emotional immaturity from a young man, part fear of the game's magnitude. When Fiji crashed out early he took the blame – in the papers, on Facebook – was dropped by the coach and told that he would never play for his country again. Needing money and a career, he had gone across to France and an academy contract with Toulon, his big brother Pio Tuwai getting all the games for Fiji and all the plaudits for his offloading and try creating. When Toulon noticed the talent that should have been obvious to all, he was offered the chance to follow Virimi Vakatawa and take French citizenship so he could play for Les Bleus instead, but that solitary sevens cap had him tied to Fiji. Now, with Pio on the slide, he had burst into our team with the same sweet timing that took him through and round defences.

Noise from the travelling hordes of Argentinian supporters, the players in the blue-and-white shirts with eyes wide and jaws clenched. The neutrals were with us, as always, and there were plenty of Fijians in the stands, blue wigs and some bare chests, one man there because he had won the state lottery in Australia, another who had been working in the mines in Peru and spent his savings driving across the Andes.

The boys with William's white strapping taped around their wrists. At the Olympics you aren't allowed to show any political or religious slogans on your kit, so that meant two layers of strapping: the first, with Bible verses and exhortations scrawled on them in black pen as always, a second layer to cover them up and carry them into battle. Argentina with talent in their ranks, me knowing that I had five men on the bench as good as any other team has in their starting line-ups.

In the first few moments, with no pattern to the game and no scores, Sami Viriviri turned his ankle and collapsed in a heap.

I thought he'd broken it, or at least torn his ligaments. We stuck him in a car and raced him back to camp, where we had a piece of equipment called a GameReady. I had crowd-sourced the funds among Fijian expat businesspeople that summer via a group called SouthBay Davui, who raised almost 50,000 US dollars for us over the three years. The kit was a red-and-black box filled with cold water and ice, attached to a sleeve that wrapped around an injured muscle or joint, designed to speed up recovery. Around £7,000 a pop, way outside our Fiji Rugby Union budget. To lose Sami for the tournament would be a considerable blow. We hoped the GameReady would live up to its name.

Josua began well. Nothing flashy, not yet, not trying to force the door open as Save had been doing, just probing and testing. Defenders knew we liked to offload and were watching for the pass on Josua's inside. Osea made the runs round the outside, so much harder to defend against, and the flow came, Josua there to score the first try of the game.

We worked together in defence too. Three calls every time one of their players hit the deck after a tackle: *polo* to go straight in and try to steal the ball, *biuta* to leave it alone and line up the defence again, *barasi* to counter-ruck, to send two men in to clear out the defenders over the ball, a third man coming into the gap to take the ball and go. Always working the *tolus*, the threes.

Calm even after Argentina score themselves, Franco Sabato crossing in the corner. We kept the ball alive, finding the offloads, Viliame Mata getting involved, those tight connections from the seven weeks in training camp starting to pay off. Jasa winning everything in the air, just as we had practised.

As a coach you keep scanning, not thinking about the challenges ahead, immersed in the immediate. Was that line break through our defence because someone's looking tired? Who should I take off the bench to tip the balance? Which one of their players looks vulnerable, so let's get our big men running at him, our sidesteppers making him feel as if his boots are nailed to the turf. Ropate, keep an eye on Vatemo for me. Naca, I want Kitione Taliga on in one minute, get him ready.

A score for Argentina would have put us in trouble. And it came, Santiago Alvarez enveloped by his team-mates after touching the ball down, us 14–7 down with five minutes to go. A time when the old Fiji would have panicked, would have run out of energy and started resorting to wild passes and dangerous high tackles.

We were still making small mistakes. A year before the little doubts might have started gnawing away inside: maybe this isn't meant to be, they're going to get the better of us here. And then they had a scrum deep in our half, looking to run exactly the same move they had used to score against the USA earlier in the day. Fiji teams of old wouldn't have watched the opposition. They wouldn't have practised defending certain set moves. And so Argentina would have scored, because their scrum-half stayed on his feet and had an unmarked team-mate lurking out the back, but we knew it was coming and covered that exact line.

Kitione on the rumble, justifying that selection ahead of Pio Tuwai, using that strong backside of his to smash through a defence that had appeared structured and organised. Osea with the conversion from right out on the touchline to make it 14–14.

Now the doubt on Argentinian shoulders. We won the kick-off. Minutes ticking down. No sense of pragmatism from us, just continuing to play that attacking open game that came as naturally to us as *lotu* and *talanoa*. And then Kitione again, finding holes where there appeared to be none, powering into a tackle and bumping his way through, driving on and away for 21–14 and the first little slice of clear air between us and a ghastly upset.

I had seen us panic in tight matches before. When the cross-code great Sonny Bill Williams had come into the New Zealand side earlier that year, his hero's reputation threw all our players off their game. In my first season when we had lost those semi-finals in Scotland and London to New Zealand, we had held leads with only seconds left and blown them with rattled decisions. Save Rawaca, on as a replacement, had left his brain in Pacific Harbour and was threatening to do the same again.

A late escape down the right wing from them. And Jerry, off the bench and as important finishing the game as starting it, sprinted across to make a spectacular tackle right in the corner, taking his man into touch, flat-out speed from a kid who used to skip training, energy all the way from someone who had left sugar behind in that dentist's chair in Suva. I went straight across to him on the final whistle. Jerry, they'll be dancing in the streets in Newtown after that.

21–14 was close but reflected how good I thought Argentina were. They were probably the third best in the tournament, and they didn't get the podium finish they deserved. With the players I kept things positive. A cup of tea with Osea afterwards, knowing that he and the team would be sorting it out amongst themselves anyway. Good to get that out of the way, Osea, no injuries, everyone getting game time. Did you have a word with Save? Yes. Ben, let's look to tighten up on defence, conceding two tries a game is too many. Osea, you've got it.

Day two. Wednesday, 10 August, four matches left in my career as Fiji coach. Ours would be the final group game, 1.30 in the afternoon, a potential quarter-final just over three hours later.

Grey clouds in the Rio air, rain squalls blowing in, good news from William the physio. The GameReady had worked its miracles on Sami Viriviri. His ankle was sore but it was mobile. He was good to play.

With that came a conundrum. Argentina had beaten Brazil, so we were through. Great Britain had beaten New Zealand. If the USA beat us, they would go through at Gordon Tietjens' expense. Should we pick an under-strength team, to get rid of the nation who had won the World Series more than any other, who we might otherwise meet in the quarter-finals, angry and out for revenge?

Not Fiji. My only gamble would be on Save Rawaca. One last chance for him to show that he could be the old Save rather than the derailed express of the past two months. I had asked him if everything was OK. Yes, fine. Osea had tried to talk to him and got monosyllables in return. Even Ropate could get no more. Save had always been smiles and enthusiasm, showing me his plate at dinner time, asking if he had done enough in training. All that had gone. He wasn't hanging around with the boys between games, he wasn't doing anything for anyone in the team.

The team was otherwise solid and ready. Jasa, Semi, Leone. Jerry, Vatemo. Osea. Save.

Early on Save took a pass, tried to do too much on his own and was tackled into touch. A few minutes later Danny Barrett ran through a series of challenges to score under the posts. 7–0 down, Save shaking his head.

Exactly as planned, we attacked their breakdown. Cut their possession off at the source, use our *barasi* counter-ruck. Osea away from one counter-ruck to bring it level. For a coach it was one of the most satisfying things you could see – an opportunity you had spotted, a tactic you had practised but kept tucked away for this specific match and challenge.

Save's demise was the opposite, dropping the ball in the tackle, trying to force it, being selfish, blowing a clear try-scoring opportunity by trying to do it all himself. I knew I would take him off at half-time. I thought too that his tournament might be over. Poor as a starter against Brazil, ineffectual as a replacement against Argentina, a one-man calamity now. More mistakes than the rest of the team combined, and not a single person among the managers or players who could get through to him. He was behaving like a child in a sulk, knowing the argument was lost but unable to admit it, shutting the door on everyone else. None of us could find the key.

The *barasi* kept us in front even after Osea was yellow-carded for a weary high tackle. Vatemo scoring off another breakdown steal, and then again three minutes into the second half. Semi in the corner for 24–14. Jerry pulling the strings, a late dash down the touchline from their winger only a little gloss on the final scoreline of 24–19.

We had played in patches with a style no other team

could match and very few could defend against. By making it look easy we were pulling off perhaps the greatest feint of all. We could run those support lines because we had run up sand mountains. We could play with freedom because the players felt safe and valued. We could be as creative as the 1970 Brazil football team because the players intimately understood the logic of each other's rhythms and talent.

US coach Mike Friday looked typically outraged. He had talked up their breakdown work all season, their toughness in the tackle. For it to be exposed as a weakness left him unable to compute. It must be someone else's fault. It couldn't be a flaw in his thinking or preparation. It must have been the referee or his players not doing what they should or my players doing something illicit.

He left telling the media that his team had not had the rub of the green. I didn't expect any praise from him. I was content with this result and the fact that in 13 meetings between his teams and mine, our boys had come out on top 11 times. Neither defeat had come in an important knock-out match.

We moved on, New Zealand in our sights later in the day. The temperature had dropped now, the clouds darker overhead.

The boys had always got themselves more pumped for games against New Zealand than anyone else. If ever it boiled over, it did so against the nation where so many Pacific islanders went to work and make money, to take citizenship and to end up in that famous black jersey rather than our white one. Those who were part of the constant drip-drip diaspora were never viewed as traitors. It was almost instead as if they had graduated, been called to a better team and a richer world.

Maybe I should have been worried. Gordon was the most decorated coach in sevens history, New Zealand the most successful rugby nation in history. But I wasn't. I thought they were playing poorly, and I was certain that they had over-trained. You could see the accumulation of all that fatigue in them as they walked around, as if constantly in search of a couch to lie down on. They were good players, some of them with an evens chance of becoming greats, but their bodies were wrecked – superstar Sonny Bill Williams already gone to an Achilles injury, his fellow All Black Liam Messam having calf problems and so only on stand-by for Rio, the talented Kurt Baker falling out with management and being left at home.

I knew they would try to cause us problems at the breakdown, to slow down our natural pace and flow. So we decided to avoid those breakdowns, to keep the ball in hand and to keep moving them around. If they were after a slow game we would play at a high tempo: our sevens-specific fitness against their marathon training.

It was a simple team selection by now. Jasa, Semi, Leone. Jerry, Vatemo, Osea, Josua. The start was chaotic, the ball bouncing around between us, passes going into space behind players. To the western coaching mentality it was unstructured panic. To the Fijian way it was letting the flow come together. Searching for the connections, having fun with the ball, playing, even in this Olympic quarter-final, with the same sense of freedom that Noel and I used to have in the back garden and round the school table-tennis table. Risk? It's only a risk if it doesn't work.

New Zealand will always work hard for one another. Stretch them, test them, run the *kotis*.

Osea took the ball midway inside their half and found

Josua coming in on that sharp opposing angle. Through one tackle, hauled down 15m out. An offload from the floor, Vatemo with men to his right, New Zealand shipping defenders that way. A dummied pass, a dart left, the last defender drawn in. Osea in space down the left wing to take the pass and dive over the line.

5–0, the conversion missed. On the touchline I always tried to remain calm for the players. After moments of patience, sudden strikes like that were hard not to react to. You wanted to grin and whoop and throw an arm round Ropate's broad shoulders.

I could see Gordon deep in thought. Working out the phases of play New Zealand needed to put together, the techniques of tackle and pass.

For Ropate and me it was like watching art rather than a computer program. My players moving his defenders around like a strange muscular ballet, a spin and a step there, a gracefulness to it all. Fishing all the time, pushing the net out over there and then drawing it back in, throwing it again further away. Waiting for the bite, for the weakness to show, for the flow to take over. Ghosts against the machine.

The Kiwi frustration began to show. Young winger Rieko Ioane picked Jerry up in a tackle and drove him dangerously into the wet ground. A yellow card, Gordon fuming.

And then their best player produced a conjuror's trick of his own. Gordon had not always trusted Gillies Kaka; too off-the-cuff, liable to say what he thought even if it contradicted the coach's orthodoxy. Now it worked – a run to our defensive line, a chip over the top, gathering the ball under the posts for a converted try and a 7–5 lead.

Into the half-time huddle. With the team in a circle

facing me, all focused, I tapped my right hand on my left shoulder. Flick off the Devil, boys, flick off the Devil.

We had talked about it in training. When you're tired and you're struggling but you need to make that run and you need to cover that space, that's when the Devil pops up on your shoulder and says, why bother, it's not worth it, someone else will do it.

This had become our visual cue. Flick him off, not today mate, you're gone.

I knew Gordon would be telling his team they had to score first in the second half. To me it was wasted breath. No one sets out to score second.

Boys, I know you're good enough to win this game but you're out of the competition in seven minutes if you don't get this right. A look in their eyes told me that there were no butterflies, only a strengthening of the bonds that bound us. A surge of resolve. Come on, let's play.

The crowd were noisy in their support for us. We were the little nation against the big boys, the locals seeing us as the outsiders and our own supporters, in their clear plastic rain capes, banging drums and waving their wet flags.

We kept probing, we kept fishing. The ball in Fijian hands, the tired Kiwis growing wearier by the moment. Ioane back on but gaps starting to open.

It was Jerry who did it. Semi Kunatani with a pass left, Osea lurking on the wing outside Jerry. Shimmying, glancing out to Osea as if the pass was coming, a dummy and a dart and Sam Dickson motionless and Ioane only able to wave a hand at his heels as Jerry accelerated away and under the posts.

It was all the reasons why I had taken that punt on him and the best of what he could be, encapsulated in a couple of seconds. Us behind, the biggest game of our three years thus far, the vision to see an opportunity where most would have shipped the pass on, a little show and go, devastating explosive pace to get away. It was what William Ryder could do at his best and exactly what made Waisale Serevi the king of sevens. Watch the ball and his feet will take him away. Watch his feet and go dizzy. Blink and he's gone.

New Zealand were good at hanging in games. Defend and defend and hope to get an opening. We were dominating possession, and we could win games with 20 per cent possession, but we weren't being ruthless, and we weren't playing the way the rest of the rugby world thought was sensible. With a minute to go and a one-score lead and having been awarded a penalty, New Zealand or South Africa would have taken a while to get the ball to the kicker, let him take a breath, mark a run-up and then boot it into touch. They would walk to the line-out to burn through a few more seconds. By the time they caught the line-out throw the match would be over.

That was the pragmatic way to do things. We chose instead not to drop a goal for an unassailable eight-point lead but to keep running it in search of a try.

Two years before I would have been shouting at them in fear and frustration. I had learned now to be quiet. In the semi-final in Hong Kong we had spurned a straightforward kick to do the same, and scored a try instead. The players understood the pulse of games and they played without the anxiety of what if.

And so when we lost the ball to give New Zealand back possession on the last play of the game and with it one final chance for them to nick it at the death, I couldn't be angry. This was how we played. A coach cannot condemn risk when it suits him yet celebrate its rewards when it comes off.

Live by the sword, feel its sharp edge. My heart was thumping.

An eyebrow raised at Ropate. We're not losing this one, are we?

With Josua blowing we had signalled for Save to get ready to come on with a few minutes to go. He refused. The rest of the replacements tore into him in Fijian. I glared at him. Get on the field. Have some control. Play for the team.

New Zealand came at us. A big tackle, the ball going loose, one of their players diving on it, Kitione Taliga up on his feet with a shout of *polo* and a scrap for the ball. A whistle from the referee, a penalty to us, should be game over.

Except Save came steaming in and tried to throw the Kiwi aside. More black shirts suddenly piling in, Save's arms up in faces, the referee shouting his number – Leave it! Calm down! 11! 11! Get out of it! – Gordon expecting the penalty to be reversed and his team given a second golden shot.

Our players were on Save like furious older brothers. Sami shoving him away – Save! Save! – pushing him backwards from the mass of bodies. Osea with his eyes wide, shouting too – Save! – beckoning him over with fury on his face. The referee to Osea – It's still a penalty. White. – Relief washing over Osea, the ball kicked into touch, the game won.

I went to Jerry first. An arm round him, never swearing because the offence to Fijians outweighs any exhortation. Jerry, that was pretty cool. Jerry all grins and talking about

273

what it would be like at home. Me with another squeeze – You looking forward to tomorrow now? – and Jerry bouncing on with the excitement coming out of every pore.

Save next: I'll have a word with you in a minute. Waiting until it was just the two of us on the touchline: I don't know what you're upset about, but don't ever do that to us again.

In the changing room Osea sat him down. Each of the boys told him what they felt. No screaming, just honest words. *Vosota* from Save – sorry – but an empty one.

We needed him out. It was a quick decision: we have one day of rugby left, an Olympic semi-final and then maybe a final to come. I don't want this bloke in the changing room, I don't want him complaining and moaning about wanting his phone back. I want him nowhere near the pitch.

William came over. Save's complaining about a sore hand. This could be our exit strategy; under the regulations, if the tournament doctor confirmed that it was an injury that ruled him out, we could bring Masivesi Dakuwaqa into the squad as a replacement.

William took Save off to have the hand scanned. Save wasted five hours by putting the wrong hand in the scanner. We came back to a result which said it was clear, tore into Save, sent him off again and got the correct diagnosis this time. Broken hand, Save out and still acting, to my eyes, like a spoiled child, Masi into the squad.

Save may have been carrying that injury for a while. He had asked for it to be strapped before the final group game against the USA. Maybe that had added frustration on top of whatever else he was carrying.

His behaviour was still unacceptable to us. To walk past

that standard would have been to insult the whole team. Only Save was thinking of himself above his team-mates.

Looking back at those games, we should have got rid of him on day one. He was a wonderful talent but his ego had taken over. You find these things out and then you have to make a quick decision on them, sad though that might be. Talent is a coach's to harness but a player's to waste.

It's a strange feeling when you begin a day that you know will define you. As I locked my room in the Olympic village, checked the lanyard round my neck for my accreditation, put the big bunch of keys in my bag, I thought: the next time I touch these keys, it will all be over. When I come back to this door I'll know. A gold, a silver, nothing at all.

The semi-final against Japan was due to kick off at 2.30 p.m., the final at 7 p.m. The previous evening I had gone down the fire escape and across the hall to hang out with Ropate, watching the day's action from other Olympic sports. We had wandered into the food hall and sat down with hot chocolates for a natter, just as if we were back in Pacific Harbour.

I had said to the boys that night to enjoy their *lotu* and get to bed. No point in going through the game for them. I would give them a couple of focused points in the morning. Ropate and I chewed it over. Japan might try something funky on line-outs, switch to a four-man set-up and run something different off it, maybe sending a man from the front looping round to try to tear the seam in the defence between back of the line and fly-half. They were good at getting defences to turn, and their coach was innovative. They would be prepared, and having beaten New Zealand in the group, they were confident.

I spoke to no one at home that morning. Natalie was at our house in Fiji but I had turned my phone off to be at one with the team. Only Ropate had his with him, our one point of contact should officials or drug-testing or Frank want to get hold of us.

I was up early and went for a stroll around the perimeter of the village. In the temporary bank was the best espresso stall in the place, run by a barista with cool tattoos. I chatted to him about those, about my plans for a tattoo of my own when this was all over, and then took my double espresso out onto the big lawn, a great rectangle of artificial grass dotted with plastic cubes and shapes you could sit on.

I sat on the ground with my back against the fence and thought about the day ahead. The boys would be in the swimming pool at 7 a.m. for a gentle limb-loosener, Naca in charge. I had wanted him to know that I trusted him and that I knew he would be organised.

I wandered over there. I could hear the laughing and splashing around as I got closer. The pool was shared with everyone in the block, so Australians of various heights and sizes were coming over to see what was going on.

Ah mate, that's the Fiji team.

Ah yeah, it's their finals day today.

Mate, I love those blokes . . .

It gave me a lovely glow of pride to see them like that – enjoying themselves, relaxed, smiling at strangers, spreading the good vibes on the biggest day of their sporting lives. We did a *lotu* right there, the songs bringing even more boys and girls to the yard. A couple scooped up water in their hands and flicked it at me. Osea gave me a hug and smiled. It's going to be a good day today.

As we walked off to breakfast I couldn't help but smile

too. Professional sports teams spent fortunes trying to get to this state: a unity of purpose, a relaxation no matter what challenge lay ahead, a happiness in how we were getting there.

With England there had been one person in the camp who had always been stressed. His anxiety had bled into everyone else. With Fiji we all felt the same way. You couldn't fake it and you couldn't force it. As we had flow on the pitch so we had flow off it. As a coach coming from England it shouldn't have worked for me, but it always had, and I loved it. It came naturally to us but to no other team. It was maybe the most powerful of our secret weapons.

We should have been under pressure, a million people back home relying on us, the favourites now to go all the way. And yet none of us felt that way. No one cared who we drew or who we played. There was a great deal that could go wrong – someone getting ill, a problem on the way to the ground, an injury in the warm-ups. Because those were the uncontrollables, I didn't worry about them. The controllables were keeping seven players on the field. Save had been dealt with. Frank had joined the team huddle on the first morning before the Brazil game and written a big speech intended for use before any final. There were no other distractions, just us as a little group moving around.

Three thoughts for the boys as we walked onto the pitch at Deodoro. Don't underestimate Japan. Go fishing. Have fun. I thought Japan would be saying: keep the ball, slow Fiji down, track their offloads. Frustrate them, get them yellow-carded.

We both got it right: 65 seconds in, Vatemo scored a beauty. Shortly afterwards, he was penalised for a shoulder charge and given a yellow.

Two minutes in the sin-bin, Japan alive. Teruya Goto into the left corner for 5–5.

Vatemo was sitting on the touchline with his hands on his face, knowing that every Fijian around the world would be shouting at him on their televisions.

No panic. I understood this team. I could see the flow coming moments before it fired; a shape developing among the white shirts, the speed building. Sometimes it broke down, but it always picked up again, because there could be only one way to play – with ambition, with confidence. And suddenly the thrust, the rapid acceleration, and Josua Tuisova was bumping off defenders and diving into the left corner.

When we were in this mood it was like watching a boxer fooling around until he got to the round when he wanted to knock his opponent out. Sometimes I even thought the players needed the stimulation of a tight match to produce their best. It was why they loved the risk and the reward that came with it. How could it be fun if there was no jeopardy involved?

Semi Kunatani thundering through to make it 15–5 early in the second half. Jerry going fishing and then doing his wonderful sidestep-jump into a hole in the defence and tearing away for another.

No more cramp for Jerry, not with the chocolate addiction long gone. He could run the length of the pitch like that and never look like slowing down until his shadow was under the posts, assuming his burst of speed and change of direction had not left his shadow lost and alone somewhere on halfway. 20–5 at the final whistle, his boots his knife and fork, his try cutting our path to the final and

278

a guarantee of Fiji's first-ever Olympic medal of any colour. Silver as a minimum, gold within reach.

We had three hours to go. Food and drink for the boys in the first half-hour, and then I climbed back into the stands to watch the rest of the second semi-final between Great Britain and South Africa. GB had fought past Argentina in the quarter-finals with a try in added time from Dan Bibby, who I had brought into the England set-up in 2012. Down 5–0 at half-time to South Africa, they fought back again, this time Dan Norton, who I knew as well as any England player, stepping inside a defender to score. Tom Mitchell, once my skipper, knocked over the conversion, and with some fine defence they held on. I liked the poetry of it all: a team full of players I had trained, with a coach who had been my controversial captain, up against the team I had poured more into than anything else. A small part of the old me against all of the new one.

Naca worked our recovery. Stretching, ice baths in the changing rooms, hot baths to flush the lactic acid out of the muscles. Simple food, chicken and rice, muffins grabbed from breakfast that morning, oranges and apples and bananas. Reminding the boys to eat and to take on water on a warm day when the wind might fool you into thinking that you hadn't lost as much in sweat as you really had.

It could have felt like the longest three hours of our lives, but we played it right: trying not to bounce around, watching from the stands a few of the classification games which would sort out the rest of the placings, but with your eyes on soft focus. Getting ready again for a warm-up that wouldn't be much more than a jog, waking up heads as much as bodies. Not shouting at them as some coaches did – Recovery drinks now! Ice baths now! Five minutes and 30 seconds until we go! – but keeping them in that golden zone, alert yet relaxed. Keeping an eye on my own energy levels with a plate of chicken and rice, popping back into the tournament organisers' office for one final espresso with Chris Cracknell and one more chinwag with the happily engaged woman and her wife to be.

It was closing in on 11 o'clock at night back in England. My mum and my sisters had been out for a Brentford tandoori and had stuck champagne in the fridge at home. Midday in Suva, the nation with the brakes on, everything cancelled for this, no one on the roads, no one in the fields. Natalie at Uprising with all our friends among the staff in the big open-sided bar. The National Stadium with a sold-out crowd watching it on vast temporary screens. Ovalau falling silent, the bars in Levuka rammed, the kids at St John's College with lessons cancelled. Labasa shut down, Vanua Levu still. Power back on in Koro after Cyclone Winston, tarpaulins over the televisions. Jerry's wife holding their young daughter up at the back of a packed room in Newtown.

I had planned out a grand speech to make to the players beforehand. I was going to talk about the destiny of our journey to the first Olympic rugby final since 1924, about how proud I was of them and the difference it would make to the nation.

I ditched it all. I looked around the changing room and they were singing and dancing. They looked like a bunch of kids in Nadi going out to play touch rugby on the beach. I don't need to say anything here. Whatever I can come up with isn't going to improve where we are.

The speech would only have been for me. Coaches like to have these moments, to feel like they are the great inspiration, that their words are going to make all the difference. It would be mere flannel. Instead, a simple thought for a simple moment: enjoy it. A wink, and sending them on their way.

It was cooling off in the stadium, about 18°C, a brisk wind snapping the flags. The big blue electronic scoreboard in the corner was burning bright, two floodlights down the sides of the pitch, one in each of the corners. On the halfway line two officials each holding a giant flag of the two nations, the match ball on a green Rio 2016 plinth between them.

The team was an easy selection. Jasa Veremalua, Semi Kunatani, Leone Nakarawa. Osea Kolinisau, Jerry Tuwai, Sami Viriviri, Vatemo Ravouvou. On the bench, Apisai Domolailai, Viliame Mata, Kitione Taliga, Josua Tuisova, Masivesi Dakuwaqa. Sami got the nod ahead of Josua because I thought Great Britain might try to turn our big man and wear him out. Only 21 years old, he handled it with great maturity. No worries, Ben, I'm sure you'll bring me on. Josh, of course I will.

In the tunnel coming out I watched the British team standing stiff and tense. Phil Burgess, the last player I signed before leaving England. Dan Norton, signed when he was young. James Rodwell, coached him at England Counties. Tom Mitchell, watched him play for Bristol University in freshers' week. Dan Bibby, spotted playing for UWIC and the North Wales Exiles sevens team. Ollie Lindsay-Hague, saw him at Milfield School, followed him through Harlequins and signed him from there. Marcus Watson, brought him into the England set-up when he got booted out of London Irish's academy.

After their semi-final I had studied them all again as

they walked around the pitch and warm-up area. They were clearly delighted to have made the final. Maybe they had now settled for that, an Olympic silver subconsciously enough of an achievement. As they stood in that tunnel, edgy and upright, our boys jogged through, laughing and joking. I actually thought Osea was going to pat the referee on the backside. At the last moment he lifted his hand and went for the back instead.

GB had already warmed up on our designated side of the pitch. Whether it was deliberate or accidental, they weren't for moving, even when we asked them. When Chris Cracknell tried again, he was told, Don't be that bloke, Chris. It happens in rugby sometimes: one team thinking maybe this will mess with the opposition heads, refusing to move when asked in case it is seen as being subservient. I couldn't be bothered arguing. Let them play their little games. We put two cones down while GB went through a full fierce set of drills, hitting tackle-bags, doing hard sprints; a few skips for us to get the calf muscles going, heel flicks to warm the hamstrings, sideways strides, jogging backwards. The boys knew all the commands, a couple put on an English accent to announce them and we all laughed again.

I knew other coaches thought we were either being lazy and unprofessional or had lost our minds. Everyone else was sprinting and crashing and panting. My sports science degree had taught me a great deal about the body and Fiji had taught me more. It would be the attitude we left our warm-up with that would be critical, rather than the number of tackles we had practised.

In the stands I could see Frank and his entourage. Princess Anne a little further along, there to present the medals, a patron of the Scottish Rugby Union for half her life. World Rugby president Bill Beaumont, athletes from other sports come to cheer on their team-mates. A little jolt through the guts. A reminder that this was an Olympic final, that the world was watching.

GB coach Simon Amor walked round not looking anyone in the eye. I didn't mind that. I never liked the insincerity of the pre-match good lucks and good games, when you both knew that neither meant it and that luck shouldn't come into it, so I walked round the back of the Great Britain dug-out to get to ours. In my black rain jacket and black shorts I was still feeling a preternatural calm. Not thinking about everyone watching on television in Fiji and Britain, watching instead as the players came out from the tunnel onto the pitch.

GB walked. We ran like kids hearing the school bell and dashing into the playground. Osea leading the way with a big grin, Jerry behind him. At one point all seven of them were perfectly in step, arms and legs moving at exactly the same rate, unified in mood and in movement. They came together in the huddle and raised their right hands high, palms piled together, a pyramid of muscled arms.

We had spoken about attacking the kick-offs. I thought GB would be weak in the air compared to us. We wanted to counter-ruck as much as possible too, to *barasi*, to attack them in white waves.

I expected excellence. We got perfection.

Flow from the first kick-off, gathering the ball deep in our own half, flinging it left, Jerry finding Osea, Osea careering across halfway. Leone taking it on, Jerry picking it up from his feet and going left, Osea taking the pass 30m out, faking inside and then scorching round the outside to reach out with the ball in both hands and touch it down over his head as the tackle came in.

Fifty-five seconds gone. Not a single British player had touched the ball since the kick-off. Fijian supporters with blue wigs and bare chests leaping around in the stands.

Flow throughout the team, ambition and pace and anticipation and power. GB had conceded one try in the half an hour of knock-out rugby they'd got through so far. Two minutes later – two minutes in which they were yet to get into our half – we worked the ball right to Sami Viriviri. Smashing through two tackles, Jerry sprinting down the wing, outside the last desperate defender, round and under the posts.

Three minutes gone, 12–0 up.

Sami charging again, a feint and an acceleration, defenders falling off him like burrs off a bear, Jasa running onto the flat pass for try number three. Straight from the kick-off, Dan Norton unable to hold on to the high ball, Semi grabbing the rebound and flicking it inside for Leone to canter over.

Less than eight minutes gone. Four tries up. Bedlam in the stands.

I was watching it unfold with greed – let's get an absolute shedload of points on the board here – and with a dreamy aesthetic pleasure. When it mattered most, in the crescendo to it all, we were playing the rugby I had been striving for the last three years, through all the struggles and doubts and darkness. It was beautiful and it was terrifying, aggression mixed with art, a relentless stampede that was impossible to resist.

Semi Kunatani crashing through the middle. Straight through two red shirts, another trying to lasso those huge legs, but Vatemo was outside him to take the perfectly weighted pass and outsprint Tom Mitchell for the corner. You almost felt sorry for Tom: flat-out in pursuit, unable to narrow the gap, tossed around as he dived vainly at Vatemo's feet like a toy rabbit in the mouth of a greyhound.

29–0 at half-time. Had we landed all our conversions, it could have been 33.

It was the most flawless half of sevens rugby I had ever seen. Five tries to nil, GB not once in our half with ball in hand. Scoring at will, through guile and through strength. An unstoppable force, a beautiful chaos.

I could hear 'We Shall Overcome' being sung in Fijian and then in English in the stands. Nothing to say to the players in the huddle except keep turning the screw. Ropate trying to keep a grip on his emotions but his eyes dancing and his fingers twitching.

Running back out. A brilliant *barasi* counter-ruck as Britain tried desperately to attack from deep. Semi stealing the ball and going up the middle, Jasa on to the pass to go between the posts. Rather than putting the ball down, Semi looked up, saw Josua a few metres back in support and casually threw it back for the kid to join the party.

We were 36 points up and only 4 minutes to go before Britain scored their only try. Even then we went straight back up the other end, ransacked another ruck and saw a second substitute, Viliame Mata, reach out a big paw to slap the ball down for our seventh try.

I turned round and saw all those around me in tears. Leone sitting on the bench with his hands over his face. Osea doing the same.

I thought about my dad. This is where those spin-passes in the back garden took me. You hope you will always have

285

other achievements in your life but you know too that the rankings have just been reset.

I felt grateful, that I could enjoy the moment, that I could get all our subs on so everyone could get a slice of the Olympic final. I wanted us to play on, to give the ball to those fresh men and let them enjoy themselves rather than kick it out when time was up. Keep the flow going for another few blessed moments. Play for the points, for the chance to bring 50 up, play on just for the love of it.

We kicked it out. Some players in each other's arms, some on one knee with heads buried in forearms, Vatemo lying on his back with the ball clutched tight to his chest.

Ropate and I walked slowly onto the pitch. Up to each player in turn, a tight hug and a whisper in the ear.

You are an Olympic champion. You.

FIFTEEN

Those were my most emotional moments, the whispers in each ear. My most cherished one was the embrace with Osea, my captain crying with happiness on my shoulder. The rest of it? Beautiful protocol.

The organiser part of your brain cannot switch off. I made sure the boys all had their tracksuits on for the medal ceremony. Ropate pulled them up off their knees and away from the supporters and lined them on the long podium to wait for their golds.

As Princess Anne went down the line, taking medals from the official to her right, each player knelt in turn. It was the first time in Olympic history anyone had received a medal in that fashion. Some people thought it was the Pacific islanders genuflecting in front of a white woman, others that it was some sort of hangover from the colonial era. But this is how Fijians accept gifts. Put it down, get lower than the person giving it to you, clap twice with cupped hands. No one had told the Princess Royal but she understood from previous tours of duty – two cupped claps in return, her smile mirroring that of the players.

I stood 20m away, a little flashback of the journey that each had taken fizzing through me as the players received their medals in turn. There was a sense of contentment, more so than an ecstatic happiness. Relief, as much as anything, that we had made it, that every idea and hour of training and plan had been worth it. A thought of what might be happening back in Fiji and how Mum would be in her Brentford living room.

I didn't want to be in the celebratory team photo. I wasn't quite sure what do to with myself. And then all the players started waving and calling, and Frank piled right into the middle of them, so I strolled over and stood at the side. At which point Apisai bent down and lifted me on to his shoulders, as he had done as we celebrated our two World Series titles. I patted him on the head, remembered it was the height of rudeness to do that to a Fijian and opted for a slightly self-conscious clenched-fist salute instead.

Frank slapped shoulders and backs. He then pretended to punch Leone. We all flinched. I couldn't imagine another head of state doing the same. But then, which other head of state would be at the centre of all the team photos, and which nation had waited quite as long for this moment as Fiji?

Halfway around the world, a week-long party had kicked off. The state broadcaster in Fiji had immediately begun replaying each of our matches en route to the final; people were yelling and whooping as they watched as if it were all in real time again. Across the archipelago streets and fields were heaving with revellers in cars and on foot and dancing around. Schools were closed, feasts were being prepared, fatted pigs were in for a cruel surprise. *Kava* was being served exclusively in tsunamis.

Protocol. Osea and I had to do a winners' press conference – it was by far the biggest number of journalists I had faced. In a weird way, retelling the stories of the players, of the obstacles they had surmounted to be there, allowed me to find fresh pride in what they had done. I was sharing my love for them. I wanted the world to know.

In the changing room there was a sense of camaraderie and weary gratification rather than wild-eyed celebration. It was like that scene from *The Shawshank Redemption* when the inmates have been tarring the prison roof in the hot sun, and Andy Dufresne somehow persuades the sadistic prison guard to bring them all cold beers. Tired men sitting on the floor, dirt and sweat on their faces, shirts sodden, all looking around at each other with wonder in their eyes.

Another protocol: you celebrate an Olympic gold with the biggest night out of your life. Frank was certainly going to push on; he organised cars to take the players from the athletes' village to the temporary Fijian High Commission in the shadow of Sugarloaf Mountain. Josua, Jasa and Jerry are all teetotal and opted to stay in the village. Others preferred to mark the occasion by marching straight into the free McDonald's and filling their boots.

I was happy for them to take their pleasure where they chose – cold beer, caipirinha, double cheeseburger with fries and Olympic gold. I was shattered. Normally I would have been craving a beer too, but by the time we got back, media duties done, it was gone midnight. I celebrated by unlocking the door to my single room again and sliding under the thin, scratchy Rio 2016 complimentary duvet. My phone, finally back on, would buzz relentlessly with messages for the next 48 hours. I left it in my bag. I could read them in the morning, when they would have me smiling even more.

It was probably the best night's sleep I've ever had. Not a twitch, not a troubled thought. Waking up totally rested, smiling. My first thought: we won the gold...

We stuck around in Rio for a week, all but Save, who flew home alone without a medal, not wanting to wait for it, not wanting to hang around. The sports-obsessed kid in me tried to see everything I could. Every night of track and field, cycling at the velodrome, handball, basketball. South Africa's new Olympic 400m champion and world record holder Wayde van Niekerk came to hang out and join our *lotu*. He and Osea fast became good friends.

We all just wanted to get home, back to our families, back to the villages, to the real celebrations with the people who had backed us every day for the last three years. No matter that our players of 6ft 7ins and 16 stone and heavy limbs were crammed into the back rows of economy flights. We were Fiji bound. A change of plane in Auckland: an offer from Air New Zealand to upgrade me to business class. I offered it to one of the bigger lads; the stewards found out, asked us to give them ten minutes, and moved the entire team forward. Fully made beds, three hours' precious sleep before a welcome like no other.

You could see the people out on the runway at Nadi as the plane came in to land. When we came to a stop you saw the thousands piling out of the terminal and into the streets beyond. An ocean of pale-blue flags, a sea of hugs and kisses and garlands of flowers. They took us to Prince Charles Park for a packed-out welcome reception and then a flight to Suva for the same again on an exponentially bigger scale. The bus ride from airport to Grand Pacific hotel normally took 25 minutes. We were lucky to do it in two hours, and that was with full road closures and a police escort. Every street, every building, every balcony and every tree, people piled high and hanging out, all cheering, all waving.

The Grand Pacific has a long white balcony. Like Charles and Diana after their wedding, we lined up and waved back at the heaving streets below. Families waiting for us, Jerry's young daughter and wife, Semi's surrogate mothers. Viliame Mata's father Sitiveni had flown back from his posting in Iraq. I saw a woman in a full burqa celebrating next to a little Indian kid next to a huge Islander. All those disparate and often divided parts of the nation united by this moment, everyone proud to be Fijian and to share it with everyone else.

Natalie was there too. It was great to see her, even if in my head I was wondering what would come next. I wanted to look after her; she had done it all for me, moved her life across the world, been there by herself for large periods of it as I gave everything to the team instead. We had dinner and I slept again like a dead man, too tired to talk, too tired to worry.

That was the warm-up. Frank had declared a national holiday for the following day. In an open-top bus we meandered through streets that appeared not to have emptied since the previous day. The National Stadium on Queen Elizabeth Road had been at capacity for hours. Frank was there on a raised stage at one end, his wife with him.

So too was the Fijian president, George Konrote, an affable old boy who was usually never allowed to be at the same event at the same time as Frank.

Flags everywhere, in every hand. The team and management in pale-blue shirts, flowers in our hands. On the bus in from the airport I had seen old Fijian internationals by the side of the road, joining in the carnival. I saw Eminoni Nasilasila in the stands. I hoped Isake Katonibau and Pio Tuwai, Alifereti Veitokani and Josua Vici were there too. If it hadn't been for all the players in that training camp at Uprising we would never have won gold. Those 17 bone-on-bone matches there were harder than any Olympic game we played.

I was asked to kneel on the stage, and the president formally awarded me the Honorary Companion of the Order of Fiji, the highest civilian honour in the nation. The players followed with honours of their own. Frank stood by a plinth, and the stadium fell silent:

Today is a milestone in the development of our nation. Precisely 60 years after Fiji first went to the Olympic Games in Melbourne in pursuit of gold, silver and bronze, we have finally done it. And it is gold – a shower of gold, glittering as bright as the Pacific sun.

To Ben, Osea and the boys and the three team officials who have received official honours today, thank you again for what you have done for our nation. Thank you for making us proud. Thank you for filling us with inspiration. Thank you for firing our imaginations about what is possible for a small nation working together as a team.

You are all very lucky to be living in a golden age.

Forty-six years after Independence, we are finally showing the promise as a nation that most of us of a certain age always knew was there, but which we were squandering by not being able to work together as a team.

I want to talk about Ben's wider legacy by saying this: we must never be afraid as Fijians to reach beyond our shores to obtain the services of people who know more than us about something. Insisting that only Fijians know best is the surest path to national mediocrity.

Because while Fiji is a place full of talent, we sometimes need direction. Someone to train us and pass on their superior skills. And Ben, that is one of the most important lessons you will leave behind in Fiji. That whether it is a rugby coach or someone to run our ports or our civil service, we have a great deal to learn from outsiders. They have the capacity to empower us, to take us to another level. And that is what has happened with our Rugby sevens team.

Vinaka vakalevu, Ben, Osea and the boys, for giving us all a lesson on what is possible for a small nation that focuses on achieving greatness. Yours is a famous victory. A victory that will live on in the memories of our people long after everyone here today has gone.

It is a victory for the ages. A victory for every Fijian. *Vinaka vakalevu!* Thank you!

I hadn't prepared anything, not after sacking off my best-laid plans before the final in Rio. But words were easy on a morning like this:

How could we feel pressure on our shoulders, when we were being carried on the shoulders of every Fijian?

293

We went to Rio with no gold medals on this island, we now have 12.

With 12 comes 12 role models, 12 people that can help set a legacy, 12 people that can help to inspire the youth of Fiji, 12 people that can tell you all that anything is possible with hard work.

The boys here have a real chance to do all those things and have that gold medal, that responsibility, to inspire not just in sport but in every area of life where Fijians can stand tall.

My contract officially came to an end on 1 September. Before then there was one more piece of madness to enjoy. Uprising was part of Serua province. At a meeting of the chiefs, they decided to make me an honorary chief too. My name would be Ratu Peni Raiyani Latianara, my reward three acres of land, 160m of it prime beachfront, jungle sweeping up the hills behind.

There was already a permanent police presence outside my house. We had been left alone before the Olympics, but now all restraint was gone. When I walked around the streets I got mobbed for autographs and selfies, which as a ginger man with glasses was hard to adjust to. At home the doorbell would constantly be rung by well-wishers and photo seekers. For the ceremony the police came in force. This way sir, you might enjoy this.

I was taken to the field, dressed in a Fijian shirt and a *sulu* skirt. All the women of the village stood in front of me. I had been told to expect this, and then the etiquette to follow. One of them would be carrying a *tabua*, a whale's tooth. I would have to find it.

They all ran off. Live on television, I had to chase after

them. It was somewhere between *It's A Knockout*, *Benny Hill* and a courtship ritual – the women disappearing in a large peloton, some of them in ginger wigs, me trying to find some of my old 400m hurdles speed endurance to hunt them down, cheering from all around.

I spotted the woman who I thought had the tooth. She was the one in the centre of the peloton, the yellow jersey being protected by her pack of domestiques. With a burst of pace I closed in on her. Like Semi Kunatani charging for the try line, she stuck out a straight arm and fended me off.

The peloton engulfed me as I finally got hold of her and the tooth. A great mass of laughing women, wigs slipping over their eyes, whale tooth held triumphantly to the skies. It wouldn't have worked at Twickenham.

I did wonder in those moments if I was making the right decision to step away. The Fiji Rugby Union were still half-hoping I was going to stay on as coach, despite the flight I had booked back to London. They were yet to advertise my position.

Serua did feel like *vale*, like home. Maybe, had the FRU been more malleable, if my relationship with Natalie had been a perfect one, I could have kept going. But I had found out with England that you cannot always choose the manner of your eventual departure nor its terms. What better ending could there be than a nation's first-ever Olympic gold?

The FRU chief executive John O'Connor escorted me to Nadi airport with my suitcases. Ben, I guess that means we have to advertise it now? I got taken by the airport staff into departures. A choir had gathered to sing me off. Embraces from those I knew, hugs and handshakes from baggage crew and check-in staff and ladies who came out from behind their concessions.

I was shattered as I climbed on board. I looked out of the little window at the smiles and waves and flags. A surge of relief again that we had done it, that we had been successful. A small memory back to the moment I had landed here three years before, jetlagged, intimidated and uncertain. All fast-forward in between, all memories now and about to fade into the slipstream. Nothing about me could ever be the same again.

Nothing would be the same for any of us.

Ropate stayed on as sevens team manager for another six months. There was once again no salary for him, only the per diems he would get for overseas tournaments. After the World Series leg in Cape Town he received a letter from the FRU: we've heard that you might be thinking of stepping down as manager, so this is to officially tell you that you have been relieved of your duties.

Same old problems. He decided to set up a haulage business, the perfect forum for his talents. I gave him some seed money for it. I had decided too to use the land I had been given to build a little holiday place, employing locals from the province that had made me a chief. I wanted Ropate to project manage the construction. I could think of no one better. I missed him more than anyone else; a week never went by without us talking on text or Skype.

Chris Cracknell, another critical cog in our final success, returned to the UK. He carried respect from the team, several of whom had played against him in his days with England, as well as the good wishes of the older local women, who had wistfully nicknamed him Brown Sugar.

Like me, he had needed to escape London and to hit the reset button; Fiji suited him, and his lifestyle suited Fiji. He could question me, and that was great for me. I could try to mentor him, and that worked for his future plans.

Osea played that first new season but found himself substituted earlier and more frequently. Whether it was someone on the Fiji Rugby board wanting to knock him down a peg or two, or the new coach looking to stamp his own mark on the squad, he was left training on his own, ostracised once again. I offered to find 30,000 Fijian dollars to support him for a year while he tried to get back in, but it became clear the door was closed, even though the team's results suggested they were desperate for his peerless leadership.

I had always known that whatever you build in Fiji can fall apart within weeks. There is no legacy in Fiji, only another day and another struggle. I tried to get him into Loughborough University so he could study and play, go to the Commonwealth Games in 2018 and then maybe the World Cup in Japan in 2019. One conversation with the new coach closed that door. There would be no way back.

He got married. I flew back to Fiji for the ceremony. All the boys were there, at the Pearl Resort in Pacific Harbour. His father, former special forces, now minister, spoke through his tears about how it had all been fated: the new coach trusting his son, his son the single most important player for the coach, a journey to gold that was scripted from above.

Osea is now in the USA with his new wife, a contract to play for the Houston Strikers in a new 15-a-side league, his Green Card in place and his first child on the way. He and

I, bound together for ever, reborn through one another. I had found my voice; Osea had found his calling.

Jerry Tuwai stayed in Fiji. He had offers to switch to the 15-a-side game, contracts from a second-division team in France, but he turned them down. Two children now, a home-boy who doesn't want to go away. Still in the team, still a talent like few others. Looking after his money, wanting to leave his kids with more than he had, dreaming of a farm in his father's home province on Vanua Levu, where he can grow *kava* when the time comes to put away the boots and find another knife and fork to feed the family.

Vatemo Ravouvou is still on his epilepsy medication and still epilepsy free. He was selected for the Fiji 15-a-side tour of the northern hemisphere in the autumn of 2016 but was barely used and became bored. He is playing sevens again now, desperate to travel, aware that if he doesn't have rugby in his life then mischief can catch up with him fast.

Semi Kunatani returned to his village to be greeted by a cardboard cut-out of him on the road in that was bigger even than him. Playing in the back row, he could become a real star at the World Cup in Japan. None of it ever went to his head.

Sami Viriviri sent his money home to his mum and siblings and then, with the cash from his contract with Montpellier, built himself a house. He called it Montpellier. He had a daughter just after the Olympics. He called her Rio.

The new coach dropped him from the sevens team. He came close to a deal in the English Premiership with Leicester, then Gloucester, and then in the Pro 14 with Edinburgh, only for them all to fall through. At his age he needs to be playing. With his class, anything else would be a woeful waste.

Apisai Domolailai stayed in Fiji and still plays with the sevens squad. He is still obsessed with horses.

Jasa Veremalua is trying to get a contract overseas. In the meantime, he is training as a manager at the Hideaway Resort in Sigatoka, up against those wonderful sand dunes.

Leone Nakarawa moved to Racing 92 in Paris and is doing brilliantly – playing well, earning good money to send home.

Viliame Mata, Big Bill, got a deal with Edinburgh and has made his debut for the Fiji 15-a-side team.

Masivesi Dakuwaqa, our one-eyed wonder, got a deal playing rugby league with the NRL's Canberra Raiders, thanks to Jarryd Hayne's kind words.

Kitione Taliga went to France on a punt with Stade Français; the FRU were so slow to grant him permission to play that he had only a few matches to impress and was not taken on. He's playing now for the Fijian Drua 15-a-side team in Australia's domestic National Rugby Championship.

Save Rawaca failed to turn up for his lucrative deal with Saracens, the best team in Europe. Sarries had taken my word for him when offering him that contract and spent thousands of pounds on visas and flight tickets. When he blew it, I felt as let down by him as I had in Rio. He had a chance at La Rochelle and failed to take it, getting overweight and missing out on a spot with the Flying Fijians too. He was a wonderful talent, but his ego got in the way. He listened to bad advice from those around him, unable to handle no longer being the number-one star, a rapid descent that none of us saw coming. He is now at Bayonne, trying one more time, his wife sending me an email apologising for his past behaviours. I hope the penny drops for him, as the talent is there and he still has time.

Josua Tuisova, the kid who took Save's place in Rio, is now at Toulon in France, with every club in the world after him. He is a global star and will do even more at the next World Cup. I went to the south of France to visit him. As always he was perfect, no dramas, no mistakes, no ego. Everything about Josh gives you a warm glow. It was a joy to coach someone with his physical attributes and skills.

Pio Tuwai was arrested by the police in October 2016 and charged with assaulting his new girlfriend. At the subsequent trial he pleaded guilty, was ordered to pay her damages and given a domestic-violence restraining order. In January 2017 he married a different woman, a nurse from Lomaiviti who was training in New Zealand's North Island. With a travel ban in place after his conviction he was initially unable to join her. I wrote him a reference. He is now hoping to get a contract to play sevens in Japan, as always an incredible talent who struggles to steer a rational path through a tumultuous life.

Frank Bainimarama remains Prime Minister of Fiji. The next general elections are due in 2018.

When your phone rang with a call from Frank or his PA announcing a call, it always made you feel nervous. Your heart beat a little faster. You wondered what you might have done.

In that first year I now think he was changing as much as I was, preparing himself for the first free elections since his coup, me trying to drag the team into the present and then the future. As our relationship developed I grew to respect him; while we never became close, in our conversations he was reasonable with me and committed to the team. If I needed something serious I knew I could call him. The darker stuff was there, but I never saw it myself, and neither did those around me.

Before I left I was promised a Fijian passport, beautiful and blue. It would make a big difference with my plans to set up a charity there and begin work on my land. It hasn't happened yet but I am still hopeful. Frank and I exchanged birthday greetings on email, and when I returned to Viti Levu in 2017, he was warm with his welcome.

The ripples from our win in Rio continued to spread. After a short corporate speech I gave in Dubai one night, a gentleman came up to me, asked me where the team was staying and went round to give each of them 1,000 US dollars. Another heard that many of their parents had never seen them play abroad and told me he would fly 40 of their friends and family to the next tournament in Dubai and put them all up in a good hotel for a week. Wherever I travelled in the world, the love people have for Fiji and its sevens team shone through. Everyone's favourite second team. A lot of people's flat-out number one.

Natalie. Natalie and I are no longer together.

She had travelled back from Fiji to London a few days before me. When she did, it became clear that it had been Fiji holding us together, not pushing us apart. I think I had known for a while but been unwilling to confront it, scared of what it would feel like, selfishly worried about the effect it might have on the team.

We were different. We always had been. When our cogs meshed we drove each other on. When they were displaced, we ground against each other instead. We wanted different things, and neither of us could change who we were, no matter how much we once thought we could.

301

She would say that the job was everything to me. That I found it hard to switch off. It was always the next challenge, the next player to find, a problem to solve. Always tournaments to focus on, a battle to fight. I wasn't someone who could compartmentalise. If the rugby was going wrong it would affect my mood in all areas of my life. She would say I wasn't warm enough with her, that I should have been more tactile, more openly affectionate.

I did try and make it work. When we split I must have thought about it a hundred times – is this right, shouldn't we get back together? The old Catholicism still lurking in there somewhere, a feeling that marriage was for life and divorce was a failure. A sense of disappointment that I was going to be that person. I'd always thought I would never give up.

But I knew. You cannot be happy if you are not being true to who you really are. You can't stay together for tradition or for regret.

It was a simple divorce. There was no need to use solicitors. The house had already been sold.

The decree absolute came through on 2 August 2017. The overwhelming feeling that summer day in London was one of reflection: what we had done together, the happiness at the start, the hopes that had slowly seeped away. Knowing it was the right thing but that sadness was inevitable too. Hoping she was dealing with the day OK.

We haven't seen each other since. I really hope she is seeing someone else and that they are giving her what she wants. Planning holidays, big nights out, love and attention. She is a kind, caring, warm-hearted woman, and she did nothing wrong in our relationship, only tried to make it work.

When I went back to Fiji the coconut wireless had done its job. The old ladies in the villages told me they would be holding interviews to find me a suitable *yalewa*, a girlfriend. I haven't taken them up on the offer yet.

Another ripple, another seemingly impossible consequence. In April 2017 the Reserve Bank of Fiji issued 2 million special $7 bills. On one side of the note was the picture of us celebrating on the pitch in Rio, two rows of players, Frank in the middle, Ropate on the right, me on Apisai's shoulders with my fists apologetically clenched. On the reverse was an image of Osea in full flight, ball tucked under one arm, big grin on his face, a little seated me to the side, resting my cheek on my fist.

On the same day they released a million commemorative 50 cent pieces. On one side, the players in the arms-raised huddle and the words FIJI RUGBY SEVENS * GOLD OLYMPIANS. On the other, me sitting on top of the highest dune at Sigatoka, rollers coming in off the Pacific behind. The inscription ran around the bottom: BEN RYAN * SEVENS HEAD COACH.

I suppose I had brought change to Fiji. Now they had change with me on it.

If you haven't ever bought something with money featuring your face, I can tell you it's fun. It didn't last for long; everyone in the country seemed to want something to commemorate it all, and the notes and coins became a rarity within weeks. I've kept a few for myself.

In the months that followed I explored lots of opportunities, consultancies with various sports teams and governing bodies across the world, working with companies on their leadership and internal cultures. I investigated the possibility of setting up a Super Rugby franchise in Fiji so that the best of the Pacific islands talent could stay at home and make money playing there, developing the game across the islands rather than haemorrhaging talent to New Zealand and Australia and France. I found sponsors and I found some support at World Rugby, but it trampled on too many toes at the Fijian Rugby Union. I thought about stepping across to 15-a-side coaching but sensed I might find it too restrictive and predictable. I loved the variation that I had and being my own boss as a sevens coach. I hoped I hadn't already achieved the best that I could do.

If I had changed something in Fiji, then I was a different person too. Those tribulations and successes had made me a far better coach and leader. Driving this was the realisation that the love was back, where it had been when I first started coaching senior rugby at Newbury.

I had lost that passion with England. I had seen things I didn't like all around me and just assumed that was what professional rugby had to be like. It sneaked up on me, making me more materialistic, worrying about status, developing, like the others, blind spots to what I really cared about.

This is what happens to so many of us. We get dragged into a life that isn't fulfilling us or getting the best out of us. You don't realise that you have become a bad version of yourself because no one tells you.

I had been unhappy and unable to recognise it. Fiji blew all that away. Three years of relentless work, of failures and disappointments as well as success, of tragedy and great friendships and bonds that I could never have imagined. Three years of enlightenment, thousands of miles away from everything I knew.

Fiji showed me what I was good at. It slowed me down and cut away the old distractions and panics. Winning gold validated the stuff that I believed in and wanted to be: treating people with respect, giving them room to grow, having good values, being authentic. Winning by being nice.

Contentment can be hard to find. For me it is there more often than ever before. My mum, my sisters, my friends tell me when I see them. You're you again. The kid, the sports nut, the coach who cares.

And so now I let my thoughts fall once more. Where will I be in another three years? I think about happiness rather than a particular job, staying true to what I believe in instead of a certain salary, helping others achieve the best they can. I think about the simple pleasures now I'm back in London. Loving the people around me properly, grateful for my health and happiness. Fiji changed me, taught me more about myself at an age where I thought I knew all the big stuff. I still want the sense of peace that it gave me, but its beaches are too far from my true home. While I will always go back, London is where I want my next chapter to begin.

And I think about my best friend.

I don't know if Noel saw what happened in Rio. I don't know if Noel is still around. If he is alive then he will have been in and out of prison and he will be even more of a changed man.

I don't care. I still want to catch up and see him. Talking to each other – this is what's been happening, remember the games in the back garden, the table-tennis at school, the five-a-side parties? We would connect there. We would get answers.

Maybe he will read this. Maybe this is not the end but a new beginning.

My tattoo. The one I discussed with the barista in the Olympic village, the one I got done in the Bowery in New York at the end of the Olympic year.

Blue ink on the inside of my right forearm, there for ever more.

Vei Lomani. Love one another.

Acknowledgements

I'd like to thank the following people.

For my rugby journey: 'Capt Mac', the first coach I ever had – you started it all. Paul Hopkins, the best teacher I ever had. David Christie, for giving me my first teaching job. David Smith, for giving me my first opportunity in professional coaching. The many, many good people at the RFU.

Coaches along the way I met and who inspired me: Vinny Codrington, Pat Lavery, Wyn Ellis, Pete Halsall, Tony Rodgers, Paul Turner, Mark Ring, Ged Glynn, Phil Keith-Roche, John Kingston, Brian Ashton, Neil Rollings, Dusty Hare, Ed Morrison, Paddy O'Brian, Steve Hill, Stevie Gemmell, Stuart Lancaster, Chris Dossett, Paul Kitovitz and Kevin Bowring.

For friendship and support: Mum, for her love and bacon sarnies, and for the support – up in the middle of the night to watch us play on TV, reading the *Fiji Times* every day to keep up with all the news. My sisters Lizzy and Sarah. Sean, Iain, Cary, Matt, Jamie, Pete, Canster, Gez, Monty, Kate, Hannah, Damien, Crackers, Jez, Burdo, Burky, Si, Scrunter, Twitford, Charlie, Mazza, Felts, Andy, Terry, Damu, Morgs, Nadine, Nathan, Rusty, Brett, Rich, Mike Popata, Kenny, lubes, Moira, Paddy, Spoorsy and Fi. The late and great Beth Coalter. To Natalie, for all the love and support you gave me through sickness and uprooting. You were always there and I wish you an amazing life ahead. I'll always be thankful to you.

On my Fijian Journey: Oscar, Ropate – thank you for everything. Naca, William, Jen, Bela, Tani, Jeremy, Crackers and Mat – the dream team! Bruce, for the friendship and constantly sending out good vibes. James, Rene and the Uprising Beach Resort – at the start when I needed help, you guys were there. Culden, for helping me to negotiate those first early steps. Skinny Bean Café, for providing me and Crackers unlimited espresso. Natalia, Jeff, Kim, Sophie, Logan, Janice, Kelly, Alana and all the Larsen and Bentley clan for friendship, boneless chicken curry, unlimited supplies of Fiji Gold and laughter.

Natalie, Ben and the Pearl. Robyn and Doug, great neighbours and friends – Paleo Red Wine nights were the best! Roddy, Jim, Liz and the UK High Commission – you were always there to support me. Peter Mazey and his crew – Vinaka! Shane, Angie and the Fiji Airways massive – I couldn't have asked for better friendship and support. The people working and living in Pacific Harbour and Serua, a place that feels like home. To all the Fijian journalists who called me in the early morning or middle of the night. To all the hard-working office staff at the FRU.

To all the players I've ever coached, and the coaches and staff I have worked with – thank you for everything.

To Paul Murphy and his great team at Orion, and to David Luxton and Mark Spoors, for all your hard work on the book.

Finally, to Tom Fordyce, who made this process a joy

and the book a reality. He writes so brilliantly and our catch-ups in almost every coffee shop in Bloomsbury and Soho to unpack my thoughts, feelings and emotions to tell this story were always so uplifting.

Vei Lomani.